Supervising the PhD

FRED'S

Supervising the PhD

A guide to success

Sara Delamont, Paul Atkinson
and Odette Parry

The Society for Research into Higher Education
& Open University Press

Published by SRHE and
Open University Press
Celtic Court
22 Ballmoor
Buckingham
MK18 1XW

and 1900 Frost Road, Suite 101
Bristol, PA 19007, USA

First published 1997

A catalogue record of this book is available from the British Library

ISBN 0 335 19516 4 (pbk)   0 335 19517 2 (hbk)

Library of Congress Cataloging-in-Publication Data
Delamont, Sara, 1947–
    Supervising the PhD: a guide to success / Sara Delamont, Paul
Atkinson, and Odette Parry.
        p.   cm.
    Includes bibliographical references (p.) and index.
    ISBN 0–335–19516–4 (pb). — ISBN 0–335–19517–2 (hb)
    1. Doctor of philosophy degree—Great Britain.   2. Faculty
advisors—Great Britain.   3. Universities and colleges—Great
Britain—Graduate work.   I. Atkinson, Paul, 1947–   .   II. Parry,
Odette, 1954–   .   III. Title.
LB2386.D45 1997
378.2'4—dc21   97–569
                                                                          CIP

Typeset by Graphicraft Typesetters Limited, Hong Kong
Printed in Great Britain by Biddles Ltd, Guildford and King's Lynn

This book is dedicated to Amanda Coffey for being the easiest PhD student Paul and Sara have (so far) supervised.

Contents

Preface and acknowledgements

Writing this book is an act of *hubris*. No one with any sense would claim to 'know' how to be a successful doctoral supervisor, getting students through with friendship, integrity and emotional stability intact. The self-confidence of the doctoral supervisor can be destroyed by one 'failure': one person who fails to submit, or whose thesis is rejected by the examiners, or even one who never gets going but fritters the registration period away. We chose to write this book because we had done two research projects and our data on PhD students and their supervisors were extensive, because we had lived through a period of change in the British PhD and because we felt our experiences were worth sharing.

We have of course learned a great deal from our own doctoral students over the years – not least from our mistakes, which they have had to suffer. Paul Atkinson would like to acknowledge in particular John Beynon, Robin Bunton, Amanda Coffey, Andrew Lloyd, Evelyn Parsons, Andrew Pithouse, Stuart Todd and Patricia Taraborrelli. Sara Delamont would like to thank Mary Darmanin, Jane Pilcher, Teresa Rees and Jane Salisbury. Paul Atkinson and Sara Delamont have supervised over seventy-five short (20,000) dissertations for five different masters degrees, plus other MPhil and PhD theses. They have examined higher degree theses in twenty-two different UK universities, and Sara Delamont sat on the social science higher degree committee of the CNAA for its last five years. All those students and colleagues have contributed to the experiences drawn on in this book.

The chapter titles and opening quotes are taken from Dorothy L. Sayer's (1935) *Gaudy Night*, which includes many apposite remarks on the perils of academic life and research. The edition used is the 1972 NEL version, and page references are to that text.

The Economic and Social Research Council funded the research upon which we have drawn in this book, with two grants: 'The academic socialisation of doctoral students in social science disciplines' (T007401010) and 'The academic socialisation of doctoral students in natural science disciplines' (R000233120). We gratefully acknowledge the support of the

Research Council. The views expressed in this book are the authors' and do not represent policy of the Economic and Social Research Council. We are grateful to Bob Burgess and Chris Pole for frequent discussions on both projects.

Sharen Bechares and Karen Chivers word processed this text for us. Angela Jones transcribed the tapes in the original research project.

I

A most persuasive piece
of argument

When I was at Flanborough College, examining for the professorial theses in York University, there was a man who sent in a very interesting paper on a historical subject. It was a most persuasive piece of argument, only I happened to know that the whole contention was quite untrue.

(Sayers 1972: 330)

Supervising doctoral students is one of the most satisfying things that anyone in higher education can do. Watching a new scholar become an independent researcher, conduct a project, write up the results, present them at a conference and see the first publications is a wonderful experience. Guiding a new scholar into your specialism is intrinsically rewarding and the best way to ensure that your own work echoes down to the next generation and beyond. Building up a research group, with doctoral students and postdocs (postdoctoral fellows) is even more rewarding. Our aim in this book is to convey the joys of successful supervision, offer advice on how to maximize the chances of your students being successful and foreshadow problems that can arise, by forewarning you and offering you both preventive measures and remedial ones. We hope that experienced supervisors can learn from the book, although newcomers are its main target. Our basic philosophy is that good, pleasurable supervision is based on self-consciousness, not intuition or flying by the seat of the pants. The whole idea of the book is that successful, pleasurable higher degree supervision is based on making explicit to yourself, and to the students, what the processes and issues are. Many of the problems that arise stem from supervisors thinking that students know things they do not know, or vice versa, or both.

We have organized the book so that it follows the progress of a student through from starting out as a doctoral student to careers after the viva voce examination. Not all theses proceed in the linear way in which we have organized the book, but the linear structure works well enough for the book. Thus, we start with how to ensure that the students get off to a good start, and end those chapters relevant directly to the process of supervision with the development of academic life after the viva. The eleventh chapter opens up with the place of doctoral supervision in the career of the lecturer, and the role of the graduates in the academic department and the wider university. These issues take us to considerations beyond the intrinsic satisfaction of higher degree supervision. Readers of this book will be acutely aware of the extrinsic rewards and pressures that bear on the supervision and management of graduate studies: postgraduate students, and their numbers, are regarded as indicators of success for academic departments and their universities. Successful completion does not only mean that an individual student is rewarded, or that an individual supervisor can share in the pleasure and can experience professional pride as a consequence. Completion rates are extremely important. Research councils and the British Academy, which are the source of centrally funded research studentships in the UK, increasingly demand high completion rates (usually submission of the PhD within four years of commencement) as part of their processes of recognition. Numbers of research students and the number of degrees awarded are part of the evidence required of all departments in the UK, as part of the funding councils' recurrent Research Assessment Exercises – on which depend the core funding of academic departments and their universities.

Imagine your university is having a staff development workshop on 'higher degree supervision' and everyone present has to outline a problem – as each supervisor speaks you hear about the following vignettes.

Vignette A: Writing block in earth sciences

Wendy Jackman has been studying a saline intrusion into an inland waterway and is trying to write up the thesis. She has written the methods chapter and the literature review, but writing about her own data makes her feel sick. Her supervisor, Dr Helen Marsh, keeps saying, 'I can't help unless you give me *something* on paper' and 'Time's running out.' Dr Marsh has no idea how to help a student with a writing block.

Vignette B: 'Ignorant' supervisor in ancient history

Jules Harnest is being supervised by Dr Henrietta Francey. Henrietta says she is trying to be friendly and supportive, but she is ignorant of the methods Jules wants to use and the empirical area he is working on. He is keen to study nosebleeds in Ancient Greek medical thought, and has been thoroughly enthused by scholars using computer software to work on ancient texts. She is not familiar with the literature on Greek medical thought, admits she is ignorant but sceptical about the use of IT in ancient history, but reports that the department is so small there is really no one else to supervise Jules: her colleagues are expert on the Hittites, Roman architecture and the early church. She is the expert on the Greeks, but her main interest is marine imagery in drama. Henrietta has not read the literature Jules is reviewing, and she reports that Jules is openly wondering how useful her comments will be. Henrietta asks the group how much research she is morally obliged to do on Ancient Greek medicine and whether she should go on an IT course.

By the time you and the workshop leader have heard about problems like this, being a PhD supervisor seems to be impossible. They might not be problems you have encountered yourself. You may find it hard to imagine a higher degree supervisor being unversed in relevant aspects of the student's research – and in the laboratory sciences such a distance between supervisor and student is rare. You may find it hard to envisage that 'writing up' could be a major problem for any higher degree student (although the problem is fairly widespread). Nevertheless, such problems, and a fair number of others like them, are quite commonplace in academic departments. Even if you have not had to grapple with such issues yourself, there is no guarantee that some such professional and personal problem will not occur in the future. Moreover, if you are going to mentor other academics, and you are going to train the next generation of academic supervisors, then you may find it useful to think about such issues. Indeed, it is one of the limitations of graduate work in the United Kingdom that, given its tradition of individual effort and apprenticeship, with little explicit reflection on the processes and products, we rely too much on our own experience, and too little on more general principles. The aim of this book is to offer some advice and suggestions for avoiding problems, and solving them as and when they arise. We are not focused obsessively and exclusively on 'problems' and the more negative side of academic supervision. We must reiterate that we regard successful supervision as intensely satisfying: the development of a successful working relationship with a higher degree student is one of the high points of academic work. But such working relationships – however successful the outcome – are developed over time, and cover many facets of academic work. It is rare indeed for there to be absolutely no hitches, no hiccups, no disagreements. However gifted the student, however distinguished the supervisor, the process requires work and attention. When we discuss 'problems', therefore, it is not in order to depress the reader, or to suggest that the enterprise is intrinsically fraught or flawed. Rather, we wish to give our readers the opportunity to reflect on these issues in such a way as to avoid problems, and so maximize the personal and intellectual pleasures to be gained.

Let us take the second of our vignettes, about the 'ignorant' supervisor. Suppose that Harriet Francey goes back to her department determined to tackle her problems. First, she sits down with Jules and 'comes clean' about her problems. This clears the air between them and they agree on a set of compromises. Henrietta goes on an IT course, and then she and Jules attend a day conference on IT and ancient history, at which several experts are speaking. Henrietta discovers several old friends there, together with their doctoral students. Jules comes away with a useful list of doctoral students in other universities he can network with by e-mail, so that he can keep in touch with other people using the same analytic tools. Henrietta starts to use IT herself, and discovers that it can enhance her work. Her next book on Aristophanes starts to move faster as she deploys her new skills. She and Jules agree on a short list of central texts in Ancient Greek medical thought that she can be expected to read, and she works through those. Meanwhile, she arranges for Jules to have a few meetings with a scholar in another university who is a UK expert in Greek medical thought, getting him a travel grant to go there. Jules relaxes, feeling more confident about Henrietta, and Henrietta starts to plan a paper on medical metaphors in Sophocles. When you meet Henrietta a year later and ask after Jules, she is reinvigorated and cheerful. Their action plan has resulted in a year's productive work for Jules, while Henrietta has nearly finished her book and written her paper. What were being presented as intolerable burdens for Henrietta have now turned into research opportunities.

This book presents hitherto unpublished data collected by the authors from supervisors and higher degree students during two research projects, and the authors' own experiences, as supervisors and as the successful completors of three PhDs and one MPhil between them, to provide guidance on how a successful supervisor can maximize the student's chances of completing a thesis quickly and efficiently.

The two research projects were conducted between 1989 and 1993 in the UK. The first was on social scientists (in town planning, social anthropology, human geography, urban studies and development studies), the second on science (artificial intelligence, biochemistry and physical geography and environmental sciences). Data from interviews and observation gathered in these research projects are drawn on here. The findings from the projects are not all rehearsed here (but see Parry *et al.* 1994a, b, 1996). The available data include interviews with over fifty supervisors taped and transcribed. In addition to those research-based insights, we draw on a good deal of practical experience as supervisors and in working with graduate students in a variety of social sciences on their own skills and research problems. We have, for many years, run a course for doctoral students at the University of Wales, Cardiff. We have worked with students from sociology, criminology, psychology, education, planning and other disciplines (our direct experience is not confined to the social sciences: we also have experience with students in earth sciences, chemistry and pharmacy). We meet those graduate students in a series of weekly workshops, in order to go over a number of core skills and processes over the course of a research project. These are intended to inculcate many of the 'craft' skills of academic life, and to help those selfsame graduate students to go on to become well informed supervisors when their turn comes. We try to make those workshops as practical as we can, with handouts and worksheets. Some of these have been reproduced as figures in this book, such as Figure 4.1 in Chapter 4. We use them to illustrate our general points, and to share with our readers examples of the kind of resources that can be used in constructing such 'skills' courses.

Throughout this book we have tried to blend advice for supervisors – places where we say 'Do this or your students will suffer' – and findings from academic research. We have offered advice only on points where our experience and the research findings are in agreement: that is, where the experiential and the empirical are mutually supportive. Our basic belief is that supervising is a skill, or set of skills, that can be learnt and can be improved with practice. We want this book to be a cheerful and optimistic one – our aim is to parallel the enthusiasm communicated by Becker's (1986) *Writing for Social Scientists*.

We have written the book, and conducted the research that partly informs it, primarily in terms of the PhD. The doctoral candidature and the research processes that go with it inform most of our discussion. Of course, such candidates and their concerns by no means exhaust the range of higher degree work, or the kinds of supervision that may be involved. In addition to a relatively small number of masters degrees exclusively by research (the MPhil in many cases), there are now very large numbers of taught masters degrees that include a part-requirement dissertation (typically in our own institution with a limit of 20,000 words). The substantial growth in such masters degrees in the UK has meant that 'supervision' is now a much more pervasive aspect of academic work in virtually every department. The scope of such short dissertations is, self-evidently, much reduced from that of the PhD. The requirement of an original and major contribution to scholarship is not relevant. The conduct of major pieces of empirical research or the promotion of significant theoretical development are not feasible or relevant. Nevertheless, they do require supervision, and their supervision calls for at least some of the same skills as does that of doctoral students. Our discussion of issues, problems and solutions should not, therefore, be seen as outside the sphere of relevance for academics concerned only with students at the masters level. Many aspects of supervision are generic, and we are aware of that fact.

Ethics and confidentiality

Throughout the book there are illustrations taken from our experience, and examples from our research project. All the illustrations and examples use pseudonyms for people and places. The illustrations feature research students of ours and our friends in Britain and the USA, and they are hidden behind pseudonyms taken from Agatha Christie. Sometimes biographical details have been changed to protect the student further – for example, a person who was a Welsh rugby international might be described as a 10,000 metre athlete. The informants from the two Economic and Social Research Council (ESRC) funded research projects have also been protected by pseudonyms: all the supervisors are called Dr X, all the students have a forename and a family name. Thus Dr Throstle is supervising Jason Ingersoll. All the universities are also protected by pseudonyms. We have also used some data from a study conducted for BERA (the British Educational Research Association) by Eggleston and Delamont (1983), and the students who responded to that survey are also protected by pseudonyms from Agatha Christie.

The structure of the volume

Chapter 2, 'Caught and held by a cobweb', shows how to help students move from their undergraduate or taught postgraduate phase into the research postgraduate phase. The specific focus will be on helping students to design a *manageable* project, i.e. one which can be done single-handed in three years by a beginner.

Chapter 3, 'The balance between tradition and progress', is about a balancing act. Once the student has a sensible project, it has to be timetabled and planned, and (if empirical) the research design has to be established. This chapter focuses on the delicate balance a supervisor has to strike between ensuring the planning is done but not undermining the student's autonomy by 'taking over' the research.

Chapter 4, 'Old manuscripts', focuses on the literature review. This chapter shows how a good supervisor can ensure that the student reads widely enough, and writes an interesting literature review, while still getting on with the data collection. Many students 'drown' in the literature: the good supervisor is alert to that danger.

Chapter 5, 'Heavy and thankless task', deals with supervising data collection. The good supervisor, who will him or herself have negotiated access, chosen methods and done his or her own data collection, can help a student to avoid the worst mistakes. This chapter focuses on how successful supervisors can deploy their own experience to help their students.

Chapter 6, 'Disagreeableness and danger', is focused on how the supervisor can keep up the students' motivation and work rate through the sticky patches. Completion of the project is as dependent on keeping up motivation and effort as it is on academic excellence. The difference between academic success and failure quite often comes down to perseverance and overcoming difficulties. The supervisor needs to be alert to potential problems, and needs to think about how to encourage students to carry on, surmount problems and submit their work.

Chapter 7, 'The contorted corkscrew', is about the acquisition of a variety of tacit competencies, broadly concerned with judgement and 'taste' in postgraduate research. In addition to technical issues of research design, data collection and so on, supervisors and students need to focus on broader issues of academic socialization within the relevant discipline.

Chapter 8, 'An emotional excitement', is all about writing. Turning data and notes into a completed thesis defeats many students. There are few books on writing, and nothing on how a supervisor can help a student to master writing, and even learn to enjoy it.

Chapter 9, 'A lack of genuine interest', deals with choosing examiners and preparing for the viva. Many candidates are scared of the 'unknown' aspects of doctoral examinations. This chapter explores how a good supervisor can reduce anxiety by organizing 'mock' and practice vivas, and provide useful advice on handling the real event. It also addresses the vital issue of how to select appropriate external examiners, so standards are maintained but students also get a reasoned verdict.

Chapter 10, 'The brave pretence at confidence', focuses upon how the supervisor should be 'moving them on: launching their careers'. This chapter deals with the supervisor's duties to help students publish, build a strong curriculum vitae and seek jobs.

Chapter 11, 'A rather unpromising consignment', deals with selecting high degree students and building a research group. This chapter will deal with the selection of research students: vetting applications, interviewing candidates and matching students and supervisors to maximize the chances of thesis completion. Then it turns to the role that a research group plays in the career of the successful researcher.

We see these as the main issues with which a British supervisor has to be concerned. The institutional frameworks with which we deal – on the basis of our research and also from our professional experience – are from the United Kingdom. This is not, however, an exclusively British, parochial view. Our perspectives are not applicable only to graduate study in UK higher education. Notwithstanding national differences in funding, organization, examining, completion rates and completion times, many of the issues are generic and cross national boundaries. The evidence from other industrialized countries suggests that many of the basic issues are similar there: indeed, the findings of the most thorough cross-national study are that disciplinary identities are more powerful than national differences. That is, doctoral supervision in physics in Japan has more in common with doctoral supervision in physics in Germany than with history supervision in Japan. A brief summary of that programme makes our case for the international nature of basic supervisory problems, and serves briefly to locate what we have to say against that international backdrop.

International comparisons

In 1987, the Spencer Foundation funded a three-year research programme in five countries (Japan, the UK, West Germany, the USA and France) on the ways in which graduate education and research were related (Clark 1993). The research programme produced analyses at the national level of 'the historical development of higher education and science' (p. xxii), and of the contemporary structure of funding, of research and of higher education. More intensive investigation of archetypal disciplines – history to represent humanities, economics to represent social science, and physics to represent the sciences – took place in all five countries, with the addition of engineering in Japan and the biomedical sciences in the USA. The national level analyses were based primarily on published data, the intensive investigations on interviews with 'faculty, graduate students, university administrators, and, if necessary, personnel in research institutes' (p. xvii).

Burton Clark's dream for this comparative study was that 'cross-national comparisons' would 'lead to a richer understanding' (p. 378). He saw the main issues facing the five countries studied as the rise of mass participation in higher education, the labour market demand for advanced education, the expansion of knowledge and the increased government role in patronage and supervision of research. These four trends have led, Clark believes, to common tensions: between concentration and diffusion, between locating research in non-university settings and maintaining it there, and between bureaucratic control and autonomous competition. The five nations investigated during this Spencer programme vary considerably in the ways in which their higher education had responded to the four trends, and in the ways in which the resultant tensions were showing. Clark argues that, in 1990, 'the future of British academic science is quite problematic' (p. 369), because the 'tension between university and state is great' (p. 369). An expanded version of the British section has been published in Britain (Becher *et al.* 1994) as a separate monograph. Coincidentally, while the Spencer Foundation programme was drawing to a close, the British ESRC was launching a research initiative on the social science PhD, which has also been published (Burgess 1994). Subsequently, two projects on science PhD students and their supervisors were also funded by ESRC. In 1995, the UK finally had a substantial body of data on doctoral study, remedying a long-recognized deficiency (Winfield 1987).

Superficially, the five nations have very different systems of graduate education. France has the CNRS system, as well as the 1984 reform of the doctoral degrees, which led to the single doctorate followed by the *habilitation*. The USA has the largest and most diverse system, yet when Gumport (1993: 265) collected a vivid comment from a doctoral candidate – 'According to students, some days are better than others: "Some days you're a peon. Other days you know how . . . and you're king for a day"' – it could have come from any doctoral candidate anywhere.

The Japanese section will probably be the most like *terra incognita* to readers who may be surprised to learn that Japanese graduate education 'is small and relatively weak' (p. 297). Only 6 per cent of the first degree graduates go on to do graduate work, and 'earning the doctorate is not a . . . routine part of the early stages of an academic career' (p. 311) in the humanities and social sciences.

Shining through all the national differences are the commonalties of disciplinary cultures. The everyday experiences of a doctoral student doing physics are more similar to those of another physicist across countries than they are to a historian in her 'own' culture. Japanese history candidates experience supervision in ways very similar to historians in the other four countries. The supervisory cultures and the existence or absence of a laboratory setting for research are more important for the life of the individual student than the particular nation state, despite Traweek's findings on physics (Traweek 1988). The dilemmas facing supervisors are very similar across the industrialized countries, and we hope this book will be relevant in all of them.

The problems of hypothetical supervisors opened the chapter. We end it with some real supervisors discussing their task, and the tensions they feel.

The problems of supervision

The scientists and social scientists we interviewed discussed sensitively how they had to find a balance between heavy-handed dominance and a 'hands-off' neglect of their students. Among our respondents were several who confessed that they were not good at handling the delicate balances required.

Dr Netley, a social scientist at Boarbridge, told us:

> It's very difficult to get the right balance between how much you teach them and how much you let them get on with it.

His colleague, Dr Munsey:

> If I feel the student wants to be hand-fed, i.e. he wants me to do half the work, that's not on. I look for the independence of personality in addition to motivation. They should be academically capable and physically capable of doing the data collection and analysis, with some guidance obviously, but I'm not prepared to give up more than 10 per cent or 15 per cent of my time to a study if I find they keep knocking on my door every day, asking me to provide them with information and data.

These accounts of the supervisory relationship draw on contrasts of dependence and independence on the part of the research student. Dr Coltness, of Tolleshurst, was adamant that:

> supervising is extremely difficult, let me say that. I think it's the most difficult part of my work. It's the part I enjoy least because I feel I don't do it well enough.

Central to Dr Coltness's doubts was the delicate balance:

> How much should you be spoon feeding? Should they be doing it themselves? Should I be in the library sussing out things? How much re-writing? Do you go through it with a toothcomb? [*sic*] . . . There are no guidelines at all. So I find it very problematic. How much to help the weaker ones, how much to try to keep up with the brighter ones. They are so different, they're not off-the-peg.

Dr Danson, a natural scientist at Forthhamstead, described this process:

> Once we've decided on a topic and an area of work then I think the student will gradually put more and more into the project on his or her initiative, I mean it's not a doctorate of being a technician, it's a doctorate of philosophy.

This is a particularly important distinction in a laboratory discipline: successful researchers have to be autonomous.

> Therefore you're not actually wanting someone to do something and then tell them to do something else. You're wanting them to come back with ideas, and indeed, from then on guide the project in particular areas.

Perhaps the most detailed reflection on supervision we collected emphasized the changing nature of the student–supervisor relationship over time. One of our informants, Dr Shannon, a social scientist at Chelmsworth, emphasized how the relationship between student and supervisor can, and must, change over the student's registration period:

I do think it's quite a difficult process for both parties, supervisor and student. And it changes over time. It's a very personal thing. To begin with the supervisor's in quite a strong position in defining and directing students, and they're relatively subordinate at the beginning, willing to accept your advice and direction.

For Dr Shannon, the student needs to outgrow that early phase, so:

as the student gets more and more into the subject, that relationship begins to change, because they develop an expertise which the supervisor is no longer sharing. Also they develop a view about their intellectual property which is separate from their supervisor. And it's a bit like a growing-up process, an intellectual growing-up, and it leads to conflicts at a certain point in time, as the student develops that independence.

For Dr Shannon, the time when the balance begins to shift can be likened to the stormy adolescence of the candidature:

I've always found there's this period in the middle where there is that conflict, like my relationship with my daughter, where there is a change occurring, and it's quite difficult as a supervisor to begin to 'let go' almost. You feel they're not ready for it, they're not in control, and that leads to a degree of conflict which can be overt, or could not be overt. Sometimes people will avoid seeing you – it's like that.

Dr Shannon said she had observed this period of conflict between colleagues and students.

I've seen that process sometimes with colleagues, where people don't seem to be able to complete, and I think it might need to be overtly addressed. And I think the most successful candidates are when you can be relatively open about that, get through it and then move to completion. But otherwise you can get stuck in that phase when the supervisor still tries to over-direct, over-control, and the student tries to pull away and develop their own interests. And if you're not careful you can get bogged down – the student doesn't know how to progress and you're not giving them the sort of advice they need to get through.

I don't know if other supervisors have felt this, but I do think there's this shifting relationship which is actually quite difficult to cope with.

While Dr Shannon was more articulately self-critical than many of our respondents, she was typical in her concern to do the job well. Most of our respondents talked at length about the pleasures and pains of supervision, and about their strategies for helping students. They discussed selection, upgrading from MPhil to PhD, told stories of catastrophes and successes, and were self-critical. Some of them found it enormously rewarding, such as Professor Brande, a geographer from Hernchester, who expressed the task as follows:

> I think the most important thing you can do as a supervisor is to really give them a love – it sounds curious, that word, but I think it's the right word – for what they're doing, and a sort of motivation, because I think that research is a desperately lonely business.

Dr Gastineau, in development studies at Gossingham:

> DPhils are terrible things, and I don't yet know a DPhil student who didn't go through a financial crisis, a mental crisis, a supervisor crisis or an emotional crisis, that's why it's such an appalling system.

Dr Jelf at Eastchester, a social scientist described his ideal student:

> The ideal student will write regularly, be a good friend, won't mytho-logize the PhD as a lifework, will be a source of stimulus to your own work.

This book is intended to help supervisors to diagnose and deal with the crises and build good relationships with PhD students, so that Dr Jelf's ideal is more often obtained.

Conclusion

If the reader has recognized anything we have raised hitherto, then he or she will already be aware of the diverse issues that confront the contemporary academic, who must tackle the demanding intellectual and personal task of overseeing the development of graduate students. As we shall have reason to mention later in the book, the transition from undergraduate to postgraduate can imply major changes – not only in status, but in styles of work, intellectual problems, confidence and self-esteem. Likewise, the shift from undergraduate teaching to postgraduate supervision can imply similarly significant shifts in professional tasks and preoccupations. Neither undergraduate teaching nor postgraduate supervision comes 'naturally'. The latter is not simply a direct extension of one's own research activity either. It is an important aspect of academic work in its own right. It is, moreover, a key feature of academic departments and of most academics' core duties. The institutional organization of postgraduate work has been the subject of considerable attention in the UK in recent years. The research councils have encouraged more systematic attention to the quality of post-graduate provision, and the success of graduate students. The proper preparation of graduate students for their own research, and for their own future role as researchers and research supervisors, has been the topic of considerable debate and some degree of innovation in the UK: the introduction of masters degrees aimed at the transmission of research skills and methods is but one aspect of such policy reviews. The professionalization of higher degree work should have had a direct impact on academics' perceptions of this aspect of their professional role. Higher degree work cannot be based – even if it ever should have been – on *ad hoc* or implicit criteria, approached casually in the interstices of the working week. It demands and deserves to be treated seriously as a set of commitments and demands on a par with other teaching and scholarly activity. It is our ambition to make some contribution to the processes of reflection and personal development that will help the academic – whether experienced or novice – to approach such challenges and to reap the rewards that go with them.

2

Caught and held by a cobweb: getting the student started

a tortoise-shell butterfly, fluttered out into the brightness of the window, where it was caught and held by a cobweb.

(Sayers 1972: 10)

Introduction

It is hard to recognize how terrifying the new status of 'PhD student' can be for a person starting out. Even if the student has been an undergraduate in the same university, the role and status are new; if he or she is in a fresh department and university then everything is strange. The supervisor has to ensure that the students get started academically, find their feet in the institution and adjust to the status.

This chapter has four sections. First, it deals with setting up productive working relationships with the students; then with what are reasonable expectations for you to have of them and vice versa; then it addresses some common problems that arise in the first few months of a candidature; finally, it addresses two 'unspeakable' issues, sex and lies.

'Managing' your supervisees

Having a reasonable experience with higher degree students is dependent on the relationship with you, and, if there are any, with the other supervisor(s). You need to sort out a good working relationship with your supervisee. Relationships have to be worked at, and discussed, because most of the problems stem from a failure to set out the expectations both parties have for the relationship, agree them or agree to disagree. A few supervisions devoted to discussing the best ways to work together will not be wasted. As the needs of the student will change over time, the ground rules of the relationship may need to be renegotiated periodically, but it is most important to set up guidelines early on so the student knows what to do, and how to work with you. Consider these three vignettes of different 'management' and relationship problems, brought to a university staff development workshop.

Vignette C: Dependency clash in French

Dr Benita Melchette introduces a different problem, over-dependency. Heidi Hayhoe is doing an MPhil thesis on the *Tel Quel* group. Every week she sees her supervisor, Dr Benita Melchette, and says: 'What shall I do now?' Benita reports that this makes her cross: Heidi seems feeble, and it is her thesis, not Benita's. Benita reports that she keeps saying, 'It's your thesis – what do *you* think you should do next?' But this is not helping to get Heidi to be more independent.

Vignette D: Control clash in the business school

Professor Thorkjeld Svenson reports the reverse problem: over-independence. Ben Proble is clear about what he wants to do (a re-evaluation of the 1965 'new philosophy of management' initiative at Shell UK) and what methods to use. He wants his supervisor – Professor Thorkjeld Svenson – only to point him at any literature he's missed, and read his draft thesis. Ben would be quite happy to have only one or two meetings a year. Thorkjeld wants a weekly meeting, and wants to oversee all the stages of Ben's PhD. He is an experienced supervisor, but feels puzzled by Ben's resistance to 'proper' supervision.

Vignette E: Clash of personal styles in biochemistry

Dr Wilfred Pomfret says he does not know why he has been sent on the course, but he has one annoying student, Humphrey Quint. Humphrey and Wilfred agree about the theory and method of Humphrey's thesis (he is working on photo-phosphorylation), but have a clash of personal styles. It becomes clear as Wilfred talks that Humphrey is very well organized – 10 minutes early for meetings, with a clear agenda for supervisions and a timetable for his thesis work, and he keeps to his schedules. You spot that Wilfred is a charming, but casual, person. He has usually lost his diary, he forgets things and lurches from one forgotten appointment to the next. Wilfred says he is always in the lab, but hates being interrupted by the doctoral students while he is working. You can see that when he *does* meet

> Humphrey, Wilfred could be inspiring, but he reports cheerfully that he has now broken three appointments with Humphrey (no supervision for eight weeks) *and* he has lost the draft chapter of Humphrey's thesis he's had for three months. Wilfred did not want to be at this workshop, and he recounts his problem as one of Humphrey being a 'fusspot'. You can see Wilfred would be a maddening supervisor.

In each of these vignettes, we can see that the parties have never sorted out the basics of the relationship. In this chapter we set out guidelines for making explicit how the relationship is going to work, to try to avoid such clashes and misunderstandings.

A good starting point is to get hold of Phillips and Pugh's (1994) *How to Get a PhD* (2nd edn) and read Chapter 8 yourself; and Cryer's (1996) *The Research Student's Guide to Success*, and read Chapter 6. Then get your student to read them, and then devote part of a supervision to discussing them. Because they are student-centred books you may find them offensive, but this makes an excellent basis for sorting out how you and your student will work together. Cryer includes the responsibilities of supervisors according to the National Postgraduate Committee (p. 59).

It is easy to forget that students may not know what a PhD *is*. Colin Ives, an anthropology student, confessed to Odette that:

> A lot of mistakes I've made are the result of me not asking questions and people not putting me right – they presume I must know ... I didn't know the PhD was meant to be an argument, as Dr Durtham said, it's meant to say something. I thought it was meant to be one of those old-fashioned monographs, a collection of information. When I was an undergraduate I used to think a PhD was one of those articles you get in *Man* or something, a 10,000 word article, I used to think 'they must be PhDs'.

Colin discovered what a PhD was, not by reading some in the Kingford library but:

> I just happened to be reading a book, the prospectus, one day, and saw 100,000 words and thought 'That's really long', and nobody bothered to tell me, and nobody has told me.

Note that Colin did not *ask* about thesis length, but waited to be told by 'someone'. He had not read any recent theses in the library, or been briefed on the requirements. He was in his third year when we interviewed him.

The growth of taught courses for doctoral students may reduce the number of students like Colin, but only if the course includes some very explicit coverage of very basic 'facts'. Our experience is that students like

Colin who most need explicit coverage of basic issues, like length, structure and function of the thesis, are most resistant to taught components, regarding them as 'irrelevant' to their own individual project. A wise department makes sure that some basic material is covered in a course, that a document with fundamentals is issued to all students and that a supervisor also deals with them. Similarly, supervisors who wish to survive their careers unscathed by appeals and complaints will ensure that their students have, and are urged to read, the formal rules governing the degree for which they are registered. However, this does not ensure that students hear, far less that they understand, what is covered.

Example 2.1: Marie Morisot and the failed upgrade

Marie Morisot had done a taught masters in the department, on a part-time basis, including a 20,000 word thesis. The department policy is to register such candidates initially for an MPhil. When she applied to be upgraded to a doctoral candidature two years later, she was refused. At this stage Marie complained that she had never received decent supervision, that her supervisor had never explained the difference between an MPhil and a PhD, that she had never known what was required for either and that no one had ever told her that she needed to develop a theoretical perspective. Because our department runs a course for MPhil and PhD students, taught twice a year, first in the daytime for new full-time people, and then in the evenings for the part-timers of all years, at which handouts are issued, including the university's formal documentation, and because Marie had attended it, we were able to say formally that those complaints were unjustified.

What follow are, first, some guidelines for a good relationship and, second, reasonable expectations, which may prevent you discovering after several years that you have a Colin Ives on your hands.

Guidelines for a good relationship

Discuss with the supervisee how the two of you will work, separately and together. Explain how you like to work with your PhD students, and see if they are going to be able to fit in. If they seem recalcitrant, find out why, and reach a compromise.

The best time of day to meet

Are they morning people or night owls? Which are you? Would 7.00 a.m. be a good time? Would 6.00 p.m. be better? Resolving this will enable you to discover their biorhythms – watch their faces when you suggest 7.00 a.m. – and their domestic circumstances. If there is a new baby, a crack-addict teenage child or an elderly parent to be cared for, you need to know, so that you can plan realistic meetings. Similarly, if your student is circuit training twice a day, or too hungover to focus before lunch, or coaching A level candidates every evening, you need to know that too. In the end you and the student need to find a regular slot, at a time of day when you are both awake and alert, so you can supervise the student. If you are a morning person, and the student only wakes up after dark, then an alternating slot may be the best compromise: one week you are awake and the student is not, the next you are flagging but the student is bright eyed and alert.

Example 2.2: John Cavendish

Sara had a part-time MPhil student called John Cavendish, who was the head of a rural primary school fifty miles from Cardiff. John's wife, Mary, was a member of the Welsh women's netball squad. They had two small children. Supervisions were fixed to take place on Saturdays when the netball squad had training. The Cavendish family drove to Cardiff, left the children with their grandmother, and separated for John's supervision and Mary's squad training. This worked perfectly well: John got his MPhil.

Scheduling the meetings

Initially a new student needs a weekly meeting, even if it is brief, because it is too easy for a novice to drift. However, it is sensible to discuss, probably termly, whether the meeting schedule is meeting both your needs. A longer gap may not be harmful, but given that there are inevitably periods when you are not available, about thirty supervisions a year is a sensible target. If you are not going to have a regular, timetabled slot, then the issue that must be settled is: who will set up meetings; and if it is the student, *how*? If you are senior and have a secretary, does the student see her or him to fix a supervision? If not, does the student bang on your door? Leave you a note? Phone you at home?

These may seem pathetic questions, but students cannot know how to arrange to see you unless you explain and set the rules. It is all too easy for a student to drift, hoping to catch you in the corridor, when he or she really needs a supervision. The following comment, made by a man doing a PhD, is not unusual:

> Four tutors have supervised my study. Supervisor No. 1 left to take up an appointment overseas after one year. Supervisor No. 2 left to take up an appointment elsewhere after one year. Both were extremely

busy men. As a part-time student I was loath to take up their time. When writing or telephoning for infrequent appointments I seemed to be in rather the same position as a National Health hypochondriac with ingrowing toenails pestering a neurosurgeon. I'm sure the supervisors did not intend it to be so.

(Jimmy Thesiger, a PhD student in Education)

An agenda

It is an excellent idea to have an agenda for supervisions, agreed in advance. It is important, though, to decide who decides the agenda. Here the sensible answer is probably both of you. Sometimes you need to set it: to say clearly: 'Next week, please bring X and we'll discuss it.' At other times, the student needs to set it, so you ask 'what do you want to focus on next time?' and then follow the agreed agenda.

Mechanics: confirmation and cancellation

One of the worst things about supervision is the broken engagement. For a supervisor, a 'no-show' student is absolutely maddening, especially at 7.30 or 8.00 at night. For a student, the 'vanished', absent supervisor is simply horrid, especially if the student is a part-timer who has travelled into the university at some cost and expense. All supervisor–student pairs need firm arrangements written down, and clear cancellation arrangements. Undergraduates may never have needed an appointments diary; as a doctoral student they do. You may need to recommend buying an academic year diary, carrying it and entering appointments. The one produced by the *Times Higher Education Supplement*, which has lots of useful addresses in it, would be a good buy, and you can recommend it to them when the annual advertisement appears. Once they have a diary, and the habit of entering meetings, you can *negotiate* the mechanics of confirming and, when necessary, cancelling and rescheduling meetings.

Example 2.3: Paul's confirmation policy

Paul has a clear confirmation policy with all part-time higher degree students. They phone Paul's home the evening before the supervision appointment to confirm it. This has two functions. If Paul has to cancel, he can do so, rearrange the meeting and deal with any immediate problems on the phone. If the student cannot attend, he or she can cancel, reschedule and seek telephone help. If the supervision is confirmed, both Paul and the student explicitly remind each other they are going to meet. This means both turn up, and if either has to prepare, there are still a few hours before the actual supervision to do so.

When such arrangements are not made, there can be confusion and bad feeling over broken or missed appointments. Sometimes, however, a more complicated cancellation arrangement is needed.

Example 2.4: Cynthia Murdoch

Sara had Cynthia Murdoch to supervise for a 20,000 word thesis. Cynthia lived 50 miles (80 kilometres) from Cardiff, where Sara works, and had a full-time job. The supervisions were scheduled for 7.00 p.m. Frequently Cynthia got stuck in the traffic on the Severn Bridge and it was 8.00 p.m. before she got into Wales at all, and she was still 20 miles from Cardiff. After several frustrating missed encounters, Cynthia and Sara agreed that if Cynthia had not arrived by 7.30 Sara would go home, assuming Cynthia was not able to reach Cardiff. Equally, if Cynthia could see that she would be more than 30 minutes late she would either give up and go home or phone from a call box to give her new arrival time. Cynthia got her MScEcon.

The annual cycle

What is your annual, termly, weekly, cycle like – when will you be free to concentrate on them? Research students cannot be expected to know, unless you explain, that when you have a research council grant application to prepare, or a hundred exam scripts to mark, or a major conference paper to write, you have less time and attention for them. A few minutes explaining what the pressures and deadlines in your annual cycle are always pays. Make sure they know when your busy times are, and set up the formal, longer meetings for the quieter periods. Learning about deadlines for grant applications, conferences, marking and examining is an important part of their socialization, so explaining your annual cycle is not only sensible, it counts as part of their training. A discussion of your annual cycle should also help them to plan theirs, so they do not book their holiday for the same week you need them for intensive supervision.

Mutual availability

Sort out a timetable of the first term, first year and whole thesis period – check mutual availability. It's no good them relying on you, the supervisor, reading 50,000 words in July if you are going to be in Australia then. It is particularly important to be open about long absences – maternity leave, sabbaticals, field trips – and serious disruptions, like being head of department or dealing with the A level results and admissions in August. Then, if the student is worried about not being supervised, you can agree to set up telephone or postal supervision, or bring in a second supervisor, or set up a support system for your absence.

Expectations for the relationship

Try to be as explicit as you can about what you hope to provide for the supervisee: methodological help, advice on the literature search, theoretical ideas, help with computing, visits during foreign fieldwork, debugging of equipment, practical tips, good references when they are applying for jobs, or tea and sympathy. If possible, try to be equally explicit about what you cannot, or will not, provide. If you are acutely aware that your computing skills are inadequate, say so, and promise to help the student to find the computing skills and advice he or she needs from elsewhere. If you are ignorant of the academic literature on a topic, the student needs to know how to seek help from a colleague to make up for your ignorance. If you hate conferences, do not go to them and cannot put students in contact with networks in the discipline, they need to appreciate your efforts to despatch them with your colleagues to make this up to them.

During the research project, Odette interviewed a woman who expected very close, friendly relationships with doctoral students. Dr Challoner, at Tolleshurst, described her intensely 'personal' supervisory style as follows:

> All my students come over for dinner, they know us as individuals and as a family. Eunice, who comes from Canada, has spent two Christmases with us. Bill, who was a Zambian student, his grant ran out and he had nowhere to live so he lived with us for six months to finish. So I guess my style is different.

This struck Sara very forcibly, because she finds it hard to combine personal friendship with supervision.

Example 2.5: Evelyn Howard and Rita Vandemeyer

Evelyn and Rita were both overseas students funded to do PhDs with Sara. She explained to both of them that they would need to make friends in Cardiff, because she did not mix socially with graduate students, preferring a professional, academic relationship. Evelyn found a circle of women active in local green campaigns, and shared a flat with one of them, so she soon had a full social life in Cardiff. She completed her PhD. Rita found it hard to make friends, stayed in a university room she disliked, and withdrew after eighteen months.

It is particularly important to have clear expectations about the students' writing, and to communicate them to the students. Be clear about when written work is expected, when they will get it back and the sorts of help you will give with it. This is particularly important with students whose first language is not English. If you are not prepared to correct grammar, stylistics and spelling, then the students need to know this early on, and you need to steer them to a source of help. Losing student work is unforgivable. Keeping it for weeks is nearly so. If you *know* these are faults of yours then stress that they must *always* keep back-up copies, and the two of you must work on scheduling you enough time to read, comment on and return what written work they hand in.

Example 2.6: Alfred Inglethorp

Alfred was a PhD student of Prof. Bauerstein and had given him a thesis draft in January 1975. In January 1976, he came to see Sara to say Prof. Bauerstein had not read it, admitted he had not read it, claimed to be 'too busy' to read it for the foreseeable future and was not sure where it was in his office so could not return it. Alfred's employer wanted to know when he was planning to submit his PhD, Alfred wanted to revise his draft with supervisory advice and was in despair. Sara suggested that Alfred wrote a polite note to Prof. Bauerstein pointing out that he had had the draft for twelve months, which was unacceptable, and that Alfred made an appointment with the head of department, ostensibly to ask him to explain the problem to Alfred's employer. Alfred saw the head of department and discovered that most of Prof. Bauerstein's students had been ahead of him with the same complaint. The head of department appointed new supervisors for all Prof. Bauerstein's candidates; Professor Bauerstein resigned his university post; Alfred submitted, and got his PhD.

Keeping a written record of the supervisory experience signals that you have high expectations of it: that you expect it to last. Keep an agreed record of decisions you have both taken, and make sure you keep a copy in your files. This is particularly valuable if you are ill, or on sabbatical, or away for any reason, and a substitute supervisor has to be involved. It is also invaluable if you end up involved in an appeal or other legal/disciplinary proceedings. It will also help students when they write up the thesis, because key decisions will be 'minuted', in your files and in theirs.

The supervisor will, depending on the discipline, probably hope that the student will generate publishable findings. It is also useful to decide what will happen about publications by the students (whose name goes first etc.) early on, long before there *are* any publications. In humanities and social sciences it is not usual for research students to publish much before submission; nor is it usual for the supervisor to be included as an author on conference papers, or publications before or after submission of the thesis. However, in science and technology, where joint publication is much more common, the students need to be made aware of the conventions of the discipline, the laboratory and the research group. If the custom of the lab is that *all* publications carry the professor's name, and the supervisor's, the sooner the students understand that, and the reason for it, the better. Sorting out this issue allows you to set out the expectations that the students will finish, will produce publishable work and will succeed, and to explain the politics of publication for the individual, the research group and the department.

Example 2.7: Dr Hersheimmer

Paul and Sara were sitting at lunch in the Cardiff staff club with scientists from several departments. One of them pointed across the room to a man, Dr Hersheimmer, eating alone. 'Dr H is too ethical for his own good. He is really gifted, but he doesn't publish enough. He won't put his name on his students' papers – insists they publish on their own. It's killed his career.'

If you work in a discipline where such a comment could be made, it is important that your students know this from the outset.

Expectations: reasonable and mutual

The more you sort out your expectations, the better the relationship is likely to be. As part of the negotiations of a relationship, you have a right to set out your expectations for student conduct. Figure 2.1 sets out a number of such expectations, which might form the basis of an explicit departmental code of practice. If you are not doing the things in Figure 2.1, your students will have legitimate grounds for complaint.

Praise and criticism

In the early stages of a supervisory relationship it is very easy to destroy a student's self-confidence by criticism, or to give him or her a false sense of security by too much praise. Students can expect an evaluation of their progress, constructive criticism, and advice and reference to others for some kinds of help (e.g. a specific method, a particular theory). Because criticism always hurts, it is important to discuss how necessary it will be for you to criticize them, how you will try to be constructive and how you will try to praise their successes too. Using some examples of how you have been constructively criticized in your career is often helpful.

In the next section some of the problems supervisors and students face when starting out on a new candidature are discussed.

Figure 2.1: Reasonable expectations

A supervisor can expect a PhD student to:

1 Turn up to appointments, prepared for them.
2 Write regularly, and share the draft material.
3 Tell the truth about work done and not done.
4 Keep in touch – socially, practically (holidays, sickness, change of address etc.) and academically.
5 Most importantly, do the research tasks that have been mutually agreed and scheduled.

In return, students can have expectations for their supervisors:

1 Regular supervision. A reasonable student can expect to see his or her supervisor twenty to thirty times a year (if full-time), for a private, one-to-one discussion of the research.
2 Written feedback. A student can expect to have draft material read, and returned with *written* comments in a reasonable time.

Problems and difficulties in the starting out phase

There are several sources of problems in the starting out phase. These include those owing to the inexperienced supervisor, the inexperienced student and the failure to get the relationship going. It is important to remember that for many students doing a higher degree involves them in structuring their *own* work for the first time in their life (Hockey 1994b). Most have come from school, where their time and their curricula were very largely structured by teachers (and parents), to an undergraduate degree, where time is organized and deadlines are quite short. The full-time student suddenly has an unlimited time horizon, and a task of overwhelming and unknown complexity. The part-time student has to find time in a life that is probably full anyway, and schedule the academic task. Encourage your students to read Chapter 4 of Cryer (1996) on 'settling in'.

One of the biggest problems is that many supervisors are inexperienced (Hockey 1994a). Dr Morrow, a social scientist at Boarbridge, described her early inexperience – 'so six months after I'd arrived I was supervising three people which I found deeply terrifying' – in order to contrast it with her current expertise, by the time of our research. In most British universities there are no requirements that supervisors are trained, or that they learn to supervise by doing so jointly. Dr Morrow's experience – she got a lectureship in geography and was immediately allocated three doctoral students – is common in arts and social sciences. In science and technology the new supervisor has almost certainly been helping doctoral students

throughout her career as postdoc, and is more likely to slide smoothly into
the role.

If you are a new supervisor it is worth asking if your university has a
training course, and if not, applying to be sent on one elsewhere. Failing
that, a discussion with a popular or successful supervisor in your department, or a meeting of younger staff over lunch to discuss tactics, should
help you to get started.

The vital thing to recognize is that new students will, inevitably, flounder
in the first weeks, and it is the supervisor's job to give them some tasks,
guidelines and activities. Dr Morrow had learnt that this was an important
role for the supervisor, and by the time of her interview she was much
more confident in her supervisory skills:

> when the student starts they feel very lost and lonely . . . poor students
> with a desk and a filing cabinet, and they were sitting there looking
> at it and what were they supposed to do next? So I'd always try to give
> them something to do – read certain articles, review them in written
> form. And that's something I know about myself, I'm not very good
> at commenting on verbal discussions – I need something in writing,
> however scrappy. Then having got some flavour of how they work and
> where they were at, I would try to set various projects for a term's
> duration.

In this way, Dr Morrow aims to respond to the individual student, but also
to set up a framework. Similarly, Dr Palinode, lecturer at Portminster in
an applied social science, described his own PhD experience at Boarbridge:
'I know supervision is always problematic, it's a problematic relationship,
but the quality of supervision I had at Boarbridge I didn't think was very
good at all.' Dr Palinode's use of 'quality' here does not seem to depend
on special connotations of quality assurance and the like. It seemed to
reflect more the lack of attention and lack of direction he had experienced as a doctoral student. He stressed that he had been lost and isolated, especially in the early days of his doctoral experience:

> I think you need to be able to talk to a breadth of people who are not
> necessarily close to your subject but understand generally, and can
> give information that can help, rather than being in the lost position
> I was . . . But the first day you arrive, there you are with a blank desk
> and you think 'what do I do now?' And I spent the first six months
> deciding what I was going to do . . . I think it's quite important to be
> settled in, and for people to help you early on. I think the doctoral
> programme, although you can't see it at the time, is quite useful – it
> depends – it could be argued that you should do a year's research,
> understand the processes of doing it and then do a research meth-
> odology programme, and then do the PhD.

Dr Meade, now on the staff at Boarbridge, claimed that when she did her doctorate there several years before, 'when I was doing mine it was very much being thrown in at the deep end . . . it was a jump from undergraduate work. I started off with one supervisor here – excellent academically but in fact just let me carry on in my own sweet way.' Similarly, a lecturer in artificial intelligence at Illington, Dr Panthing, said he began with a total lack of knowledge of what a British doctorate should be:

> I would say also I did not have a clear idea of what a PhD was . . . I had not read enough of them . . . I never had a clear, I don't think I had a clearly focused problem . . . I was always sort of exploring a lot of things, and I didn't have a clear question in mind that I was attempting to find the answer to . . . I think in effect I probably had about enough work for two PhDs.

He juxtaposed that past lack of understanding with the experience he has today, as a supervisor. Dr Panthing says of his work with doctoral students: 'I try and help them firmly identify a problem, explain to them that their research field is a life-time occupation, but the PhD is just a milestone and should be focused. Get it done, get it over with, and move on.' This is a typical contrast between the lecturer's own past biography, when no proper guidance was provided, and his own supervisory role, offering proper advice and support.

It is easy to think that a bright, high achieving, undergraduate will become a bright, high achieving, doctoral student by magic. A department's concern to attract good students, and the limited choices open to doctoral candidates, may have unintended consequences:

> the 3rd year undergraduate cannot be expected to know how anxious many departments are to attract good students and that this sometimes leads them to give too rosy a picture of their ability to ensure that a student working in a particular area will have the necessary facilities and be supervised by someone with sufficient knowledge in the field.
>
> (Rudd 1985: 64)

Certainly we found, in more than one case, that students who had been 'high flying' undergraduates were not necessarily suited to exigencies of doctoral research. The following account, provided by a home recruit whose registration period had elapsed, suggests that self-recruitment is not without its own risks: 'I was a star pupil in my [undergraduate] year, and I think that has a bearing upon my difficulties because I'd always been able to do it and everybody thought I'd be able to carry on like that.' The following comments from doctoral students, the first four interviewed by Odette Parry in the early 1990s, the fifth writing for Eggleston and Delamont (1983) in the early 1980s, reveal how unsettled new doctoral students can be.

Ben Safford described his first months as an unsettling experience: 'the whole thing seems very daunting, you don't know where your niche is, or if there is one for you.' Bryan Faul said, 'I suppose I expected a lot more structure', and Nick Minakis commented, 'you tend to be thrown in at the deep end' echoing generations of his predecessors. Laurence Fournier, a third year, captured the student's dilemma: 'a lot of them have the idea of being suspended between a student who just absorbs things, and an academic who produces it, and that suspension gives them all kinds of paranoias and neuroses – suspended between these two slots.'

Finally in this section, we offer a long extract from a written response to an enquiry about postgraduate problems. Michael Seaton was a doctoral student in education responding anonymously to a request from BERA:

Working in isolation in comparison with the situation as an under-graduate. This was a problem I was not remotely equipped to deal with because as an undergraduate I had worked alone whenever possible, always choosing dissertation work in preference to lecture courses, and thrived on it. I obviously failed to realize how important I had found being part of a group, both in terms of exchange of ideas and for reasons of 'ego' or morale – affirmation that my work and ideas were acceptable or even good, recognition that when I didn't understand something nor did a lot of people. The second big problem was my expectations of myself. I find it impossible now to work for hours every day, to make a real onslaught on the work as I used to when an undergraduate. This caused me weeks of total panic, a feeling that I had completely lost my ability to work. I think I have gone some way towards realizing that this is due to the different nature of the work, but it is a recurring problem and still some-times seems overwhelming. I was not at all prepared to solve this problem and I had worked extremely hard as an undergraduate and thoroughly enjoyed doing so. I am working towards solving it by con-gratulating myself when I work a five-hour day rather than feeling a failure because it isn't twelve hours. This 'psychological' approach doesn't always work! Another problem is a feeling of insecurity in academic terms due to carrying out research which is supervised and will be examined in a department (or part of one) in which the discipline (history) is different from that in which I did my first degree (sociology and education). I am rather nervous that this leaves me particularly vulnerable to attack.

A more practical problem than all of these was the initially enorm-ous one of how to actually go about carrying out a piece of [histor-ical] research. This problem related not to the research topic, how to develop it etc., nor to any profound theoretical or methodological problems, but extremely simple things like, well where do I go, what do I look at? The only way to describe this adequately is that for the first few desperate weeks I felt I wanted someone to say, look, next week take the number ten bus and do ... [whatever]. My supervisor and other members of the department were always helpful and friendly, offering constructive advice, but *never* on that level. I felt nobody remembered the experience of not actually knowing 'how to do research'. Of course one can't be spoon fed, in fact I probably seek minimum guidance from my supervisor, but I do feel that some sort of 'Idiots Guide to Starting Research', either written or verbal, would have been a great help in that initial period.

These are all problems which I sometimes feel are solved and which at other times threaten to drive me to navvying as an alternative! The biggest help is the knowledge that most research students feel the same way. I sought help mainly from friends and from lecturers I knew well from my first university: simply because I didn't want to 'impress' my supervisor – who is always, sympathetic and helpful – with my obvious stupidity!

Confidence-building and confidence tricks

No matter how able the student, there are times, especially in the early periods of the research, when the supervisor may have to build and support the student's self-confidence. Indeed, in many cases, the supervisor's main task is to reassure and motivate the student rather than supplying detailed advice on the content of the thesis itself.

Imagine yourself in a staff discussion of postgraduates and hearing about the case in Vignette F.

Vignette F: A lack of self-confidence

Dr Jamie Smuth, from the English department, tells the group about his student Mirelle Feldster, who began a PhD with him six months ago, to do a study of gothic influences in the fictional work of Winifred Holtby. Dr Jamie Smuth has just told her to redraft the chapter that she had been working on for four months – on Holtby's war service and the literature of the First World War. Mirelle wept and ran out of the room. Dr Smuth was paralysed with embarrassment, had no idea of what to do or say, but discovered from another student that Mirelle is under the impression that he thinks she is incapable of the level of work needed for a PhD. She believes that she is probably not clever enough to do a PhD, and keeps worrying that she is not doing the right things. In fact Jamie is excited about Mirelle's work, and thinks she is perfectly capable, but does not know what to do next.

Jamie Smuth obviously needs to signal more clearly the nature of his criticisms: he needs to find ways to separate his comments about this particular piece of work from any negative estimations of his student's general abilities or the nature of her chosen project. He also needs to make more clear the general standards or criteria he is adopting. A student needs to know that searching comments that are based on the highest possible standards of scholarlship, intended to bring the student's own work up to that very high level, are not intended to imply that he or she is entirely incompetent and 'not up to it'.

It is hard to realize how insecure many students are about their own potential to achieve higher degree standards. It is enormously easy to destroy their fragile self-confidence and perhaps to demoralize them. Vignette F is a dramatic one, but not impossibly so, as Example 2.8 shows.

Example 2.8: Owen Griffith

Owen Griffith was a PhD student of Lucien Bex. One day, Meredith Crale, a PhD student of Paul's, found Owen in the men's lavatory, ripping up his thesis draft and burning it in the handbasin, strip by strip. Owen had decided, after a supervision in which Prof. Bex had criticized one of his chapters, that he might as well destroy his work and 'pack it all in'. Meredith seized the remaining draft by force and took it to Paul's office for safe keeping. Paul found Prof. Bex and persuaded him that Owen was in need of either an explicit recommendation to withdraw, or an equally explicit statement that he really was capable of a PhD and that this weak draft was only that. Prof. Bex had had no idea that Owen was so vulnerable.

The experienced, successful supervisor knows that there are times when the student must be told that the work is fine and that he or she is doing well, because it *is* fine for that stage of the registration and the student must move ahead. Criticism, even unvarnished realism, can at such points demoralize and demotivate. The American sociologist Harvey Sacks once pointed out that in everyday life 'everyone has to lie'. Tact and reasonable behaviour dictate that we do not always tell the whole truth. In that sense, supervisors often have to 'lie'. You may be fortunate enough always to supervise students of outstanding ability, whose work never falters, and who never lose momentum or suffer from any doubts. In such circumstances, there is no need for careful management of the stark truth, perhaps. In many cases, however, there is need for a more strategic management of advice and criticism. Judicious 'white lies' will allow the student to move on, and if he or she is really any good, he or she will see that more needs doing later. (We return to the development of academic judgement and insight in Chapter 7.) We are not suggesting that the supervisor should blindly encourage students whose work is clearly inadequate, or who are heading in quite the wrong direction. Clearly, such delusion is in no one's interests, and misdirected work needs to be aborted at the earliest opportunity. Equally, no supervisor should express totally inappropriate approval for work that is clearly below par. But advice and criticism need to be managed in order to encourage the competent student to develop sufficient self-confidence to embark on and sustain several years of demanding, independent work. The wise supervisor will cultivate phrases such as 'I'm very pleased with this', 'This is coming along well' or 'This is an excellent basis for the PhD', which are unambiguously favourable, but omit the qualification 'for a person in the first six months', or 'when it has been revised six or eight times'. The sensitive supervisor will realize that, at the wrong time, thoroughgoing and detailed criticism of work in progress can undermine the student and bring the progress to a dead stop. Most students, like most academics, need to have their self-esteem supported: supervisors need to cultivate skills of confidence-boosting. Failure to do so can damage the working relationship and hold up progress.

We are not advocating an abandonment of critical standards in supervisors. As we have suggested, purblind enthusiasm for anything and everything, however poor, is clearly inappropriate. But students need the clear and supportive endorsement of their supervisor, who in turn needs to be able to distinguish between authoritativeness, even assertiveness, and damagingly negative criticism. Students need to be given 'permission' to embark on their research, while guidance and evaluation need to be applied with a careful touch. One needs to bear in mind that even the most able of students need reassurance about the quality of their work, and that if they do not get it, they are unlikely to progress. (The same applies to most of one's academic colleagues, of course.)

Sizing up the student: cue-consciousness and the supervisor

There is one further issue that the good supervisor may wish to address early on in the relationship. That is, sizing up whether the student is 'cue-conscious' or 'cue-deaf'. These terms derive from research on final year law students studied by Miller and Parlett (1976), adapted by Eggleston and Delamont (1983) for higher degree students in education. Miller and Parlett divided the law students into three types: 'cue-seekers', 'cue-conscious' and 'cue-deaf'. The cue-seekers were the fewest in number, and they 'deliberately interacted with the system'. In other words, they asked staff about the form and content of their examinations, they found out who the external examiners were and what they specialized in, and they set out to impress the lecturers with their ability and level of interest. The 'cue-conscious' were alert to hints about assessment, but took no active steps to acquire such organizational knowledge. The 'cue-deaf' did not believe that impressing staff was relevant, nor did they hear cues when given out. They believed that hard work and virtue were rewarded. The cue-deaf tried to 'revise everything' because they had not heard any of the guidance about selectivity and did not trust themselves to 'spot' topics. The cue-seekers used the data they had amassed to inform very selective revision strategies. So, for example, a cue-conscious student would look at past papers, and then say to a lecturer, 'Regina *v* McKay hasn't come up for several years, has it?', to try to test whether it was worth swotting up that case. The cue-seekers were disproportionately successful in getting first class degrees.

Eggleston and Delamont (1983: 39–45) used the same threefold categorization to characterize research students surveyed for BERA. Twenty-one of 84 respondents were classified as cue-deaf about the examination of their degree. We have already quoted the example of an extremely cue-deaf research student, Colin Ives, earlier in this chapter. We shall return to the appropriate ways to handle the cue-deaf student in later chapters. Here we wish to stress that it is useful to decide quite early on whether a new postgraduate student is at the cue-seeking or cue-deaf end of the spectrum, because if she or he *is* cue-deaf then the supervisor may need to make many aspects of the whole higher degree period more explicit than might otherwise be necessary. These personal or intellectual styles are not absolute differences, and do not have to be thought of rigidly as if they represented personality types. But they capture some differences that can have far-reaching consequences for how students approach their work and how a supervisor needs to work with them. Just as the anxious student, or one whose self-esteem is fragile, needs careful encouragement, so the relatively cue-deaf student may need to have things spelled out rather more explicitly than might otherwise be the case. A failure to appreciate the nature of cue-deaf student styles can lead to misunderstanding and frustration on both sides. The supervisor may assume that a student will have 'picked up' what he or she needs to know about procedures, obligations and so on; the student may fail to do so, and may feel aggrieved if the supervisor did not explain things with sufficient clarity.

Personal and working relationships

The relationship between a higher degree student and his or her supervisor can take many forms. We have already suggested that it is necessary to establish clear, productive and mutually convenient arrangements for the supervision. Without a firm basis for everyday work, supervision is likely to become frustrating and difficult for all parties. Beyond that, the degree of personal commitment is likely to depend on personality and the nature of group dynamics in the research group, the department or the faculty. Some research students and their supervisors establish close collaborative relationships, and personal friendships, that may last for many years after the higher degree itself has been completed. Indeed, the networks and invisible colleges that characterize a great deal of academic work are often formed on the basis of such relationships. The stream of higher degree students you supervise, the research groups you may build around you, can form the basis of long-term collaborative arrangements. Those networks are part of the successful academic's 'cultural capital'. Such relationships and their value are not confined solely to the academic world. Research students from industry, public sector agencies and so on can also be extremely important members of the research network – again, providing opportunities for further collaboration, research access, professional advice and so on.

Active research groups, with a critical mass of higher degree students, postdocs and more senior academics, are more characteristic of the natural sciences than the humanities or social sciences. (We return to the issue of fostering research groups in Chapter 11.) Here it is worth noting that the existence of a formal research group – often vital in providing the right working environment in the laboratory disciplines – provides a framework for the promotion of more sociable and personal working relationships as well. The development of graduate schools and formal training provision in the humanities and social sciences may help to provide similar kinds of social environments. Nevertheless, in those latter disciplines, the higher degree student's work and progress are more likely to be based in more individualistic relationships with one or two academics.

In all cases, but especially when the supervision is based primarily on a one-to-one relationship, it is important to establish at an early stage whether it is 'working'. Crucially, if it is not working out productively, then remedial action needs to be taken as soon as possible. It is standard practice in contemporary quality systems for there to be an explicit procedure for a change of supervisor. Admittedly, in small departments, and with highly specialized research interests, this may not always be easy. But it is more useful to recognize and address problems at an early stage than to press on regardless and to ignore clashes of personality, working styles, intellectual orientations and the like. In the subsequent chapters of this book we shall be introducing a variety of 'problems' and their possible solutions, and we do not dwell on them here. It should, however, be possible for a student and her or his supervisor to address any identifiable problems and incompatabilities without blame or recrimination: it should be seen and handled as a practical issue concerning good working practices. A head of department, or director of graduate studies, or sub-dean, or whoever is responsible for such matters, should have procedures to hand, and should be empowered to intervene constructively.

It is clear from our interviews with students and supervisors that the degree of personal friendship and commitment varies enormously. Some supervisors keep their students at arm's length, and restrict themselves to formal relationships. Others enjoy and encourage greater degrees of friendship and intimacy.

That brings us to one potentially delicate set of issues: sex and the supervisor. It arises in a minority of cases, but it does arise nevertheless, and can crop up in three possible ways: sexual harassment, sexual relations between student and supervisor by consent and sex in the project.

Sexual harassment

In the BERA research, Eggleston and Delamont (1983) were told of one sexual harassment case by Geraldine Marsh, who wrote:

> My original supervisor has a reputation for making passes at female students. When this happened to me, I found offence was taken when I gave what the supervisor considered to be the wrong answers to his questions. The relationship grew worse, and I changed my supervisor.

In our experience, we have known one male lecturer who behaved in a way that distressed three women higher degree students, one of whom claimed that when she refused his advances he withdrew supervisory help. There can be misunderstandings in this area: men may not realize that their behaviour is harassing, especially if they are from a different culture, class or religion from the student. There is the occasional disturbed student who sees sexual harassment where none existed, or where none was intended. It is hard to be friendly, sociable and supportive in a relationship with a power dimension. In general, those who wish to avoid accusations of sexual harassment should never touch a student unless invited to, be very careful when telling jokes or using endearments, avoid asking about students' personal and emotional lives, and try to ensure that social events and travel together are chaperoned. The problems with sexual harassment overlap those of consensual sexual relationships with students.

Sex and the student

There is a power dimension to supervision which complicates the idea of any *consensual* sexual relationship between student and supervisor, either gay or straight. Our feeling is that if a sexual relationship develops the student ought to have another supervisor. The guidelines for doctors and patients are a useful model for supervisors who feel an intimate relationship developing.

Sex in the project

There can be problems if the project is about sex, and/or if the supervisor and student disagree about sexual issues. Phillida Salmon (1992: 115) recounts a case of the latter kind:

> Another student whom I undertook to supervise was an apparently pleasant and conscientious person who brought evidence of high academic ability. Nonetheless, there was something about his research approach which made me feel very uncomfortable. Unwisely, I ignored these feelings. It was not until we had been working together for two years that it became obvious that his interest in his young women subjects was a prurient one. At this point I withdrew from a supervisory role which I should never have taken on.

Issues of sexual conduct are merely extensions of the more general issues we have been alluding to. They concern the establishment – the negotiation – of appropriate expectations, boundaries and mutual obligations within the supervisory relationship. They also serve to underline how significant the relationship is between the higher degree student and the supervisor. It is not necessary to develop unduly intimate personal relationships in order to recognize that there is a strong element of mutual dependency inherent in the process of higher degree work. The student is often dependent on the supervisor, not just for the formal aspects of the research – such as access to research facilities, technical advice and specific oversight of the work – but also for a host of less visible things, such as personal support and confidence-building, personal contacts and network-building. The supervisor's task is often one of striking a series of balances, between involvement and detachment, between directing students' work and letting them have their head. We turn to some aspects of that 'delicate balance' in the chapter that follows.

3

The balance between tradition and progress: designing and planning a project

It is rather difficult for us of the older generation to hold the balance between tradition and progress – if it is progress.

(Sayers 1972: 44)

Introduction

The title of this chapter comes from Sayers but the theme is echoed in many of our interviews with social scientists and natural scientists in British universities and former polytechnics about their supervisory experiences with PhD students. Dr Crupiner, a geographer from Tolleshurst, told us: 'it causes a lot of angst to me creating a delicate balance between letting them do something which is their own and giving them a good topic.' This was the most succinct statement of one of the dilemmas facing the social science and natural science supervisors we studied between 1990 and 1993. Other academics constructed their accounts in terms of similar tensions and dilemmas. They described tensions and balances at every critical stage of the research process: not only topic choice, but also research design, data collection, analysis and text production. At all stages supervisors expressed a pull between their desire to exercise tight control and to allow the student the freedom that comes from non-interventionist supervision. The academic staff variously express the tensions and contradictions between the imposition of supervisory control, on the one hand, and the granting of licence to students to pursue their own ideas, on the other.

Dr Nuddington, a social scientist at Boarbridge, said he was much less directive than some of his colleagues:

I have colleagues who will lay out a very clear-cut routine for the student to stick to – I'm a little bit more casual than that. I don't

really believe in regimenting the students too much, because if I do
that I'll impose my will on them too strongly – it's supposed to be
their PhD, not mine.

For the natural scientists, who were more likely to have teams of doctoral students and 'postdocs' working on closely related problems around
a funded project, there was a tension between the individual thesis topics
and the overall research programme. As Professor Nankivell, a natural
scientist at Ottercombe, explained to us:

> In my mind I constantly try and weigh up the balance of supervision
> that is required and I've come to the conclusion that it depends on
> the individual, especially with my experience with the MSc person
> who needs his hand held all the time. Now I could have been really
> blunt with him and kicked him out but that wouldn't have benefited
> him but it would have benefited me because I would have got the
> research done that I had hoped, so I'm always balancing my own
> intentions, research in hand and trying to develop the individual's
> research skills, and I find it a difficult balance to strike.

The appropriate balance between organizing the PhD for students and
watching them sink or swim on their own has been altered by the policy
change. Today the funding bodies are imposing sanctions on institutions
whose students do not submit inside the time limits. This was leading
some of our respondents to report that they had altered their supervisory
pattern. One such was Dr Crupiner, a social scientist at Tolleshurst:

> Sometimes a PhD student doesn't want to see you because they want
> this to be their own stuff and there's always a dilemma about saying
> to a student, 'This is a great topic, this is what you should do', and
> I'm more inclined to do that these days because of the time limit,
> whereas in the past I'd avoid it. It's caused a lot of angst.

Similar views on the increasing pressure from ESRC and the difficulties of
the delicate balance can be seen in the interview with Dr Wishart, a social
scientist at Latchendon:

> the PhD programme should really be a marriage of your interests
> and the student's interests. You develop together. Now I'm conscious
> of the pressures that are coming from the ESRC to churn over PhDs
> in terms of three or four years, but I perceive the PhD as something
> that is essentially your starting point in a long career . . . As a super-
> visor I'm not saying 'You must produce Chapter One in four weeks,
> get them all done in ten months.' I much prefer to allow people to

choose their own pace and in a sense to me that's a part of the learning process of being a PhD student. I think it's a lonely existence for many but I think they have to push at the limits, they have to engage the supervisor. I can push them to a certain extent, I can say, 'OK, what have you been doing for the last two or three weeks?', but in the end I'm going to put barriers in their way and they're going to have to jump over those barriers. I'm not necessarily going to demonstrate how to jump over those barriers. Some are smarter than others in terms of how they proceed with the problems of jumping over those hoops. Others are less certain and need more direction, more of a helping hand.

What must be avoided is described from our interview with Dr Mincing, a natural scientist at Ottercombe, who described his own experience as a student:

> My supervisor . . . hadn't had any experience of PhD students before and he took on four at the same time. And we all sat there in his room for the first year virtually doing nothing, twiddling our thumbs and accomplishing very little indeed.

This chapter is about helping students and supervisors away from 'thumb twiddling' and towards making a productive start on research design and the production of the thesis. If the student has courses to attend, then discussing the content of these, and any written or oral assessment requirements associated with them, provides a ready-made agenda for early supervisions. Going over the course content will serve three functions. First, it enables the supervisor to check that the student is actually attending the classes! Second, it gives the supervisor an idea of the content of the courses and how far they are relevant to the individual student. Third, the candidate's response to the courses will be revealing about the student's strengths and weaknesses: if he or she sees all discussions of ethics as irrelevant, or rejects all coverage of methods other than the one he or she has chosen, then the supervisor has to widen his or her focus.

A checklist for early supervisions

The following issues are sensible ones to focus on in early supervisions, when you are overseeing the students' early days. In the handout we use in Cardiff we state that when choosing a thesis topic, 'There are six main criteria to bear in mind, and you should discuss your topic, bearing all six criteria in mind, with your supervisor as soon as s/he is allocated to you.'

Figure 3.1: Proposed timetable for social science PhD programme (specimen, faulty, timetable for a survey of health workers)

	1997	1998						1999						2000				
	OCT	DEC	FEB	APR	JUN	AUG	OCT	DEC	FEB	APR	JUN	AUG	OCT	DEC	FEB	APR	JUN	AUG

1 Literature review

2 Establish contacts with community, identify social and health services, community workers

3 Prepare pilot questionnaire:
(1) Design
(2) Translation
(3) Pre-test
(4) Administer

4 Main research:
(1) Refine questionnaire
(2) Organize fieldwork
(3) Administer
(4) Editing and coding
(5) Computer analysis

5 Analyse research findings

6 Assembly and writing of thesis

These six criteria are enjoyment, timetabling, thesis length, feasibility, methods and theoretical perspective.

Will I enjoy working on that topic?

Students have to be strongly motivated to complete a thesis. They must be allocated to or choose a topic that interests them and fires their imagination. If the thesis subject bores them, it is not likely to get finished. A good supervisor asks students some searching questions about motivation to investigate their particular topic, and expects students to evaluate their own commitment to the topic. It is important not to confuse your own enthusiasm for a research topic with a student's. Beware of attributing your own intellectual and personal agenda to your graduate students. Equally, one's own agenda should not be allowed to pour cold water on students' research plans inappropriately.

Timetable

The supervisor is likely to be more experienced than the student, and therefore more realistic about the timetabling of research projects. Ask the student to focus on the following. How long has the student got to finish the thesis? By what date does it *have* to be handed in? What are the earliest and latest dates for submission? When do you and the student actually plan to complete it? Then encourage them to draw up a timetable, and think about designing a project that fits into the time they have. In our own classes with graduate students, we find it helpful to work with specimen research timetables like those given in Figures 3.1 to 3.3, full of deliberate mistakes. In class, we have the students work through such a timetable, find the ten mistakes, and learn from them how to make their own realistic schedules. A realistic timetable is a great help, an unrealistic one is depressing; so ensure that they review theirs regularly and keep them realistic. The three specimen timetables reproduced here – one for a social survey, one for a piece of geographical fieldwork, the third for a history project – have been carefully designed to be riddled with common faults. If all of them are wrong for your students, it is not difficult to prepare one that will allow them to 'spot the mistakes'. We have not spelled out all the errors here, but the most obvious ones in the social science project include concentrating too much data collection over Christmas and New Year, and leaving out any time for piloting the computer analysis of the questionnaire results. The geology one includes doing fieldwork at high altitude when snow would be several metres thick. The history one fails to allow any time for getting access to the archive. All three have the common flaws of a literature review that stops too soon, and a 'write up' that starts too late.

Figure 3.2: Proposed timetable for earth science PhD programme (specimen, faulty, timetable for research in Switzerland)

	1997 OCT	1998 DEC	FEB	JUN	AUG	OCT	1999 DEC	FEB	APR	JUN	OCT	2000 DEC	FEB	APR
1 Literature review	———													
2 Pilot fieldwork at 3,700 metres		———												
3 (1) Analyse pilot results (2) Plan main study				—										
4 Main data collection at 3,700 metres					—									
5 (1) Sort and classify specimens (2) Code data									—		—			
6 Computer analysis											—			
7 Analyse findings												—		
8 Assembly and writing of thesis													—	———

Figure 3.3: Proposed timetable for history PhD programme (specimen, faulty, timetable for a biogaphy of Elizabeth Twining)

	1997	1998						1999					2000		2001
	OCT	DEC	FEB	APR	JUN	AUG	OCT	DEC	FEB	APR	JUN	AUG	OCT	DEC	FEB	APR

1 Literature review: published work

(1) Twining family

(2) Victorian philanthropy

(3) Middle-class women

2 Access

Negotiate access to archives

Prelim. visit to archives

3 Time in archive

4 Analysis of notes made in archive

5 Write thesis

Length of thesis

The supervisor has a duty to prevent the student embarking on an over-ambitious programme, which would involve collecting far more data than anyone could ever use. The supervisor knows the word limit and *should* know roughly what size and shape of project will 'fit' neatly into that word length. Get the student to focus on the maximum length the thesis can be. Plan the research so it can be written up properly within the word limit. As the supervisor you should be able to help the candidate to plan a study that can 'fit' into the limit prescribed for the relevant degree registration. As is shown by the example of Colin Ives, set out in Chapter 2, it is easy to think students know what a thesis is and can plan their own work accordingly.

Example 3.1: James Peel Edgerton

Sara was supervising James Peel Edgerton's MEd thesis on Welsh children's literature. The word limit on the Cardiff MEd thesis is 20,000 words. James's first draft was 60,000 words, so 40,000 words had to be cut. This took several months and was heartbreaking.

Feasibility?

There is also the issue of feasibility. Novices may have no idea about the related issues of practical feasibility and 'political' feasibility. Ask the candidate to consider the following kinds of questions: be brutally realistic. Will you be able to get to the field site? Will the data be available? What lab equipment will you need? What advice is available? What software exists? As a supervisor you may be more alert to practical and political problems than the students. Going out into the field to do geological data collection, for example, can take much longer than a novice imagines. Theo Karras, a geology PhD student at Ottercombe, found that on his first field trip: 'it took a long time to actually – just to get my eyes to be able to see things in the rocks that you are meant to see.' He was more realistic in his plans for his next one, although he foresaw new problems: 'I think I'll have to hire a car because it's a very big area and I'll have to drive . . . and I've explained all that to NERC and they've said they don't pay for cars.' Supervisors, more advanced students and postdocs may be helpful at the planning stage. Encourage the student to discuss the practicalities with more experienced colleagues.

For social scientists negotiating access to a setting or drumming up enough respondents is a typical problem of feasibility. In the South Wales area, local education authorities in the 1970s and 1980s would not allow anyone to conduct research involving IQ tests, or inquiries asking pupils to rate their teachers' abilities. Knowledgeable supervision could prevent students wasting time designing projects based on either focus. For a historian, access to data may be difficult, but it may also turn out that the data do not exist.

Example 3.2: Thomas Beresford

Thomas wanted to work on the records of the 1920s Spanish mineworkers' unions, but discovered that, to avoid persecution by Franco's secret and political police, trade unions had systematically destroyed their records after the Civil War.

Methods

The fifth criterion is the choice of research methods. The student needs to be able to master the necessary methods, to enjoy using them *and* to have intellectual confidence in the results that these methods generate. Ask students to focus, honestly, on the following. Does their topic involve methods of data collection *and* data analysis that they: (a) *believe* in; (b) can use, or can learn to use? They need to select a method of data collection they trust and can learn to be an expert in, and methods of analysis they believe in and can master (with help). Such methodological choices are especially pertinent in the social sciences and some aspects of the humanities, where epistemological issues are contested, and methods of data collection and analysis carry with them a good deal of theoretical and philosophical freight. In the natural sciences, choices of method are normally rather different kinds of consideration. Normal scientific practice rests on methods that are more taken-for-granted within particular networks or research groups. For the graduate student, the issues are more likely to confront them as practical ones. Is the correct technique for my chosen problem available in this lab, or in this group? Where do I go to learn new techniques, if I need to? Here the task of the supervisor is more likely to involve checking that the student has mastered the necessary techniques, or is receiving the best possible advice and training. Similar issues arise quite frequently for social science supervisors and students, and among humanities students as well. Students may have to cope with particular skills in acquiring data: the historian may need to learn or improve a foreign language, the specialist knowledge required to decipher manuscripts, computer software and so on; the social scientist may need to acquire skills in a variety of data collection techniques and analytic procedures – including computational skills. Not only is it important for the supervisor and the student to establish what methodological skills will be needed, it is even more important that they jointly establish *how* they will be acquired. Formal training courses cannot be guaranteed to cover all the necessary issues, and supervisors need to recognize that they are not omniscient, and need to seek out the best sources of help and advice for their candidates. In the laboratory sciences, expertise is often passed on from postdoctoral researchers to the new generation of research students, while the supervisor offers more general advice. In other disciplines too, up-to-date methodological advice may be available most readily from research fellows and other junior academics.

Theoretical perspectives

The sixth criterion may not apply in all disciplines, but in many there are theoretical perspectives to be considered. The student needs to be happy about her or his theoretical perspective, intellectually committed to it and able to master it, before the thesis is too far advanced to change either the theory or the research design. Again, this is especially significant in the humanities and social sciences, where broad theoretical and epistemological issues are hotly contested. In such contexts, 'theory' has a very different function from that it has in most laboratory science, and implies a general perspective, determining choices of problem, choice of approach, identification with a particular intellectual tradition and so on. For many students, it is unrealistic to speak of a 'choice' of orientation on this scale. By the time they embark on graduate research work, many have become committed to a particular intellectual style, and have adopted a theoretical 'position'. In our view, graduate students become identified with such theoretical stances too early and too firmly, adopting them as articles of faith rather than subjecting them to critical scrutiny. Often, of course, the working relationship between student and supervisor is founded on a commonality of perspective, and such shared views are not always conducive to a critical reflection on fundamental assumptions. Nevertheless, students need to be encouraged to work critically within particular paradigms, and to resist the adoption of a given perspective while they remain in ignorance of alternative, even competing, orientations. Enthusiasm and blind faith are not the best foundations for scholarly inquiry, and a supervisor may have to act as devil's advocate and sceptical inquirer in order to force the student to reflect on her or his chosen perspective.

The importance of ethics

Students may not realize the importance of ethical issues. Social science research students, for example, may not realize how carefully they need to protect their informants. Students do not have to intend to behave in unethical ways in order to find practical difficulties: the unintended consequences of research – especially on controversial issues – often call for a good deal of careful thought. Inexperienced students may find it hard to think through all the possible ramifications and implications of their work. Supervisors need to ensure that their students are thoroughly acquainted with ethical guidelines and requirements – especially formal guidelines relating to laboratory work (especially with animals), professional codes of conduct, legal requirements (such as the Data Protection Act in the UK, and similar legislation elsewhere), the requirements of national or local ethics committees and so on. Students whose experience does not extend beyond the undergraduate degree, and who have never had to undertake independent research, may well need explicit and systematic reviews of ethical guidelines and their practical consequences. To some extent, such considerations also spill over into more general considerations concerning the 'politics' of the research. Where a research problem has special topical importance – and that can arise in many disciplines – a student may need to think about the possible consequences, public and personal, of the research.

This is an area where a student may learn from a 'cautionary tale', such as Example 3.3.

Example 3.3: The external's brother

Ralph Paton had conducted interviews with twenty admissions tutors to architectural schools as part of his PhD. Sara, one of the externals, noticed nothing amiss. However, the other external, Ruth Kettering, opened the viva with the complaint that the respondents had not been carefully enough disguised: one was her brother, a well known architect, and she was sure everyone in architectural education would spot him immediately. Ruth referred the thesis for Ralph to redraft in ways that would disguise her brother.

The doctoral training now required in the UK includes a compulsory course in research ethics, but students may not necessarily apply what they have learnt to their own work. Because some of the ethical issues can be foreseen by the supervisor, they can be discussed and planned for at this early stage. If the project will need an animal licence, or involve the Data Protection Act, this needs to be discussed at the outset. The student can also start to write about the ethical issues while they are fresh in both your minds.

Research design

When your students design their thesis projects, you should also be ensuring that they are thinking ahead. They should be planning the general shape of the eventual thesis as well as making a rough timetable, of the kind we have already recommended, of how they are going to research the topic. Get your students to show both to you as their supervisor and get an agreed research design, thesis plan and work schedule. These will need regular review, and probable revision: it is helpful to discuss the plans and timetable at regular intervals throughout the life of the project.

Because research design is extremely subject-specific, there is little generalized advice that we can give. However, it is always important for the supervisor to remember that students are novices, and will not necessarily know how to design a piece of research in their discipline: they are being supervised in order to learn how to design and conduct research. It is often helpful to get students to argue against the particular techniques they plan to use – in other words, to understand the limitations of whatever methods they choose. In a laboratory context, they need to learn from recently completed postdocs about how their external examiners challenged the research group's approach, in order to help them to gain a broader perspective on the pros and cons.

In the social sciences there are, quite literally, hundreds of books on research methods, and many on design, so the supervisor can encourage students to use the literature to inform their decisions. Social science students may need your expert guidance on how data generated from the different methods are analysed in order to start learning the relevant techniques. Social scientists also have to think carefully about sampling, negotiating access to a research sample or population and ethical issues, as well as choice of method and design. Increasingly the supervisor needs to warn about how long some procedures will take, and about the need to keep a diary recording the processes of decision-making and the design phase.

Both arts and social science students need to be writing even at this early stage, and we have suggested some appropriate writing after the next section, which deals with access, and is primarily for social scientists.

Helping them to get access

Frequently students can get access to the data/research site/population without help. However, it is nearly always useful to encourage them to discuss access with you, and to write up that phase as they go. We use the handout reproduced as Figure 3.4, which we are including here primarily for supervisors in the social sciences. Because access to a research population is so crucial to social scientists, we run whole classes on that topic.

For humanities disciplines, the relevant material may be in the public domain, but if it is not, the student may need the supervisor's help. If

Figure 3.4: Access

Getting access to do your research can be time consuming, needs care, must be discussed with your supervisor and must be documented. It should be written up as you go along, while the scars are fresh.

Textbooks on ethnographic methods spend whole chapters on access, e.g. Hammersley and Atkinson (1995) *Ethnography: Principles in Practice*, and Burgess (1984) *In the Field*. Books on questionnaire design don't usually discuss access so much. Even if you plan a questionnaire study, read one of the chapters in an ethnography book on access to sensitize yourself.

Basic points to bear in mind

1 Does your study need to go to an ethics committee or an LEA committee, or into any bureaucracy?
  This needs *checking out* – you need to discover what the rules are, and what procedures have to be followed.
  Then you need to allow time to go through such hoops.
  And you need to discuss with your supervisor how to present yourself to that bureaucracy.
2 Who are the 'gatekeepers' for your research? Ask around to see if particular named people will make the decisions, and see if anyone you already know has connections to them. If someone in the department was at school with the gatekeepers, or your old headteacher knows them, or they did an MEd in SOCAS, or the gatekeeper's spouse was in the same cricket team as your supervisor's cousin ... use the network.
3 Think carefully about how letters are written. Should they be hand-written or word processed? From home or college? (Make sure there are no spelling mistakes!) How much should you say about the project in the initial letter?
4 If you are going to *meet* a gatekeeper, think carefully about how you dress for it. Your self-presentation *could* lose you the access.
5 Don't make promises you can't/won't keep.
6 Remember that access is a process, not a single event.
7 Keep a diary of the process; keep copies of all documents.
8 Write up the access negotiations as you go along while they are fresh.
9 Read some accounts of access proceedings. There is a good one in Linda Valli's *Becoming Clerical Workers* (1986), and another in G. A. Fine's *Shared Fantasy* (1983) (the access processes are often in the methods appendix).

you were supervising a historian trying to write a biography of Elizabeth Twining, and you had been at Oxford with one of the current generation of the family, you can write an introductory letter for your student. One example of providing help through an 'old boy' network is the case of the Bassington-ffrench archives.

Example 3.4: The Bassington-ffrench Archives

In the 1970s, Mary Debenham, a colleague of Sara's, was writing a book about the nineteenth-century education system of Norwich and Chester. The Bassington-ffrench family had been pioneers of technical schooling in Chester, and Sara had known William Bassington-ffrench at Cambridge. She wrote to him, and he passed on the request to his grandfather, Thomas. Mary Debenham was able to do a life history interview with Thomas, who recalled his father and grandfather setting up the technical school, *and* get access to private family papers.

Many novice researchers in arts and social sciences are caught out by the length of time that negotiating access can take. As funding bodies increasingly press universities to get students completed in three years, there is less time to 'spare' for lengthy access negotiations. Paul's own career shows how times have changed.

Example 3.5: Prolonged access

When Paul was starting his PhD he began access negotiations with a Scottish medical school, asking to do participant observation on the wards. He eventually got access (Atkinson 1981, 1984), but it took a year. In those days of relaxed attitudes to submission dates this was not seen as a major problem by Paul or Paul's supervisor – Paul waited, doing other things. Today, no supervisor could allow a student to 'waste' a year.

For many students the design phase is followed by a hiatus, and they can lose momentum. While some supervisors like the student to work on the literature, for others, the step after design and starting access is a pilot study. In science disciplines, the student may need to learn to use, or start to build, the equipment needed for the experiments. Our preferred 'next step' is to encourage students to start writing parts of the methods chapter, so we discuss that next.

The methods chapter

For many social science research students, the methods chapter is a good one to write early on, and a useful 'test' for the supervisor. If the student needs help with writing, then the sooner the supervisor is aware of that the better. Equally, if the student writes well, then praise for the draft material will be a great motivator. Encouraging the student to plan, and draft, the methods chapter early on is a wise move. We use the handout shown in Figure 3.5, with an attached worksheet (Figure 3.6).

To help social science students to think about what their methods chapter can and should contain, we ask them to role-play being an external examiner, and to discuss in small groups what they would expect to find in a thesis.

The worksheet reproduced as Figure 3.6 is obviously designed for sociology PhD students: the second example is a reference to Barbara Heyl's (1979) work; the others are invented. Both Figures 3.5 and 3.6 can be easily adapted by a group of colleagues to fit many disciplines.

Figure 3.5: The methods chapter or appendix

Somewhere in the thesis there must be a discussion of your methods – a whole chapter, part of a chapter or an appendix.

This should contain four elements:

1 Discussion of the academic literature on the method(s) you used.
2 Reference(s) to at least one other study that used the same method(s).
3 An account of how it/they worked when you used it/them (which should be *honest* but not self-indulgent).
4 Copies of all your research instruments – in an appendix.

Items 1 and 2 are necessary to show that you have studied the literature, 3 and 4 are essential for anyone who wants to replicate your study.

1 Make sure that you show that you have understood the pros and cons of the method(s) you have chosen. All methods have advantages and disadvantages – you need to show that you realize that.
2 There are two kinds of literature you can refer to here – *either* published studies *or* the 'autobiographical' accounts people write. Both are useful. Methods are usually discussed in the appendices of published books – check them out as you read.
3 It is difficult to get the balance between reporting what you did in sufficient detail and being too fussy/detailed/boring. In the first draft, put down *everything* and then get your supervisor to help you cut it down. *Don't* pretend it all went smoothly according to the textbook if it didn't, *but* equally try not to make yourself look *too* incompetent.

Write early and write often

This methods chapter is one that you can start writing early in the registration period. As you take each step, write a draft section about it. Doing this while it is fresh in your mind and filing them carefully is very prudent and sensible.

Figure 3.6: Worksheet on the methods chapter

Imagine you are the external examiner for a set of theses. One of your jobs is to vet the methods chapter. Taking each of these examples, make a check list of what information you would need/expect to find in the methods chapter.

1 A survey – using a postal questionnaire – of primary headteachers in two LEAs on their attitudes to race and gender equality.
2 Life history of a brothel keeper (madam) using several interviews.
3 An analysis of diaries kept by sweet shop owners.
4 Open-ended interviews with people coping with migraine.

A flying start

If students undertake all the tasks suggested in this chapter, by the end of their first three months of registration they should not only have made a flying start, but be well aware that they have done so. Remember to praise students explicitly for the fact that they have made a good start – they cannot 'know' they are doing well unless you tell them. As we emphasized in Chapter 2, the establishment of a sound working relationship, the building of trust and mutual confidence and the establishment of sound routines are all important ingredients in building the foundations of sucessful supervision. In this chapter we have stressed various ways in which that foundation can be built on: getting students off on the right footing and establishing the basis of the research itself. While higher degree students should not feel pressured into premature fieldwork or other kinds of data collection, it is clear from many of the interviews we conducted, as well as from more anecdotal evidence from colleagues, that it is all too easy for research students to drift and for valuable time to pass unproductively. Moreover, if students start to feel aimless, or feel that their work is not progressing, then self-confidence can be damaged. If, on the other hand, students can be encouraged to make a 'flying start', then confidence will grow, research plans can be progressed realistically and supervisor and student will both feel positive about the research process.

4

Old manuscripts: the literature review

after a fruitless rummage in a cupboard ... she dragged out an ancient trunk, unlocked it and flung back the lid. A close, cold odour. Books. Discarded garments. Old shoes. Old Manuscripts.

(Sayers 1972: 9)

Introduction

Whatever the discipline, the PhD student has to get to grips with the literature, and learn how to find it, read it, assimilate it and write about it. This chapter deals with helping students to find the literature, make a permanent record of it for themselves, read it intelligently and write the review of the literature. It also deals with teaching them to cite and prepare reference lists correctly.

It is easy to overestimate the level of library skills that students have. In the research on students we have done, we regularly find people who did not know that inter-library loans existed, or other *basic* things, like where the back numbers of journals were shelved. All departments should organize sessions on library and information use run by specialist staff from the library or information centre: if yours does not, then you should fix up training for your own students. However, it is only reasonable to discuss with the librarian what can be covered: the best librarians in the world will not know what your students need unless you have run through relevant issues with them. Setting up training sessions with the specialist librarian(s) is always beneficial to students, especially if your university is not in the same city as a copyright library.

Helping the student with finding the literature

Encourage your students to make friends with the relevant library and information staff. Warn them always to be polite and patient, and to

remember to thank library (and computer centre) staff and to acknowledge their help in everything they write. Failure to get such personnel on
the student's team can cause missed opportunities, as in the case of Bryan
Martin.

Example 4.1: Bryan Martin

Bryan Martin was doing an MPhil on the experience of role conflict among
further education college principals. He complained a good deal about the
library, but never discovered that the head of the education library, Jane
Wilkinson, had done a PhD herself five years before on FE principals, and had
an enormous reservoir of knowledge about the local FE sector.

When a good relationship is established, there can be far-reaching
consequences. When Sara worked in the School of Education at Leicester
University, the specialist librarian, Roy Kirk, was active in the professional
association, LISE (Librarians in Institutes and Schools of Education). When
Roy, Sara and one of the library staff – Barbara Barr – discovered that
there was no published bibliography or union list of histories of girls'
schools, Roy got LISE to sponsor Barbara to research and produce one,
which they then published (Barr 1984). That union list is still the basic
research source for anyone working on the history of women's education.
Here a close working relationship between a young scholar and experienced librarians had benefits for everyone.

Many undergraduates have not become familiar with the range of periodicals in the discipline, so research students need to find out which are
the most important journals relevant to their thesis: by asking not only
you, and the specialist library staff, but also postdoctoral researchers and
your colleagues. Discussing the new journals, the most authoritative ones,
which ones are in the hands of small cabals, which accept a wide range
of perspectives, is an important part of orienting them within the literature. You can help by discussing where you publish, which periodicals
you subscribe to yourself and which ones you have to get on-line or on
inter-library loan, and why. This is often the first opportunity to talk about
the learned societies, and about academic publishing houses.

Undergraduates will probably not have used theses before, so this is
another category of literature the research student needs to focus on.

Other theses

There are three categories of thesis that it may be helpful to steer your
students towards. Your own doctoral thesis is often fascinating for your
students: to see how the field has changed, to realize that you yourself
were once a rank beginner and to remind them that you were young once.

If you were a PhD student at the place where you now teach, your students can read it easily. If not, then you might put a copy in the postgraduate room, or offer to lend it to selected candidates. If there are publications from your PhD, such as journal articles or a monograph, you can suggest that your students should compare the thesis and the publications to see how the same data appear in the two formats (Richardson 1990).

The second category of theses your students need to read is successful ones in their discipline in their university. They need to get a feel for the length, format, style and scope of past theses in the university they are registered in. Try to steer them to excellent examples, and discuss their responses to them. Again, if there is a recent graduate of the department who has published from doctoral research, the PhD student can compare the thesis and the publication(s). If your department or research group has produced several 'generations' of doctoral students developing a research tradition, explain to new students that external examiners will look for the local school of thought in their literature review.

The third category of theses the student may need to consult is those in other British (and American) universities. Steer them to British theses, which are listed in the *Index of Theses*, and American ones, which can be traced from *Dissertation Abstracts International.* The library staff will be delighted to show postgraduates how to use these indexes.

Abstracts

Undergraduates are unlikely to have used any of the on-line or published abstracts. Most libraries subscribe to several sets of abstracts and post-graduates should learn to use them. These are useful, but a student can be swamped by the sheer volume of previous scholarship. Two respondents to the Delamont and Eggleston (1981) survey, from the same university, reported that

> Students pioneered and established a link with the ERIC information retrieval system with help of computer centre staff. Department didn't want to know until the feasibility work was done.
>
> (Charles Enderby)

> The literature search remains a never ending headache. The infinite extendibility of the academic enterprise means it is very difficult to know when to stop. What is a reasonable literature search very much depends upon the topic and the problem. I am extremely ambivalent about specialist indexes as they are both an aid and a torment . . . The library here is very poor . . . Access to the literature is fairly straight-forward. Although I do have to shamefacedly admit that I have never come to terms with *Dissertation Abstracts International.*
>
> (Ronny Devereux)

On-line and computer searches

It is important that your students find out how to do computer searches, how much they cost (if anything) and what they are allowed to do that is paid for by the department. The facilities here and their capabilities are changing so quickly that your students may be ahead of you already, but they may not. If this is an area where you feel fully confident you can show your students what to do, but if not the specialist librarians are best placed to help them – your role is to remind them to ask nicely.

This is an excellent topic for a seminar or workshop, with the students doing theses sharing their search strategies. If there is a taught course, with sessions taken by the library, it can be followed up by academics. If not, a good supervisor can usefully get all his or her students to pool their ideas. As the technology changes, it is plausible for a supervisor to plead ignorance of the latest wrinkles, and appear to be asking students for help – thus ensuring that they get clued up. You will know you are succeeding when they start to bring you references for your work that you have missed.

The literature search is a good opportunity to start the student's acquaintance with the politics and practicalities of publication in your discipline. If your field now works mainly by e-mail and electronic publishing, if pre-prints are vital, if conference papers are central, if certain journals are of much higher status than others, this is the time to help the student discover that for himself or herself. Sooner or later the research student needs to know which are the best sources of new ideas in the specialism, and looking for literature is one way to learn that.

Helping the student with taking notes

Student may lack skills in taking notes on their reading, perhaps not knowing what to record, and they may be hopeless at organizing and storing their notes on what they have read. It is important that you help them to recognize that the quality of their thesis will depend on how adequately they research the field in which they are going to write their thesis. The quality of the notes they take on what they read is an important part of mastering/mistressing any field. Figure 4.1 is a checklist of things students in social science should put into their notes, which we give out at Cardiff. It should be straightforward for any supervisor to produce an equivalent in his or her discipline.

Many of the things in Figure 4.1 may seem crushingly obvious. However, students frequently have no idea that they will need all this information if they cite the publication in the thesis. Most undergraduate students have never looked at the technical bits of a book, or journal, such as the

Figure 4.1: Specimen checklist on note-taking

Your notes should always include:

1 Full bibliographical details.
  (a) the full name(s) of the author(s).
  (b) the title of the book/article.
  (c) the date published originally (so you know whether it is an old or a new study) and of the edition you are using.
  (d) publisher, place of publication (if it is a book).
  (e) name of the journal/book and volume and page numbers (if an article).
2 The library catalogue number (e.g. LC5146.H27) so that you can find it again (and even the ISSN or ISBN number).

In addition you should check, and note:

3 Is it an original study, or a report of other people's work? (Primary or secondary source.)
4 Is it empirical (has data in it) or theoretical or polemical? (Argumentative.)
5 What methods were used? (computer modelling, experiments, field measurements etc.)
6 What theory is cited?
7 What are the author's conclusions? (i.e. what did she or he find out/prove?)
8 On what date was the research *done*? (It may be many years before it was published.)
9 The number of informants/subjects sampled, the response rate(s). The breakdown of the sample by age, race, sex etc.

ISBN or ISSN. Encouraging new postgraduates to focus on such things helps their career. Our experience is that few students have ever noticed that books have ISBNs, or got into the habit of recording all the details of a reference. A workshop on the practicalities of notetaking and recording all the details is a good point for British supervisors to introduce the CVCP categorization system for collecting publication details from universities, and explain it.

Supervision of the student's recording of the literature is a good point to introduce discussion of software, back-up systems and horror stories about lost quotes. There are several good software packages available for storing references, and also for keeping indexed notes on the literature. It is useful to get students an introduction to one or more of these, to see if they are enthused by them. If the student prefers to keep notes on file cards, on paper or in notebooks, ensure that this *is* a genuine preference and not computer phobia. Either way, stress (repeatedly) that computerized records need to be backed up, with the back-ups kept safely in a different place from the originals, *and* that hand-written records can, and should, be photocopied or carboned, with the back-ups put in a safe place. Remind the students of this periodically. Our department has a safe, in which we ask, even urge, students to place their back-up disks, but few of them bother except when there has been a burglary, theft or fire that has destroyed the work of a fellow student. Stories of colleagues wasting hours trying to track down a quotation or citation that is central to a text but has got detached from its proper origins are useful as cautionary tales.

Example 4.2: Anne Beddingfield

Anne was a PhD student with Paul and Sara at Edinburgh in the early 1970s. By the time she came to submit she had a job in another city, and thirty incomplete references in her list: missing publishers, page numbers, initials, dates etc. Sara spent three days trailing round libraries in Edinburgh filling in those missing details for Anne.

When we tell this story to our students they are sceptical about it, so it is necessary to set up concrete examples of the miseries caused by 'lost' citations to drive the message home. If you or a colleague can afford to employ a new PhD student to check the bibliography of one of your articles or books for publication and there are some 'missing' references, this is a neat way of training them to be more precise themselves without them noticing.

Finding the literature and recording it is not the end of the story.

Helping the student to read

Professional librarians can help students to find relevant literature, and they or the local computing experts can help them to record it. Only the supervisor can train students to read professionally, in a way different from their successful undergraduate reading strategies. Researchers are, first and foremost, readers. The appropriate sources, and the techniques of reading them, can be learnt in the research group in science: perhaps by hearing a more advanced doctoral student or a postdoc pull together the key issues in the relevant journals. Gilbert and Mulkay (1984) is an account of how journal articles on oxidative phosphorylation were read by other leading and young biochemists. The doctoral student has to learn how to read the relevant literature, and write coherent accounts of it. In the humanities and social sciences, reading, defining relevance and producing the review of the literature is a more diffuse task, with more scope for individualized styles of attack. The literature review is not only a ritually positioned chapter in the thesis: that review is also the source of hypotheses and the entry to other worlds. Delamont (1992) devotes a chapter to reading which can be recommended to social science and humanities students, but there is no equivalent guide for science students. For arts and social science students there are three types of reading to be done: reading on the topic, contrastive reading and analytical reading. Novice students need to recognize the three types and plan their reading to mix them. Reading *on* the topic is the only kind that most people think of doing, yet it is the least interesting. Students need to be encouraged to do all three types. Delamont (1992: 11–17) offers worked examples of the three types of reading relevant to four different educational research projects. Here we have exemplified the three types of reading with a sociological topic, a history project and a literary one, which leaves readers in other disciplines to imagine their own.

A sociological research project

Eileen Brent is going to study the Corfiote community in Cardiff. There are about 25,000 people of Greek and Greek Cypriot origin in Cardiff; within that is a substantial Corfiote minority, some of whom are unusual in being Roman Catholic, not Greek Orthodox. Eileen's reading *on* her topic is pretty obvious: material (a) on Corfu, the Ionian islands, Greece and Cyprus; (b) on Greek emigrants to Britain, Australia, the USA and Canada; and (c) on other 'Mediterranean' immigrants to the UK, such as Cypriots, Maltese, Italians and Portuguese. Her supervisor should be able to steer her to these literatures without difficulty. Eileen's reading for contrast might include:

1 The literature on other immigrant groups from other faiths and ethnic groups, such as Muslims from Pakistan or Rastafarians from Jamaica.
2 The literature on Roman Catholic versus Greek Orthodox beliefs.
3 Studies of other multiracial ports, such as San Diego.
4 Novels of exiles and minorities.

Her reading for analytic categories might include whatever anthropological or sociological theorists she and her supervisor have agreed upon, plus those espoused by the leading authors of other studies of ethnicity in the UK, and especially in Wales.

A historical research project

Greta Onlsson is planning to centre her PhD on the life of Elizabeth Twining (1805–1889), an educational and biological pioneer. Her reading on her topic will clearly include everything on Elizabeth, her sister Louisa (the pioneer of social work/workhouse visiting) and their family; Elizabeth's friends and colleagues, her enemies and opponents, and the pupils who attended the school she ran. The reading for contrast might include histories and biographies of male educational and biological pioneers; of women equivalent to Elizabeth in the USA or Australia; or studies of other commercial 'dynasties', such as the Bulmers, Cadburys or Rothschilds. The analytic categories would probably come from feminist history (or from self-consciously anti-feminist history).

A literary research project

Donald Ross is going to study images of science, scientists and engineers in the novels of Trollope, Mrs Gaskell and George Eliot. His reading on the topic will start with the novels (probably in Trollope's case only a selection of them), central texts of literary criticism and histories of 'popular' science in the nineteenth century. The reading for contrast might include histories of science and engineering in other periods (such as Ancient Greece) or other cultures (such as China); contemporary literature with scientific or engineering themes; or studies of other issues in nineteenth-century fiction (such as slavery, illness or religion). The reading for analytic categories would be literary theory.

The general message of this section is that students need guidance on how to read appropriately for their discipline. They need to understand how scholars in their field read and assimilate the relevant literature. Some students read too widely, and need to be brought back to the central purpose of the thesis. Others bitterly resent time spent on anything not *directly* relevant to their own definition of their topic, as this respondent of Rudd's (1985: 93):

> One was offered, for example, texts to be read by beat poets like Allen Ginsberg, or novelists like Norman Mailer, who interesting writers though they are, didn't seem to me, and still don't seem to me, to have the level of seriousness of Herman Melville, or Nathaniel Hawthorne or of Mark Twain.

If this man's supervisors had good reasons to expect him to read Mailer and Ginsberg, they had not explained them clearly, or convinced the candidate. Enthusing the student to read creatively and professionally does not get the literature review written. That is your next task.

Helping the student with writing the literature review

Do get the student to check – by looking at some relevant theses in your area – how many words are usually spent on reviewing the literature in successful past theses. In a 20,000 word MSc thesis it may only be about 2,000–3,000 words. In a 40,000 word MPhil, 5,000 words will probably be ample. In an 80,000 word PhD, 7,000 words on the literature may be plenty. Many theses have reviews that are too long and unfocused.

Example 4.3: Jane Finn

Sara was the examiner for Jane Finn's PhD, which was 100,000 words long. The literature review was over 200 pages long, arranged chronologically from 1800 to 1976 (although the thesis was presented in 1989), and was incredibly boring. The examiners agreed that this long march through a diffuse 'literature' gave entirely the wrong impression of the thesis, which was actually quite good.

The problem with helping novice scholars to prepare their literature review is that very few research students have thought about what the finished product is for. You need to explain that the literature review should: (a) show the reader that the student is capable of searching for relevant material, summarizing it, arranging it by some theme and relating it to his or her own work; (b) show that his or her study is original *or* is a principled, conscious replication of a previous one.

Few students recognize that displaying the ability to synthesize the literature is one of the skills they will be judged on. Yet the evidence is that many examiners see that synthesis as a crucial part of a good thesis. (We give examples in Chapter 7.) The supervisor can alert the student to the main dangers associated with the standard thesis literature chapter. There are three main dangers. People can leave things out, be out of date and be boring. Try to ensure that your students avoid all these dangers, using the following strategies.

- To stop them leaving things out. Remember to ask your supervisees, the library staff and other people to keep their eyes open for all studies relevant to all the people you are supervising, as well as encouraging students to do the same. A colleague may spot something relevant to your student in a journal, but will only tell you or your student if you have encouraged her or him to do so.
- To stop them being out of date. Remember that your students need to *keep* reading. They cannot review the literature at the beginning and leave it. They should keep reading until the thesis is finished and then to prepare for the viva. Journals are crucial, so encourage them to keep an eye on *Current Contents* and its equivalents in your discipline, as you do.
- To stop them being boring. This is the worst danger. Help your students to arrange their reviews by themes, not just in long lists or sequences. Encourage them to highlight the findings that are relevant

to their thesis. Most importantly, the supervisor has to train the student to be critical of the literature, not just to report it.

This may be particularly difficult for students who have been educated in the Islamic/Koranic tradition, or the Confucian/Mandarin one. In both these ancient educational systems, apprentice scholars are required to memorize and absorb the work of masters for many years, and are not expected to attack and criticize the scholarly corpus. Eickelman (1978, 1985) has written eloquently about the Islamic/Koranic tradition, while Wilkinson (1964) and Hayhoe (1984) explore the Confucian/Mandarin one. Moving to the robust Anglo-American tradition, where young scholars are required to criticize the publications of leading authorities, can be confusing. Supervisors can become frustrated by an over-reverent tone, suspect a lack of ability in the student or worry about plagiarism when they receive careful summaries of published work rather than the robust criticism they want. Students can be perplexed by the cool reaction to their painstaking efforts. Neither party realizes that these are different scholarly traditions meeting in mutual incomprehension. Once a supervisor has read about the student's own scholarly tradition, she or he can discuss with the student what the differences are and help the student learn to produce UK-style texts. If you are supervising students who have been educated in countries with a Koranic or Confucian scholarly tradition, then it is well worth your time to do some reading about it: an understanding of a different tradition leads to an improvement in supervisory skill. You will be able to open up the differences in traditions for explicit comparison.

When a student does a good literature review it is a very satisfying product. At best it can lead to a publication.

Example 4.4: Bartholomew Strange

Sara was the external examiner of a PhD by Bartholomew Strange. It was an excellent thesis, and fell into two potential books. The empirical material was ideally suited to a monograph, which his supervisor, Prof. Leidner, was able to place with a publisher. Sara could see that the literature review and methods chapters contained an outstanding overview of how one particular data collection and analysis method had been used in three different ways in related disciplines. She knew that a leading scholar, Anthony Cade, was planning a series of methods books, into which Bartholomew's work would fit perfectly. After the viva, Sara wrote to Prof. Cade, and he commissioned the book from Bartholomew.

Not all literature reviews can become books, but many of them can generate a research note or a journal article, perhaps written with the supervisor. This is worth exploring with promising students, because it provides a real incentive to think about the literature, and if an article is submitted, the referees' comments provide useful feedback on the thesis, even if the article is rejected.

Teaching citation and referencing

The literature review is an excellent point or stage to train the student in citation and referencing. These are skills candidates will need, and the sooner they learn them, and deploy them automatically, the better. There are three aspects to this: the technicalities of citation, the politics of citation and the construction of the reference lists and/or bibliography. It is important to explain to students why these things matter, because most undergraduates will not have been forced to master the technicalities and will be innocent of the politics. This section deals with the technicalities first, and then the politics. It may be necessary to warn, or even threaten, students with the possibility that their thesis could be referred for an inadequate or incorrectly presented bibliography. This may even be the appropriate place to raise the spectre of plagiarism, and ensure that the student knows that the best way to avoid accusations of plagiarism is to be meticulous about citation. Unpicking a student's citation problems may also reveal more serious issues, as in the case of Alice Ascher.

Example 4.5: Plagiarism or poor citation?

Alice Ascher was doing a 20,000 word thesis at the end of a masters degree. In her literature review, she appeared to have got her citations wrong, confusing contributions to edited collections and secondary references (her bibliography was full of entries such as: i.e. Smith, 1926 cited in Jones, 1989: 32). As Sara tried to help her sort out her citations, it became clear that the literature review was full of citations to readily available sources Alice had not read first-hand, and indeed had been written without any first-hand knowledge of several key sources central to her theme. Discovering and unpicking that mistake, and sending Alice off to read the original texts of her central authors, took several weeks. Then Sara discovered that Alice was apparently unable to distinguish primary sources from secondary ones or from textbooks, or recognize the difference between writing a book and editing one. Trying to ensure that Alice understood plagiarism then had to be built into several more sessions. Here an inadequate list of citations was the warning signal about underlying scholarly problems.

Many students have not realized what they are doing when citing references, and need to have it explained that a reader in fifty years' time should be able to trace everything they used from the bibliography. The best way to reinforce this message is to show them how maddening it is to try and trace the sources of a sloppily referenced text in your own field (we leave it to you to make the selection!).

Students may also need to have the issue of intellectual ownership explained to them: they will not know 'naturally' the difference between the author of a paper, the editor of the volume it appears in, the translator of a foreign text or the compiler of a bibliography unless the nature of these different scholarly tasks is made explicit for them. Both these aspects of intellectual ownership and the consequences of ignoring them make excellent topics for student workshops – preferably based round an exercise relevant to the discipline. The case of Bella Duveen can be used: again, in a subject-specific example.

Example 4.6: Bella Duveen

Sara externalled a PhD by Bella Duveen, which was on women and sport. The bibliography contained an unacceptable mixture of items; for example, an academic monograph was juxtaposed to an interview with Jocelyn Hoyte Smith from *Athletics Weekly* or a *Radio Times* article on Rachel Hayhoe Smith, as if they had the same status as sources. When the examiners raised this in the viva, Bella did not accept it as a problem: she was apparently unable to distinguish them as types of source. Her supervisor began to squirm, as he recognized that this blind spot revealed a deep-seated problem with Bella's grasp of her discipline. Bella's PhD was referred for resubmission for MPhil only, not least because of her unscholarly treatment of the literature.

Teaching a class on referencing while writing this book, we found a masters student who was re-ordering co-authors and co-editors into alphabetical order for her bibliography. So, if she wished to cite Field and Abraham (1973) she was putting Abraham and Field (1973) in her text and bibliography.

Students whose first language is Arabic, or any other where the family name precedes the forename, may find referencing in English very confusing, and need to have it explained. It is not obvious to a Saudi Arabian that 'Banks, Olive' means one thing, and 'Olive Banks' another, and that the author goes under 'B' in the bibliography. Students from other cultures are not always able to sex authors from their forenames, and their use of 'he' and 'she' when referring to authors often needs careful scrutiny. British students are not necessarily able to sex Americans from their forenames either, and this too needs watching.

We have found it useful to run a class on referencing technicalities with a worksheet which we go through in class. Ours is reproduced as

Figure 4.2, and is clearly designed for a sociology/social policy department where theses are referenced using the Harvard system. It is fairly
easy to produce an equivalent exercise for other disciplines, using the APA
(American Psychological Association) or Biomedical referencing systems,
or those required for legal, humanities or linguistic research.

The politics of citations in scientific disciplines have been studied by
sociologists of science (e.g. Edge 1979), but there has been less research
on how scholars in other disciplines use citation. In many disciplines
researchers have found citation to be gendered: publications by women
are less likely to be cited than those by men (Cole 1979). If you suspect
that any of your students are recapitulating that pattern, a departmental
workshop on sexism in your discipline, perhaps led by an outside speaker,
may be in order. Many supervisors may never have thought about their
own citation strategies or read anything about how citation works in their
own field. Working with PhD students can be a salutary experience.

As you lay bare your own practices, you may discover more about yourself and your speciality than you wanted to know. Delamont (1989b) is an
examination of the citation patterns in British sociological writing about
social mobility, while Delamont and Atkinson (1995) explores the ethno-
centric patterns of citation in British and American educational writing.
You and your graduates may be able to produce equivalent analyses of
your own specialism which could be publishable.

'There isn't any literature'

Occasionally students will complain that they cannot find any literature on
their topic. This may be because they lack vision, and are defining their
topic too narrowly, and you can reassure them and demonstrate how to
use the literature there is. If students are defining the parameters of their
literature searching in order to 'fit' their own specific topic very narrowly,
then there will indeed be little or nothing to show. If such a narrowly
defined search throws up a good deal of research literature, then students
may find it hard to identify an original and significant topic for their own
thesis: a crowded research field may prove hard to penetrate and some
redefinition of the problem may be in order. More likely is the phenomenon whereby students define their interests so specifically that systematic
searches suggest little or no literature. In that case the supervisor's task
will be help them to rethink the task: as we have suggested already, to
search more creatively, looking more laterally for creative comparisons,
contrasts and the like.

If, when you have exhausted all your ingenuity, you are forced to agree
that there really is a lack of literature on the student's topic, you may need

Figure 4.2: Exercise on bibliographies and referencing

Spot the mistakes in each of these, and either write it out correctly below, or list the mistake.

1 Jenni Williams (1986) *Spot Removal.* London: Methuen

2 Franklin, B. J.; Williams, P. Q.; and Marshall, Z ( ) (1986) *Readings on Spot Removal.* Boston:Little, Brown & Co

3 Andrews, Z. (1926) Chaos in the Streets, New Zealand Journal of Street Studies Vol 2 No 3 pp 210–236.

4 Castenada, John Antigone's Struggles Los Angeles : Feminist Press Inc.

5 Pithouse, A. J. (1979) 'Thoughts on Radical Social Work', *British Journal of Radical Thoughts* pp 12–17.

6 Delamont, Sara (1976) 'Beyond Flanders' Fields'. In Stubbs and Delamont Explorations in Classroom Observation Chichester Wiley pp

7 Zonabend, Michelle (1974) *The Enduring Memory*

8 Gage and Berliner (1984) Educational Psychology (Second Edition)

9 Berliner, D et al (1986) Teaching Teachers Thinking Journal of Education for Teaching Vol 19 No 4

10 Adamson, David (1982) 'Understanding machismo and caciquismo'. *Iberian Studies* Vol 7 No 1 pp 1–27.

11 Penny Jones and Mary Smith ( ) 'Policewomen in Corsica'. In M. Levi and A. Smith (eds) European Policing in the 1990s University of North Carolina Press.

Figure 4.2: (*Cont'd*)

12 (look at 13 as well)
Walton, R. (1985) Entry Requirements for the UCC course in social work'
Social Work Today Vol 38 No 2 pp 75–80.

13 Walton, R. (1985) *Prison Reform in Ghana* Manchester.

14 Paul Atkinson   The Clinical Experience   Unpublished PHD thesis Edinburgh

15 Beale, Dorothea (1892) My first thirty years at Cheltenham reprinted in
D. Spender The Educational Pioneers (1987) London Virago

---

to show her or him how to write creatively about the absence. A genuine absence of research literature in a specific field can provide the student and supervisor with a creative opportunity. Gaps in the research coverage can provide very telling information about the preoccupations, biases and blind spots of the research community. They may be indicative of genuine oversight of important problems and perspectives. The ambitious and creative research student can often make capital out of a negative result in searching the literature. If the absence is a significant one, it can be used to mount a principled criticism of the present state of the field. A publishable research note may be the outcome (see Delamont 1987 for a pertinent example of a research note of this sort). In any event, a creative response to the presences and absences in the literature can be used to construct literature reviews that actually map the current state of the art.

Conclusion

Throughout this chapter we have tried to indicate a number of ways in which the research student and the supervisor can approach the task of literature searching and reviewing. Our general message is that this set of tasks – which are sometimes seen as tedious chores – can be approached professionally and creatively. A failure to think positively about 'the literature' can readily lead to the sort of dull writing that too often mars the finished thesis. Experienced external examiners will probably be familiar with at least some theses in which the student has approached the job in a mechanical and ritualized fashion. The result can be a dutiful but uninspiring aspect of the work that adds little or nothing to the final product. A more thoughtful approach to the tasks, that combines thorough inquiry with a more creative approach, can be a significant contribution to the thesis in its own right, whether or not it appears as a separate 'literature review'. Rather than stultifying, the result can be an empowering overview of the state of the art, and help to place the research student's own work firmly in its proper intellectual context. It is the task of the supervisor, along with providing specific advice on searching, reading, bibliographic work and so on, to help the students to see the wood for the trees: to help them to *use* the literature to hand as part of the research process; to link the students' own work to key issues and themes in the discipline; to derive and to explore ideas through the literature rather than passively reporting it.

5

Heavy and thankless task: overseeing the data collection

> The confidante has a very heavy and thankless task. It's not surprising if she goes mad in white linen. It's more surprising if she stays sane and sensible.
>
> (Sayers 1972: 142)

The supervision of data collection is clearly a key feature of the research process, and may be one of the most problematic areas of the project. If all goes well, of course, it may prove one of the most satisfying too: there can be few more exciting aspects of the supervisor's work than to see good quality data that put flesh on the bones of a previously schematic research design.

It is in this phase of the project, too, that prior training in methods and careful preparation of the research student pay handsome dividends. Equally, all parties need to be mentally and emotionally prepared for the possibility that data collection procedures will not go smoothly. Problems of some sort are common – to be expected in general terms, but unpredictable in practice – and should not be allowed to lead to unnecessary loss of confidence, or to the abortion of the project entirely.

Gumport (1993: 265) reports of physics PhD students:

> A student might need help with techniques of instrumentation, measurement styles, or design of equipment; there may be a leak . . . One faculty member said, 'I have to set up the harder parts of the experiment myself. But when it breaks, they fix it.'

One of the students Gumport interviewed captures the highs and the lows of the data collection phase of a physics PhD: 'Some days you are a peon. Other days you know how . . . and you're King for a day.' This chapter is about supervising through the days of peonage and the days of majesty.

Equally, student and supervisor alike need to remain flexible in their general approach. Data collection in all disciplines is unpredictable. The natural sciences are no more immune from problems in getting their experiments to 'work' and in deriving useful data than the social sciences. Thought therefore needs to be given to how various contingencies might be dealt with and how research designs or data collection methods might be modified if insurmountable problems are encountered.

The following town planning student, Glen Madson from Portminster, found out the hard way about adequate preparation for data collection, and reflected on his own lack of prior experience:

> I know I made one major cock-up in the first year by approaching a particular firm about its relationship to its union. And if I'd had any kind of research training I wouldn't have done that. It was innocent, but it wasn't interpreted that way and it cut off my access to that firm completely. And because I really wanted to do that firm, I was really upset. It had taken me six months to get some kind of access and I blew it. OK, it was common sense, but common sense that had to be learned. It's difficult doing research in organizations and in retrospect I was very sloppy, but that's because I didn't have any training.

Here Glen may overestimate the degree to which prior training can guard against adverse eventualities and accidents. Nevertheless, his rueful comments capture some of the feelings and experiences of graduate students facing their data collection.

Glen's comments also remind us of issues of time scale. Data collection, at the best of times, can be a protracted process. That is so irrespective of the data collection method. It is often labour-intensive, and graduate students – unless they are part of some larger research project, with a linked studentship – have limited resources. Often they have only their own labour power. For the part-time research student, problems of time and resources can be especially pressing. For the social science student, for instance, the negotiation of access can be a time-consuming task in its own right (and we have already drawn attention to that through the example of Paul's access problems – see Example 3.5). Access to data can, indeed, be a problem for research students in any discipline.

Example 5.1: Robert Underhay's access

Robert Underhay began his PhD in a department of mining and mineral exploitation in 1984. He needed regular access to a coal mine, and this had been promised by his supervisor, Dr Cloade. Dr Cloade had routinely despatched graduates to gather data in a mine, and was not ready for what happened with Robert. When the 1984/5 national miners' strike began, Robert was confident it would end before he was ready to gather his samples. In the event, Robert waited for 17 months, unable to go down any pit, and eventually had to abort that thesis and begin a completely different project.

Research students in the social sciences, in our experience, all too often plan data collection phases that would take a medium-sized research team, with funded support, a fair time to complete. In our experience, students are far too ambitious. Ambition is commendable, but over-optimistic estimates of time and effort are not to be encouraged. A corollary is that students often plan to collect more data than they will be able to use productively.

> In training our own graduate students, we base our advice on the following maxim: 'Take your first research design, and your first estimate of how long data collection will take. Halve the volume of data you envisage, and then double your estimate of time. You may then have a more realistic and feasible plan.'

Although one should encourage students to realize that their thesis is not the final point of their research career, and that the research they do now will stand them in good stead in the future, most supervisors will recognize the syndrome of too much data. Students who have been able to complete the data collection phase of an empirical project all too often 'drown' in data. We shall return to such 'drowning' later in this chapter. For now, we want to link it to these preliminary remarks: students and their supervisors should be encouraged to think realistically and pragmatically about the scope of data collection. A well targeted, well designed empirical project is likely to yield data that the student will be able to cope with, analyse productively and turn into a successful thesis. By contrast, any attempt to tackle a research question by overwhelming it with huge amounts of data is likely to end up by simply overwhelming the hapless student. To a considerable extent, the general issue relates to *confidence*. Too many data can be collected if the student and the supervisor are not sufficiently confident – in the precision of the research design, the significance of the research questions to be addressed, the student's analytic capacities and so on. The temptation to cover all the angles, or to collect data simply because 'It would be interesting to see if . . .', betrays a lack of assurance about the research process. We feel that one of the most important things a supervisor can impart is that sense of confidence: to collect the right kinds of data, with an appropriate research design.

How many data? Students – especially in the social sciences – are often preoccupied with this question. It seems to be especially pressing for candidates preparing for the shorter dissertations associated with taught masters courses. But it is an issue for higher degree students of all kinds. The methodologist, of course, will recognize how such questions are unanswerable in a vacuum, and how they might be addressed for particular research designs. The experienced supervisor will also recognize, however, that such questions are recurrent even among students who have had the advantage of research methods training.

In the social sciences, we are often asked by nervous students questions such as 'How many informants should I interview?' Our answer is predictable: 'It depends on what you want to do.' We find ourselves explaining that a modest volume of high-quality data that are analysed in considerable depth and with methodological precision and sophistication will often be far better than a lot of data that are superficially analysed. We remind them of the adage offered by Harry Wolcott, the American anthropologist of education. Wolcott points out that he only studies one of anything at any given time: one village, or one school, or one school principal. 'But Harry,' he says people say to him, 'What can you learn from just one?' 'As much as I can,' he tells them. This is a useful maxim for students and supervisors to keep in mind, no matter what their discipline. What is important is what you can learn, not the sheer volume of data that are collected.

Getting started and keeping the faith

One of the most important functions the supervisor can perform is to maintain the student's confidence and enthusiasm. This is, of course, true throughout the research student's career (and may need to extend beyond the formal end of the candidature, as a career progresses), but it is often especially significant during the early period of empirical work. If things were easy, and research problems were soluble as soon as we approached them, then research would be much easier than it really is, and there would be little need for research training, the whole apparatus of research studentships, fellowships, supervision and examination. Research is hard and it is messy.

In sociology and social anthropology, beginning students are often disappointed to discover that the social worlds they observe do not readily yield up research problems and analytic concepts. In particular, students who have been reared on the kind of ideas that are more characteristic of undergraduate courses and textbooks find it hard to adjust to the diffuse reality of the social world. They look in vain for their cherished ideas ('hegemony', 'patriarchy', 'anomie' or whatever) and they discover that social worlds do not come neatly packaged in such terms. They see ordinary people doing more or less familiar mundane tasks. They collect data, but often become fretful and insecure because they cannot 'see' problems or processes. It is very easy for the novice student to lose confidence early in the empirical phases of the research project in the face of uncertainty or a lack of clarity in the initial results.

The phenomenon is by no means confined to research students in the non-experimental disciplines. Experimental psychologists and natural scientists will normally have been socialized into a 'puzzle-solving' view of laboratory work in the course of the undergraduate training, and even in a masters programme. While students are exposed to the laboratory, and learn practical lab skills, the kinds of experiments they perform are often more in line with the kind of science taught in secondary schools than with the kind of work that they may encounter for the first time as research students in their own right. A number of authors have now commented on this distinction between research and the quasi-experiments that are characteristic of scientific pedagogy. The latter may more usefully be thought of as demonstrations or recapitulations. Undergraduate students are not expected to 'discover' new phenomena, nor even to explore established phenomena from a novel angle. The majority of experiments that are performed in university laboratories are not aimed at novelty. Students may be 'discovering' things for themselves, but they are usually following well trodden paths. They reproduce the taken-for-granted knowledge of 'normal science'. They and their teachers usually know that provided they follow the recipes of laboratory technique, and are reasonably careful in executing their work, then they will approximate to the 'right answers' in their practical work. Moreover, pedagogical demonstrations can be constructed and carried out because the 'correct' answers are predictable (at least to the teachers concerned).

In contrast, when postgraduate research students start to embark on their own research projects, then they are very likely to encounter novel experiences: among them the fact that their experiments – their equipment, perhaps – will not 'work' in the way that their undergraduate laboratory recapitulations 'worked'. They cannot rely on their teachers stage-managing the laboratory setting so as to ensure positive results, nor can they recover failures by recourse to the kinds of pedagogical repair described by Delamont and Atkinson (1995): in other words, one cannot wish away failure by tidying up results, or going over what 'ought' to have happened, or what 'in fact' is the case.

All our biochemistry respondents had completed a practical (laboratory-based) project in their final year of undergraduate study, but, as a biochemistry supervisor confirmed, 'At undergraduate level the experiments are designed to work, that's why they're chosen.' Many postgraduates come to doctoral research poorly prepared, because the differences between undergraduate and graduate science are largely unanticipated.

Whereas, at undergraduate level, students expect their experiments to work, at postgraduate level they can never be certain. Biochemistry supervisors recognize the difficulties experienced by postgraduates in coming to terms with this uncertainty. The biochemistry postgraduates acknowledged a lack of preparation for postgraduate work, and despondency and sometimes panic when their experiments consistently failed. The following description of initiation into PhD work is provided by a biochemistry doctoral student, and is representative of the accounts provided by other postgraduates:

> The first thing I had to do was make an RNA and I kept failing. It took me three months before it started working. The thing about biochemistry is that often nothing works and the only thing you can possibly do to come to terms with that is to grit your teeth and carry on trying. It came as a big shock to me that nothing worked.

The realization that the outcomes of laboratory work are by no means certain accompanies a growing concern among postgraduates that there is nothing predictable about doctoral study and there is no guarantee that PhD requirements will be met:

> It's that it's suddenly for real. You're not playing any more but that it's completely open ended and there is no guarantee that it's going to work. It's three years of your life and it could easily go down the toilet.
>
> (Biochemistry student)

PhD students involved in experimental laboratory work felt frustrated because initially 'you can't get something to work' and 'you can get to your wits' end trying to get something to work.' We also learnt how just because an experiment has worked once, there is no guarantee that it will work at any time in the future: 'When you run a test you might do it once and it works. You do it four or five times more and it doesn't work' (Biochemistry postgraduate). Although one explanation for this was the sheer volume of variables involved – 'for a simple experiment there may be six or seven variables, for a complicated one there could be hundreds' – this does not explain why some experiments work first time and others don't: 'Sometimes you'll do something for the first time without any rhyme or reason it will work, and other times things that should work won't.' We also learnt how, once a particular experiment has worked, then in most cases it always works: 'It's funny because if you're having trouble getting something to go, when it does finally go it will work routinely.'

Learning to cope with the insecurities associated with scientific work formed an important part of the process of PhD work, particularly among our biochemistry respondents. There are a number of strategies or ways in which postgraduates learn to rationalize initial failure. One of these is by understanding that it is not personal; it happens to everyone. In reaching this understanding, the role of 'significant others' (the supervisor and other members of the research group) is crucial:

> PhDs get bad patches when things don't work out in the expected way. They can't see where it's going wrong and they don't have any

results. They mostly appreciate that this does happen and not just to them.

(Biochemistry supervisor)

Another way in which students come to terms with failure is to interpret it as a fundamental component of scientific training which is ultimately resolvable. The immediate realization that initially nothing works is gradually replaced by a certainty that in the end it will work. Although coming to terms with initial failure is seen as a 'totally demoralizing process', it is nevertheless recognized as part of learning the ropes and therefore constitutes a crucial component of 'lab experience'. Coming to terms with uncertainty therefore constitutes an important benchmark for PhD students: 'You learn to accept that nine times out of ten things in the lab don't work; and if you can cope with that you'll be all right.'

It is when PhD students first begin to produce results in the laboratory that their previous worries and insecurities are overshadowed, and despondency gives way to a growing conviction that ultimately their experiments will work:

> When you get your first results, you get really excited. You probably get more excited with the first results than any you get after. You're really pleased. And slowly you come to terms with things not working.

(Biochemistry student)

Once students come to accept the unpredictability of scientific research, it becomes a manageable component of their work:

> If you make plans it's always on the basis that everything will work, which of course it doesn't. You could say at the first attempt there's a 50/50 chance it will work, but that's being generous.

(Biochemistry PhD)

The attitude expressed above, namely 'everything goes wrong but you have to remember that's not all the time', was shared by all our respondents in biochemistry, and was accompanied by the conviction that once 'it's started to work you're on your way'.

We do not want to exaggerate the difference here. It is a well established feature of academic disciplinary cultures that research problems in the laboratory sciences are usually well specified, and research students are not cast adrift on totally uncharted waters. Research problems are typically formulated and handed down from one generation to the next. In natural sciences, for instance, one generation may establish one set of experiments, or solve one kind of problem. The next generation may then go on to refine the techniques, solve the next line of problems, develop new techniques to derive further research topics and so on. In some labs the former generation, now postdoctoral researchers, supervise the day-to-day work of the next, who are the postgraduate students.

For all that careful preparation and the cascade of problems and techniques within the laboratory, however, beginning students frequently encounter problems. Sometimes they seem not just tricky, but unpredictable and whimsical. The natural world does not appear to research students to yield up its problems and solutions any more readily than the social world.

If research students in most disciplines were easily discouraged, then they could very easily give up the whole enterprise at an early stage. On the other hand, we know that perseverance carries rewards. For the majority of students in the social sciences and humanities, patterns and results do emerge: the relevance of general theories and major concepts does start to become apparent. Likewise, equipment in the laboratory sciences does start to work, and the folk wisdom of the sciences is that once an experiment starts to work as it should, then results start to come. And once that process starts, things rarely go wrong again in a major way. Cracking the problem is itself unpredictable. Sometimes the breakthrough can come from a critical incident, or from a particular piece of reading, or from a more-or-less random modification to the equipment. It is difficult to foresee just what will start to unlock the process. And one must admit that sometimes things just never get ungummed, and the student can never get everything to work properly, or can never quite see the analytic pattern.

What is important is for the supervisor to maintain a productive balance between optimism and realism, and to shore up the student's confidence should it wobble. Purblind encouragement is clearly dangerous: no supervisor should push students to carry on banging their head against the proverbial brick wall. If things seem to be going wrong, then one must entertain the possibility that they really are going wrong and will not get any better. If a student does turn out to be pursuing a problem that cannot be cracked, trying to study an organization to which access will not be forthcoming or trailing a technique that really is not ready to be implemented, then the supervisor's job may be to help him or her to undertake a realistic appraisal of the situation, to review what has been learned from the project to date and to apply those insights to a reformulation of the problem, or a new research design, or whatever it will take to rescue the student and her or his project. On the other hand, the supervisor needs to be alert to varieties of 'data collection blues'. If the problems of data collection seem to be routine, reflecting the normal vicissitudes of research, then the supervisor's role will be different. In such cases, the most important job is to maintain impetus, to help the student to work through the various disappointments and frustrations. A good deal of postgraduate supervision can be described as a kind of 'confidence trick' – repeatedly persuading students that they can get the equipment to work, and that it will be one day soon, that the results will start to come, that they will start to find themes and patterns in their field data, that their laborious work in the archives will start to yield significant results as well as huge volumes of dull records.

Student research projects are, in different ways, acts of faith. As school students and as undergraduates we have to have faith, and we place our trust in our teachers. We have faith that the problems we have been set are soluble and are within the compass of our existing skills and knowledge. As research students we outgrow that elementary form of faith. Now research student and supervisor alike have to embark on the research project as an act of renewed faith – believing that research is possible, that new results can be obtained, that a serious contribution to knowledge will be the outcome. The oversight of data collection, especially – but not exclusively – in the early phases, requires of many supervisors that they help to maintain that level of belief. This of course depends on the kind of mutual trust that we discuss elsewhere. The student must trust the supervisor if he or she is to take real heart from such encouragement, or if there is need for a radical evaluation of the project.

We have, incidentally, discussed these issues almost exclusively as if the research process were an empirical one in a conventional sense. It needs to be emphasized that similar considerations apply to purely theoretical work. The investigator in the laboratory, the social scientist in the field or the social historian in the archive may sometimes envy the pure theorist. It is true that 'data collection' in the normal sense of that phrase is not a major problem for the theorist. That does not mean, however, that a student and supervisor may not face similar problems. The contrast between undergraduate and research work is often just as stark. The undergraduate 'theorist' learns fairly standard ways of reading and writing, acquiring a critical rhetoric to mount sustained commentaries on leading figures in the field (as one might well find in philosophy, cultural studies, critical theory or sociology). These are, more often than not, grounded in the pedagogical devices of teachers' questions, rather than researchers' questions. The transition from such recapitulation of critical commentary to the requirement to engage in original theorizing, or to cast original light on theory, can be a major one, and may be no less fraught than any other first steps. Here too the supervisor needs to temper a critical engagement with the candidate's ideas with the ability to sustain his or her self-belief. The student has to have faith that an original voice will be found, and an original contribution to the scholarly literature will be the result.

Drowning in data

As we have already suggested, initial difficulties in getting started, and getting the research to 'work', can often be paralleled by an apparently opposite problem – drowning in data and information. These are not absolute antitheses. The same problems give rise to both phenomena. The problem is especially common among social scientists. They may have had difficulty in setting up the project, gaining access and so on. But all too often they end up with reams and reams of data. The same problems seem to result – though in somewhat different guises – irrespective of whether the candidate is conducting qualitative or quantitative data. To some extent, in at least some projects, 'too many' data are probably inevitable. Where research is exploratory, and the research design to some extent open-ended, it is virtually impossible to collect 'just the right amount' of data. Indeed, it is hard to see what that might mean. The young anthropologist who spends a year or 18 months in the intensive study of a given social setting can never judge from the outset how much is 'enough'. In any case, in such research contexts, the thesis is but one outcome of the research, and the young scholar may have few chances of such long-term immersion in a field site in the course of an entire career. The data collection must last well beyond the period of doctoral candidature and submission of the thesis itself.

The problem is by no means confined to the social sciences, however. Historians may often find themselves 'drowning' in their archive or other source material. Physical scientists too may amass a great many experimental data, once their equipment is up and running.

On the one hand, the growing pile of data is welcome. It is a visible reminder of the progress of the research. Concrete results and documentary materials provide some guarantee that the research is proving 'successful'. The accumulation of lots of data can provide the fledgling researcher with the equivalent of a 'security blanket': it is a guard against the uncertainties of research in the widest sense. The results themselves may be intrinsically exciting and satisfying. Research student and supervisor alike can become engrossed in the results as they emerge. After all, there are few highs that are more satisfying than to make a genuine discovery, to demonstrate a new technique, prove a theorem or whatever.

On the other hand, the accumulation of data can all too readily leave the student (and the supervisor) floundering. When the original research proposal was formulated, things probably had a certain simplicity. A preliminary review of the literature, or a more worked-up research design, will probably have suggested some well defined research problems. The collection of substantial amounts of data is quite likely to make things seem a good deal more messy. Even in the 'precise' disciplines, measurements are unlikely to be perfectly consistent. Correlations are not always statistically significant; not all results exactly fit the curve; distributions have outliers. When the student becomes over-involved in the minutiae of data and results, then she or he may find it hard to see the wood for the trees. Furthermore, it may be emotionally hard to give up some of those hard-won data, and students may cling to them so tenaciously as to lose a sense of discrimination.

The supervisor's role at this point has a good deal to do with helping the student to achieve some sense of discrimination. She or he needs, perhaps, to distinguish once more between what is important and what may be discarded: to exercise judgement over results that may be discarded, those that are significant and those anomalous results that might just be the germ of the next exciting project. If a student has become unduly attached to the data and the findings, then a good supervisor will have to find a way to help discard some – or at least to put them on the back burner, ready to be visited once more when the thesis is safely in the hands of the examiners, or the degree safely awarded. (Getting the student to let go of the completed thesis may also be a problem, and we shall have occasion to return to that topic.)

There is often a crucial juncture in the research process when the supervisor needs to help the candidate to step back momentarily from the day-to-day grind of data collection and analysis. It may be opportune to schedule a seminar presentation, or a brief written working paper, used as a vehicle to establish a sense of what is really important, what needs to be focused on in the thesis, what issues will engage most readily the attention of the academic community, what will be regarded as especially publishable and so on. Whether or not such formal procedures are adopted (and many programmes have regular reviews and presentations built into them, of course), it is important to help the student to gain an adequate perspective on the work, to see the overall shape and pattern that can emerge, or is emerging, and to concentrate on the essentials. Poorly constructed theses are often characterized by unnecessary detail. Self-confidence is, again, vital. The student who is unsure of what the thesis is really about, or is not secure in its significance, may be tempted to try the kitchen-sink strategy – including everything that has been done, rather than constructing a selective and purposeful set of analyses.

It is crucial in this context that the supervisor's greater experience, and greater awareness of comparable standards across different institutions, can be invaluable. The supervisor should be in a position to provide just that sort of critical and well informed distance that a review requires, while maintaining the student's trust in that critical process.

How close is the supervision?

There is no right answer to this question, but the degree of involvement of the supervisor in the actual processes of data collection is an occasional problem or dilemma for the conscientious supervisor.

In the ordinary run of things, it is impossible in the majority of cases for a supervisor to be closely involved in the day-to-day, hands-on collection of data in most disciplines. Data collection is arduous and time-consuming, irrespective of whether the research is based on the laboratory, fieldwork, the library or the archive. Full-time students barely have enough time and energy to devote to their own work. Busy supervisors have little opportunity to oversee and interfere at the level of detail, even if they wanted to, or if they should.

In many laboratory sciences the 'everyday' oversight of data collection is done by fellow students, postdoctoral colleagues and technicians rather than the supervisor. Under these arrangements the research context revolves around mutual support and sharing of materials, skills and equipment. An important feature of this model is a continuity of practice, in that skills, equipment and topics are passed down through the ranks of postdoctoral researchers and research students.

These arrangements occur where the research structure revolves around one supervisor or research director, with doctoral students and postdoctoral researchers working in his or her area on topics that are to some extent related. In this context a specific set of research-related patterns emerge which inform the 'habitus' of the group. This model was offered to us in contrast to the 'traditional' model of PhD supervision in the social sciences: 'The difference between us and social science is that we tend to do PhDs through team work' (Geography supervisor). Because supervisors or research directors tend to have several PhD students at any one time, they take a back stage role in regard to practical day-to-day supervision of students:

> I think my leverage, what I contribute, is not sitting there and doing research myself but creating the possibilities for other people to do it and trying to shape the direction of what gets done.
>
> (Artificial intelligence supervisor)

The supervisor's main role as research director means that assistance with everyday problems concerning the research are resolved elsewhere: 'I don't tell her [the supervisor] the ins and outs of problems, I tend to talk to other people, call in the knowledge of others in the department' (Biochemistry postdoctoral researcher). The PhD students see the research group environment as mutually supportive:

> There are other people working on different things but there are similarities in our work, e.g. mathematics, methods and computing. There's no explicit link between projects but we almost totally rely on each other for support. It's a reciprocal arrangement that people respect rather than a role which people take on.
>
> (Geography doctoral student)

Where group members are working on different research problems there are still overlaps in the materials and techniques which they use:

> We're all working on the same sort of areas, we use a lot of the same assays and substances . . . a lot of the substances I make will be used by other people as well. If I invent a method to make something easier then they'll use it as well.
>
> (Biochemistry doctoral student)

Less experienced members of the group rely upon the more experienced members: 'If things keep going wrong then usually someone who gets it right will sort of go through the experiment one day with you' (Biochemistry doctoral student).

Under arrangements like these the supervisor provides guidance on the framework and direction of research, while experienced group members, such as postdoctoral researchers or doctoral candidates more advanced in their work, help the inexperienced PhD students on a day-to-day basis:

> Well what I like to do with students; when I was a postdoc in the lab, I liked to work very much on my own. Because it suits me. So I encourage people to do the same, I give them their own head. Because of the numbers I couldn't always be looking over their shoulders anyway. If they need day-to-day help there are others like the postdocs in the lab and they can help them. I tend to give specific advice to students. They have a definite programme. I'm not there to tell them how to use an instrument, they can find someone else for that.
>
> (Biochemistry supervisor)

Given the numbers of doctoral students per supervisor (which can be as many as ten at any one time), it would not be feasible for supervisors to take full responsibility for training graduate students: 'Most of the training of the PhDs is the responsibility of the post-docs. We couldn't do it otherwise' (Biochemistry supervisor).

The doctoral students we talked to described the very different expectations of individuals within their research groups:

> I use my supervisor to sort out my structure and any individual problems only when I feel it is appropriate and when I can't get it from Dave or someone else.
>
> (Geography doctoral student)

The supervisor is seen as above the day-to-day functioning of the research group members:

> I think we have a really healthy research environment. We don't always, or often even, take our problems to our supervisors. We're a well established group working along the same lines.
>
> (Geography doctoral student)

Because of this, PhD supervision is seen as a collective responsibility:

> I work within a group . . . a whole group of people, research associates, PhD students and technical help and consultancy help. That makes about ten people. So for fieldwork problems or day-to-day things I don't have to go to my supervisor. There's all sorts of people to draw from who did similar PhDs, and who've come through here. So it's like a big supervisory group.
>
> (Geography doctoral student)

Where relationships with the supervisor break down, this collective support can rescue the PhD, as described below:

> We had to dig ourselves out of a dodgy situation so we pulled together and were able to help each other a great deal. It was a kind of collective survival, in the face of a staggering lack of supervision.
>
> (Biochemistry doctoral student)

The collective support of the research group also functions as a buffer, for the PhD students, against failure:

> It was a large group which was my saving. I felt I could go to any-body in the group. If I had been isolated I would have been terribly demoralized and I would probably have given up.
>
> (Biochemistry postdoctoral researcher)

The onus of supervision falls upon the postdoctoral researcher:

> I think the postdocs give day-to-day guidance. My role as head of the lab is a psychologist. Experiments don't always go well and I need to cheer them up. Especially the PhD students when nothing seems to be working.
>
> (Biochemistry supervisor)

Postdoctoral researchers often take on this role as a matter of course, 'after all it was the way I was trained':

> One thing you do get as a postdoc is troubleshooting other people's problems and you do generate a feeling for what is likely to make the difference between something working and not working.
>
> (Biochemistry postdoctoral researcher)

Postdoctoral researchers themselves acknowledge this change of role and their responsibilities in this respect: 'Recently my role has changed. I'm now a research associate which means I'm a stepping stone between PhD students and their supervisor' (Geography postdoctoral researcher). Although it was acceptable practice for postdoctorate researchers to super-vise PhD students on a day-to-day basis it was nevertheless an unofficial line of responsibility:

There's two PhDs working on the model. Here I am the direct line of unwritten responsibility. It's not in my contract and I don't really see it as my role. But I help them and sort it out.

(Geography postdoctoral researcher)

The type of PhD organization that we have just described is only possible where certain conditions prevail. The two crucial features are group size and continuity of research. Only where there are sufficient numbers of postgraduates (at different stages of research) and postdoctoral researchers can the team or group model of supervision operate. Moreover, the group or team structure depends upon a continuity of funding which allows for several individuals (students and postdoctoral researchers) working in the same area both simultaneously and in succession. Under these conditions, topics or projects can logically follow on from each other, with new PhD students developing the work of previous students. In this way, a pedagogic continuity operates as skills and equipment are handed down through the research group. If we apply Hacking's (1992) analogy of the strand or rope, we can see how the interests of group members are mutually intertwined in a linear process, through which the work of individuals is shaped and developed. However, the supervisor is ultimately responsible for the intellectual quality of the PhD student's work, and cannot abrogate that responsibility.

Some research of necessity takes place at some remove from the supervisor's gaze anyway. Social anthropology probably provides the most sustained examples of distant fieldwork, although other 'field' disciplines, such as geography and earth sciences, can also depend on distant data collection. Anthropology is probably unique among disciplines in placing such a heavy emphasis on such 'fieldwork', and in stressing its solitary nature (collective 'expeditions' or research groups are not the norm). In such cases, the supervisor and the student need to establish considerable degrees of trust in each other, and a degree of faith that the fieldwork will prove successful, despite whatever vicissitudes and intellectual problems may ensue. Anthropology supervisors try to ensure regular contact from 'the field', through letters and reports from their students. This is not always possible, however, and contact may become quite attenuated, as in the case of Nina Yeager, with whom we open Chapter 6.

6

Disagreeableness and danger: keeping up the student's motivation

If you have put anything in hand, disagreeableness and danger will not turn you back, and God forbid they should.

(Sayers 1972: 209)

Introduction

This chapter deals with one of the hardest and most diffuse tasks that faces the supervisor. PhD students very often go through sloughs of depression about debt and poverty, isolation, thesis problems and poor employment prospects, which the supervisor may be able to alleviate. They also have problems with supervision which the supervisor may not recognize, and may or may not be able to solve. Take this story about an anthropology student, told to us by Dr Feste (University of Kingford).

> Yes, this is the woman I'm seeing through to the end, who's actually been supervised as far as I can tell, by everyone else in the department . . . Well, she started with not a very coherent idea with Jeremy Styles, I think – she's doing ideas of procreation and birth – and it wasn't coherent when she started out, and she was moved on to both Ian Felgate and Ralph Dorroway, both of whom she did not get on very well with, and she seems to have been through several other people, and ended up with Carolyn Brackenberry after seven or eight years – it's been a long drawn-out saga, and Carolyn's managed to get her through to the point where she's almost ready to submit. Everything's just about ready in draft, and she [Carolyn] had to go on leave, so rather than saying 'take another nine months' she arranged to bring her to me, so that she would finish by June 30. Which is the ESRC deadline, although she's missed it by several years, as far as I can tell. The department had more or less written her off, and it's quite clear from her fieldwork material, as Carolyn Brackenberry

pointed out, that she was not adequately supervised at various points, so that questions the supervisor would have said – 'Have you asked your women this?' – particularly as she was right here in Scotland, are missing from the material, because there was no one there to suggest things, so there were gaps, which even if you're in the field, you write to your supervisor and get a letter back saying 'Try this' etc. And she's had great blanks of supervision where she was on her own, so it has been a problem.

All such stories have two (or more) sides – as we can see if we match Dr Feste's account with that of the student herself, Nina Yeager. As she tells her own story:

> When I moved to Kingford there was a trend in Kingford anthropo-logy that appealed to me . . . here there was an interest in the anthro-pology of the emotions, and that sort of thing, and I think that's very central in the problems I've had as a postgraduate student.

Nina had been a postgraduate for 'eight or nine years', and this is her account of her supervisory problem. We have put the supervisor's names in brackets for the reader.

> My supervisor [Jeremy Styles] went away for a year – I talked to him in the summer and he agreed to be my supervisor and he went away that year. So the first year I started off with someone else [Ian Felgate] for a year, who I felt I had a similar approach to, so that wasn't a problem. Then when he [Jeremy Styles, the original supervisor] came back I moved back to him, that was the arrangement, but then after a year he got a job in another university so I moved back to the man I'd started off with [Ian Felgate] as a temporary arrangement, but after a year he went on sabbatical.

By this point Nina had already been enrolled for five years and her first two supervisors were both absent from Kingford, one permanently. She should, as an ESRC-funded full-time student, ideally have finished her work at least a year before. However, Nina's story has another three years to run:

> So I was then moved to another person [Ralph Dorroway] who I worked with for six months, and who's gone somewhere for a few months, so I'm now temporarily with someone else [Carolyn Brackenberry] but in the meantime I hope to finish. So that's an end to it.

Nina then outlines her problems as she sees them:

> apart from all these changes . . . the first two supervisors really I think belonged to one school, then I changed to a supervisor of a

different school and he found a lot of problems with my work, some of which I think were because I had had poor supervision. The people were interested but not very directive at a time when I needed more direction.

Odette asked Nina to run through the 'natural history' of her PhD, and this revealed a raft of other problems. Nina explained that she had spent 1984 'trying to sort out the questions that I needed to ask' before fieldwork. However,

> I got pregnant in '85 . . . I had problems with the pregnancy, so apart from having maternity leave anyway I also had time off because I couldn't work after the fifth month . . . I had a miscarriage and my mother was ill, then I was pregnant again.

Nina had not had financial problems, because her husband supported her and the two children. 'We came to an understanding that I have had the children in my thesis time and therefore he would fund me afterwards so I'd get it finished.' Having two infant children had prevented Nina from taking much part in the intellectual life at Kingford, such as the postgraduate writing group. So: 'the isolation of it is difficult. I know you get involved in an area that's very much your own, so in a sense up to that point you're intellectually isolated.'

Clearly most postgraduates do not have two children, a miscarriage and a sick parent all in four years, or, indeed, four or five different supervisors. However, nearly all students hit some problems – repetitive strain injury, glandular fever, eviction, parental divorce – as well as the thesis-related problems. All the stages – pre-fieldwork, data collection, analysis, writing up – had their problems and their pleasures. One of our geography students, Eunice Lester, in the final stages of her PhD told us:

> I'm constantly amazed because at each point of the research process somebody will come along and say this is the worst part of the whole process – from research question formulation right up to now! And somebody just said to me they felt really sorry for me because this is the most demoralizing and lonely part etc., etc., etc. And it has been a lonely process. There are ups and downs. There are times when I'm sick and tired of reading my own prose, I don't want to do it anymore. But I'm feeling positive at the moment.

This chapter contrasts some of the different problems facing science and humanities postgraduates, then outlines some strategies the supervisor can use to help students to face them and resolve them. First we deal with data collection problems.

Data collection problems

For many science PhD students the biggest academic problem is producing usable results, either in the laboratory or from fieldwork outdoors
in caves, mountains or riverbeds. We have presented in Chapter 5 a good
deal of material from biochemistry doctoral students describing how they
come to terms with the problems of producing usable results in their
laboratory experiments, and have not recapitulated them here.

The science supervisor has to help students to learn that 'real' science
is not like undergraduate work, where the results of experiments are normally known in advance. Our biochemistry respondents came to terms with
failure by interpreting it as a fundamental component of scientific training
which is ultimately resolvable. The immediate realization that initially
nothing works is gradually replaced by a certainty that in the end it will
work. Although coming to terms with initial failure is seen as a 'totally
demoralizing process' it is nevertheless recognized as part of learning the
ropes and therefore constitutes a crucial component of 'lab experience'.
Coming to terms with uncertainty therefore constitutes an important
benchmark for PhD students: 'You . . . learn to accept that nine times out
of ten things in the lab don't work; and if you can cope with that you'll
be all right.'

Learning to cope when experiments do not work properly is an important survival skill for the science PhD student. Supervisors need to
be alert for times when the failure of experimental work is demoralizing
the student. In Chapter 5 we quoted accounts of the uncertainties faced
by our respondents from biochemistry, physical geography and artificial
intelligence, and their despondency when results were not forthcoming.
Exactly the same points were made by the doctoral students in pharmaceutics interviewed by Whittlesea (1995). For example, one of Whittlesea's
informants suggested that in 'med chem science' the sole criterion of
success is the synthesis of a new compound: 'So they have to go on and
get this product out and no matter how long it takes. So it is sometimes
quite horrible for them' (pp. 68–9). Another respondent told of a friend
who was

> starting something new at the end of the year. Some experimental
> work, which didn't go very well. He ended up spending ten months
> on it and getting nothing from it. That really disillusioned him.
> (p. 70)

We have already seen that when science students start to get their first
results, they find the experience satisfying and even exhilarating. It is
when PhD students first begin to produce results in the laboratory that
their previous worries and insecurities are overshadowed, and despondency

gives way to a growing conviction that ultimately their experiments will work.

The doctoral students we interviewed tended to locate their own work within the broader context of the scientific work in their area being carried out by all the researchers in their laboratory, and to keep up their motivation by looking at the wider picture of the overall research programme: 'In this department we tend to put everything into a wider perspective so we can see where everything fits in' (Geography postgraduate). Students tended to locate their research by specifically linking it with previous work:

> I've got a model . . . which was developed by a biologist, an ethnologist, and I've made a robot to simulate that model. I've found there are a number of problems with it, so I'm constantly trying to work out what are the best ways of adapting the model to try and make it work better.
>
> (Artificial intelligence postgraduate)

The majority of our science students described their projects as taking further or expanding upon the work of others: 'I think of my work as extending what other people have done, I think it has come out from a base and it's pushed out from there' (Geography postgraduate). In many cases respondents were able to cite the specific individual who had developed their work because they had been a postgraduate in, or were still a postdoctoral researcher in, the department. This was often the supervisor:

> Once you identify a structure there's a lot you can do with it. I have the structure from her, and by looking at it and finding out what is important I take her work forward, using my own knowledge and methods.
>
> (Biochemistry postdoctoral researcher)

Equally, it might be a previous PhD student in the department:

> You can see the progress and how things are moving on. And results seem to have more of a major impact because I'm working with Pete's model and I'm extending it and seeing how its application can be valuable. That means Pete (and John who worked on the model before Pete) are very interested in my results.
>
> (Geography postgraduate)

The number of people working on aspects of the same model at any one time can vary. The following postgraduate is also working on the model referred to above. 'Pete was here then, working on a computing model. He was just finishing his PhD as I started mine. Pete got John's job when he finished.' This pattern is not only retrospective but also provides a structure for individual research trajectories:

The idea is that she is doing a PhD and was going to take over from me when I finish. Also someone else is coming to be a PhD in October and by then I'll be the postdoc on the project.

(Geography postgraduate student)

Often individuals who have been working or are still working in the same project – whether it be the development of an enzyme or a modelling program – have different funding sources:

Tim has got a joint SERC and industry grant and was funded to do his research on this enzyme. There was a person working on the enzyme before him. The first person tried to purify the enzyme and came quite close. Then a year later Tim started and actually purified the enzyme and started working on it. Now I shall be taking that work a little bit further.

(Biochemistry doctoral student)

The existence of this continuity is itself motivating for the student, but the supervisor may need to highlight the group's successes when the student is demoralized.

We found that PhD students in the early stages of their doctoral research were poorly prepared for the day-to-day uncertainty of scientific work, in that they experience a qualitative difference between laboratory work at undergraduate and graduate level. Although all our biochemistry respondents had completed a practical project in their final year of undergraduate study, this was often inadequate preparation for their later experiences as postgraduates. As noted by Collins (1985: 35), Delamont and Atkinson (1995) and others, experiments which are carried out as a routine component of education and training address questions to which the answers are already known and are constructed to produce only successful conclusions. The biochemistry supervisors recognized the difficulties experienced by postgraduates in coming to terms with this insecurity. Certainly the biochemistry postgraduates acknowledged their lack of preparation for laboratory work, and despondency and sometimes panic when their experiments constantly failed.

The realization that the outcomes of laboratory work are by no means certain accompanies a growing concern among postgraduates that there is no guarantee that PhD requirements will be met. Day-to-day uncertainty encountered by doctoral students in the early stages of their research can lead to doubts about the predictability of completing a PhD. An important aspect of the process of PhD work, particularly among our biochemistry respondents, was learning to cope with the insecurities associated with scientific work. There are a number of strategies or ways in which postgraduates learn to rationalize initial failure. One of these is by understanding that it is not personal; it happens to everyone. For reaching this understanding, the role of 'significant others' (the supervisor and other members of the research group) is crucial.

Those of our respondents who relied upon the collection, collation or manipulation of data from natural phenomena, to a greater or lesser extent, described themselves as at the mercy of natural elements over which they had no control. This applied equally to biochemistry PhD students waiting for rape seeds to germinate and geographers waiting for the rainy season: 'The reality is you get pushed and shoved, depending on the seasonality of the thing, that's very much a big problem with natural field conditions.' For the science students, the biggest source of help with these problems was an active research group in a laboratory, with postdoctoral fellows around who could, *by their very existence*, show that there is hope: that theses do get done. For intellectual problems in science the intellectually vital laboratory is the best source of motivation. For the more individualized research characteristic of humanities and social sciences, the supervisor may be the only source of help. If the social science or humanities project is going wrong, the supervisor should use his or her greater experience to help with the practical problems, or guide the student to refocus the research, or seek help with the technical problems, or get on with another aspect of her or his doctoral research until the difficulty is resolved.

Thus far we have focused on students being demoralized by their data collection. We now move on to deal with extrinsic sources of demotivation, such as poverty. We discuss a set of problems than can beset all PhD students, leading to one, isolation, that is much commoner among non-scientists.

Problems and what the supervisor can do about them

The problems discussed here are poverty, poor working habits, lack of motivation and depression, and isolation. The major problems not discussed in detail in this chapter are those related to writing, because that is the focus of Chapter 9.

Poverty

Poverty is a crippling problem for many research students. They are living in poor quality housing, with inadequate food and clothing, and certainly cannot buy books, a PC, a decent workstation, a proper typing chair and so on. This has three consequences which impact upon their research.

1 A poor diet is likely to make them ill, spotty, tired, lethargic and so on.
2 Inadequate heat, light and facilities may make work at home difficult or even damaging to health.

3 Time may be eaten away by many hours spent on low paid, possibly unpleasant, work.

All these problems are multiplied if the student has dependent children and/or a dependent spouse, and may be multiplied even further if the student is from overseas. To be a poor 23-year-old single person is one thing, to be a poor 43-year-old woman with a disabled husband and two dependent teenagers, to be a poor Tunisian with a wife and five children under 7, are different forms of poverty. The possible solutions the supervisor can offer will also vary. At its simplest, the supervisor can invite a single 23-year-old to have a square meal every week, and ensure that he or she sometimes eats 'properly' by providing food in the supervision or a basket of fruit for the graduate room. Such 'solutions' are much less possible with a mature student who has a family home.

It may be possible in some universities to find paid work for the research student, ideally even paid work that could have some relevance to the thesis. Demonstrating in the lab has traditionally been available for some science and engineering students, but is rarely paid well enough to alleviate poverty. In some universities, humanities and social science students get paid work taking tutorials or seminars for undergraduates (such work is rarely available for overseas students). Some departments have no budget to pay for such help, however. These opportunities are usually beneficial to the student's higher degree: teaching something helps enormously with one's own understanding of it. However, the income is spasmodic – work for ten or twelve weeks, then nothing – and it can be a displacement activity – undergraduates can swamp the friendly postgraduate with demands, and it is often easier to spend time with a lonely or bewildered student than tackle the thesis task.

In these circumstances, the supervisor *may* be able to find demonstrating, tutoring or the equivalent at another institution: in general our networks are better than theirs. Coaching local school children for GCSE or A level may also be a possibility – students with a family may even be able to do that in their own homes. Again, the supervisor may be able to advise students to do such work, and help them to find it. There may also be local colleges wanting A level lecturers, or a WEA/adult education set-up where the student would be able to teach. Recognizing that the student is broke, and will need to earn, and signalling that the supervisor would prefer the work to be subject-related, is more productive than the ostrich position.

If a student has dependants, it may be worth checking that the family is getting all the available support: there may be local charities or scholarships, help from the students' union or even work for the spouse which people in the university know about, but the student may not have been to see these welfare, union or pastoral offices. If the student has to take in other work, it may be desirable to try to find some *in* the university, such as proof-reading or library assistance, rather than leaving the student to stack shelves in a supermarket or clean offices.

The worst pressures of student poverty commonly occur when students are writing up the thesis after their full-time money has run out and they have not yet found proper employment, or, if from overseas, not been able to go home. The case of Hereilio Costa is not unusual.

Example 6.1: Hereilio Costa

Hereilio Costa was from Brazil. His grant had run out, but he knew that if he went back to Brazil he was unlikely ever to submit. He was reduced to selling his possessions – his watch, his PC, his car – and helping other overseas students with their written work.

Apart from the depressing effects of poverty and poor diet on health, it may be that poverty is impeding the student's thesis because she or he lacks the basic facilities to do anything on the theses at home. A good supervisor needs to enquire whether students have got a warm room to work in. Clearly you cannot be expected to heat their homes, but you can, perhaps, heat a space in the university for them, *or* buy and lend them snuggle sacks. Have they got adequate lighting? Again, perhaps, you can have ready a 'spare' desk lamp you could lend. Have they got a proper typing chair, foot rest, keyboard and a work table of the right height?

If the university does not provide PhD students with adequate working conditions, and hardly any do for part-time students even if their full-timers' spaces are lavishly equipped, a caring supervisor will check that the student is properly equipped to do the work. Getting the proper equipment, either owning it or borrowing it for the duration, can speed up completion considerably, as in the case of Caroline Sheppard.

Example 6.2: Caroline Sheppard

Teresa Rees and Sara discovered that Caroline Sheppard was transcribing her interviews, using a Walkman to play back the tapes. She did not know that there were transcribing machines with a foot pedal and high quality 'pause' facility or that our department owned several that research students could borrow. Once issued with a proper machine, Caroline quickly finished her transcribing and moved on to analysis.

Avoiding repetitive strain injury is also important, and students may need to be warned to give themselves breaks and not to spend too long at the keyboard. If the university has an occupational health expert who can give a precautionary talk on this, it could save much heartache (and other pains).

Poor or inappropriate working habits

Even when students have good physical conditions, they may be flagging because they are relying on academic working habits that were adequate or even successful when they were on taught courses with externally set deadlines and a timetable, but are woefully inadequate for a three-year stretch of self-directed research. If a supervisor suspects that this is a problem – deadlines missed, poorly presented work, an apparent lack of progress – it may be necessary to persuade or even insist that the student takes stock of his or her working habits and becomes self-conscious about them.

Students may not realize that they have to discover how they work best, perhaps by experimenting, and once they have decided what suits them, they must organize their lives to maximize the potential for achieving their best working conditions.

It may be helpful to confess to one's own problems. It can be liberating for a student if you describe how you cannot work before lunch or on Thursdays, or without a laptop, or whatever. This can be liberating for students because it reveals that even successful academics have problems (they often think that they have problems we never have), and it can lead to a discussion of possible solutions. Clearly it is not helpful or fair to load all your problems on to the student, but some admission of fallibility is often a great lubricator.

Example 6.3: Unblocking Raymond Boynton and Margaret Rushbridger

We were giving a class on writing strategies – something we do regularly. Sara 'confessed' that she can work only on scrap paper: the backs of committee papers, previous drafts by others, spoilt sheets from the Xerox machine and circulars from publishers, shops or travel companies. Facing a clean pad of file paper paralyses her. One student in the room, Raymond Boynton, suddenly looked interested. A week later he came to find Sara and confessed that he'd been blocked for ages, but had gone home, abandoned his clean pad, and started drafting on some scrap paper. It had worked – he had written 3,000 words of his thesis.

When Raymond told the rest of the doctoral students about his discovery, Margaret Rushbridger 'came out' as a person unblocked by the personal computer. She had discovered that she was paralysed by handwriting or typing, because her results seemed permanent, whereas words on the screen were infinitely malleable, and therefore she could fool herself that she was 'only drafting'.

Repeatedly we have found students who have not thought about their biorhythms, their location, their posture, their preferred facilities. They have not experimented with silence versus noise, being alone versus being in company, the early morning versus the early evening, the clipboard in an armchair versus the laptop, the pen versus the typewriter, the desk versus the kitchen table. The supervisor can usefully explore with students how to discover what their best working habits are, and then how to achieve them.

Example 6.4: Test Match Special versus Runrig or zydeco

Sara's ideal working conditions occur during the cricket season or a simulation of it. She works best to noise rather than silence, and to speech rather than music. The *ideal* working condition is a test match – a long day of speech. She has the TV on, but silent, and the ball-by-ball commentary on the radio. If something happens, she looks up at the screen, but otherwise she lets the radio fill the room with 'burble'. If there is not a real test match, then a tape of one is the next best thing – cassettes of John Arlott and Brian Johnston burbling about Derek Underwood, Alan Knott and chocolate cake. Paul, on the other hand, prefers music: not the serious music that demands attention but something that has bouncy rhythms. Companions to academic work include country and western and zydeco, Runrig and compilations from the Stax and Atlantic labels.

We often share these predilections with our graduate classes – not to try to persuade them to share our particular tastes, but to encourage them to recognize that 'ideal' working conditions vary from person to person, and the trick is to find what suits them best.

Some doctoral students may not have realized that they need to work steadily for 36 or 45 hours a week, because they were successful undergraduates by coasting and cramming in bursts. We know that students have very inaccurate ideas about what lecturers do all day (Startup 1979), so they may not realize that the production of an 80,000 word thesis in three years needs to be a full-time job. Others may be 'overworking', because the task seems so overwhelming. A supervisor can use the regular revisions of the timetable we advocated in Chapter 2 to introduce the discussion of the proper working day, week and year. It is often when investigating the student's working habits that the supervision uncovers the more disconcerting phenomenon – a lack or loss of motivation – and it is to this that we now turn.

Lack and loss of motivation

There are three separable aspects to this: (a) distaste for a specific aspect of the work (e.g. finding a site, doing analysis, writing, word-processing);

(b) temporary loss of enthusiasm of the whole task; (c) serious, perhaps clinical, depression, with a 'medical' origin or solution.

The supervisor's role in dealing with these is, of necessity, rather different. A student who is apparently suffering serious, even clinical, depression needs to be urged towards counselling or the medical profession as soon as the supervisor is worried. Dealing with an underactive thyroid, SAD, ME or a mental illness is not within the scope of a supervisor's expertise or role. The other types of loss of motivation can be tackled by the supervisor.

If students have distaste for a specific task, there are various things that can be done. Sometimes it is possible to find them help with it: perhaps they can arrange to work with another student and share the task, perhaps they can pay for some help with it, perhaps an undergraduate can be assigned to work with them, maybe there is a research assistant, associate or lecturer who likes that task and will help with it. Clearly, the integrity of the thesis cannot be threatened, but help may be the answer. Another solution is to shelve that task and do something else for a while, or start some other parts of the whole project alongside the less preferred one. One reason why students often stall at the writing-up stage is that they have left themselves with no other tasks but writing: if they had written while they did the other phases it would not be so all-or-nothing at the end. Learning to mix writing, data collection, analysis and dull clerical tasks is an important part of learning how to be a productive researcher.

Example 6.5: Jefferson Cope

Sara was supervising Jefferson Cope. He had done a masters degree based on gathering oral histories from educational administrators in his native country. He wanted to do a larger study of educational administators in the UK, again using oral history techniques. After a few months of supervision, Sara felt that he had not really understood the method, and that he needed to think much more deeply about it before conducting his doctoral fieldwork. She therefore set him to read 'classic' methods books and write about them while waiting for access to a research site. Jefferson baulked – it was too boring for words. After several months of stalemate, Jefferson went into the field. The data were not wonderful, and neither Jefferson nor Sara was satisfied with them. Jefferson withdrew. In retrospect, perhaps, Sara should have let him discover his own methodological inadequacies once it became clear that he would not or could not read the classics and face up to the issues in the abstract.

Sometimes distaste for the whole task is owing to an intrinsic difficulty with the thesis, but it may be only a symptom of wider problems in the student's life, as in the case of Amy Leatheran.

Example 6.6: Amy Leatheran

Amy Leatheran was supposed to be doing an MEd thesis supervised by Sara. She appeared to have lost all motivation and was not making any progress. One day she came for a supervision and burst into tears. It transpired that her mother-in-law was too frail to live alone. Amy and her husband had moved into the old lady's house, where Amy no longer had any kind of study where her thesis could be left out, so that she had to keep it boxed up under the bed, or any time to work on it. She had not explained to her husband or her mother-in-law that she had a thesis to write. Once this was confessed to Sara, Amy could see that if her thesis were ever to be finished, this could not go on. She went home and explained to her husband, who immediately set about converting the loft space into a study. While this went on, Amy negotiated one evening a week free for her thesis and spent the time in the library. When the study was ready, Amy set up the thesis in the roof space, and arranged to retreat up there for two evenings and Sunday morning each week. Her husband and mother-in-law had, it transpired, no idea of the problem and were thrilled when, MEd awarded, she was able to graduate at a ceremony they could both attend.

Amy had not told her husband of her problem because she did not want to worry him or seem unwilling to live with his mother. She had not discussed her problem with friends or colleagues because everyone she knew was a mutual friend of the couple, and she felt it would be disloyal. Sara was the only person she saw regularly who was not also a friend of her husband's.

If the distaste for the thesis seems serious, it is helpful to read Rudestam and Newton (1992: 134–7), who explore both emotional and task-related blocks that they have found among American graduate students. Broaching some of the problems Rudestam and Newton explore with students may reveal whether their difficulties are emotional or task-related. Cryer (1996) has a chapter on 'flagging', which the student may find liberating. It is also worth pointing out to yourself and to the student that she or he should consider taking a break, registering for a lower category of degree, or even giving up altogether. There are always some students who will be well advised to give up the unequal struggle and downgrade to a masters degree or diploma, or even withdraw altogether.

It is helpful if all the staff in the department are interested in the graduate students and enquire supportively about the work. Sometimes explicitly telling a colleague about a student's achievement and success – in a corridor or around the photocopier – can produce a spontaneous burst of pleasure which is more motivating than the routine encouragement of the thesis supervisor.

It may be possible to provide some motivational jolts to a student. If you can organize something to reinvigorate the student you will have done him or her the biggest favour or service of the whole relationship. Among the things you can try to organize are a departmental seminar, presenting a paper at another department, a conference attendance, a conference paper, a summer school, a book review, an article (probably jointly with you), a book chapter (again, in collaboration) or organizing a small workshop. All these academic activities can help to refocus the student's energies on his or her thesis topic.

If the student has to prepare a departmental seminar paper for delivery, that can be a motivational jolt. If the department does not routinely request students to present their work, the supervisor may need to set up such a seminar: perhaps in a research group or with a small audience. Asking a colleague at another university to invite a flagging student to come and do a seminar can be motivating, especially if the invitation appears to come spontaneously, 'out of the blue'. (Good supervisors do not always reveal the strings they pull behind the scenes.) An intensive summer school is one excellent way of reinvigorating students, getting them specific skills and forcing them to meet new people.

Going to a conference, or better still giving a conference paper or helping to organize a conference, can motivate a postgraduate. These things can be set up by a supervisor, who can couple a student's name with her own or that of a colleague. Learning to do a conference presentation, meeting new faces and seeing how a conference is organized can all lift the student's eyes from the immediate problem, towards the longer-term goal of completing the research and submitting the thesis.

Getting published is one of the most exciting things that happens to a young scholar, so setting up a publication opportunity for a flagging research student can work wonders.

In general, encourage the student to build in intrinsic rewards and extrinsic ones. Think about how you motivate yourself, and how you reward yourself, ask colleagues the same questions, and then get the student to focus on the rewards professionals use. We use stationery to motivate and reward ourselves. A new project is an excuse to choose a new set of folders and ring binders in an attractive pattern, new pencils, new pens, new disk boxes, new coloured disks, new ruler, eraser, pencil sharpener or whatever. Then, starting the new project is a treat: using all the lovely new things. One PhD student we know, supervised by a colleague, shares this pleasure.

Example 6.7: Hector Blunt

Hector Blunt rewards himself for completion of goals with a new pen. Each time he has gained a qualification he presents himself with a more expensive fountain pen. For his PhD this meant a gold Mont Blanc pen – so it wasn't a cheap reward. However, Hector yearned for a gold Mont Blanc so much that he did a PhD part-time while in a demanding job in two years nine months.

Isolation

All the research on PhD students has found that isolation, both social and intellectual, is a frequently mentioned problem. This was the worst problem for the students studied by Delamont and Eggleston (1981) and Eggleston and Delamont (1983) and has been reported by many other researchers (Katz and Hartnett 1976; Scott and Porter 1980, 1983, 1984; Brown 1982; Vartuli 1982; Porter 1984; Rudd 1984, 1985; Scott 1985; Diamond and Zuber-Skerritt 1986; Young *et al.* 1987; Hockey 1991, 1994b; Wright 1992; Becher *et al.* 1994). It is less of a problem for scientists in a research group with a lab to work in, but a particularly acute problem for many humanities and social science students, for part-timers of all disciplines and for those overseas students who are far from home, friends and family. It can be particularly acute for a graduate student who is 'different' from other research students in the department because of age, race, sex, religion or thesis topic.

Supervisors individually, and departments more generally, can do something to mitigate the isolation. First, it is vital to make it explicit that in one way isolation is essential. Once an original thesis project is well under way, the student has to be intellectually responsible for it and has to become the expert in the field. *Intellectual* isolation is necessary and desirable. However, there is no reason for this intellectual isolation to be accompanied by social or emotional loneliness. Indeed, students need to realize that the former is impeded by the latter. The supervisor can try to ensure that the graduate students in the department, or the whole faculty, have formal and informal opportunities to meet. Seminars on how to get published, build a CV, prepare for the viva or apply for jobs can be slotted regularly into the academic year, in addition to seminars at which students present their work to each other. If the research students do teaching, classes to help them teach better, or workshops on teaching, assessment or pastoral care can be useful occasions to bring them together. Access to a staff common room, a buffet lunch with staff or drinks after work can, also reduce isolation, as long as the students are encouraged to mix and not left in a corner. However, 'social' occasions, especially if alcohol is involved, may be alienating or even 'out of bounds', unthinkable, for overseas students from Islamic cultures, for women from cultures with strict chaperonage and for those with child care responsibilities (for whom after-hours social activities may be difficult). A good department tries a variety of ways to encourage students to mix and make friends.

Overseas students may find vital support from a university or locally based 'national' or religious society: an Indian in an Indian society, a Chilean in a Chilean society, a Greek Cypriot in a link to a Greek Orthodox church, a Muslim in a local mosque. If there do not seem to be enough students from a country to make up a society, meeting undergraduates who can speak the language can help. We had a Brazilian PhD student in the 1980s who we introduced to an undergraduate reading Portuguese and taking a course on contemporary Brazilian novels. They met for coffee occasionally and discussed current Brazilian fiction in Portuguese. Both benefited. The PhD student was able to speak in his own language and about his own culture, the undergraduate got 'free' conversation classes from a native speaker.

One important source of support for postgraduates can be a learned society, particularly if there is a postgraduate section (and if there is not, your postgraduates might *start* one). Such a forum can provide students with a network, a disciplinary identity, administrative experience, an entry on a CV, and mitigate intellectual and social isolation. Beyond the department, or the faculty, there may be scholarly communities to be joined by e-mail, on the Internet, by newsletter and so on.

Our research on geography suggests that it shows very good practice with regard to postgraduate involvement in a learned society. Many of the geography PhD students belonged to at least one of the learned societies for geographers, especially the Institute for British Geographers (IBG). The IBG has a strong postgraduate section, as Patsy Schroeder from Wellferry explained: 'To me the IBG is great!' But she felt this was partly because 'I've been involved'. She had been an active IBG postgraduate since her first year as a PhD student, and spoke highly of the newsletter, the conferences and also the networking functions. Patsy and her friends believe that 'if you want to be a professional geographer you have to get into the circuit early.'

Most of the students had not joined what were then the other two geographical organizations, the Royal Geographical Society (RGS) and the Geographical Association (GA). The RGS (which has since merged with the IBG) then had a rather old-fashioned image among the doctoral students. As Brian Faul explained:

> my own perception of it is that it seems to have gone very much towards exploration, hacking through the jungles and showing slides about it. The IBG seems more academic, it organizes a postgraduate forum which is quite useful.

Similarly, Julian Perini described joining the IBG as 'the natural choice . . . and it's cheap to join and it's meant to be very good.' Those who had not joined the IBG were likely to have been to the IBG conference, the IBG postgraduate forum or an associated conference. Of all our student groups, they were the most clearly attached to a professional learned society.

The social anthropologists we studied had no opportunity to join the anthropological equivalent of the IBG, the Association of Social Anthropologists. It only allows established lecturers with doctorates to join, and has no section or division for PhD students. Our anthropological respondents felt isolated from their peers and their superiors in other institutions, and detached from their discipline in a way the human geographers did not. This was particularly because of the IBG's inclusive policies on doctoral students. If your discipline/learned society has a postgraduate section, pushing your students towards it is a good insurance against isolation.

The specific value of postgraduate student membership of a professional association is but a particular solution to a very general set of issues. As we have indicated throughout this chapter, and indeed throughout the book, postgraduate research can be wonderfully rewarding for all concerned. But it can be problematic in all sorts of ways, personal and intellectual. While the experienced and successful supervisor will always hope for the best, he or she might do well at least to be prepared for the worst. In the face of problems, whether financial, personal or intellectual, the research student can easily flag. Motivation and self-belief can be damaged by setbacks. Academics who have successfully completed a higher degree by research will know that it is possible to overcome those personal and academic obstacles and to succeed. Likewise, experienced supervisors can point to their own graduate students and hold them up as positive role models. They and their students will need reminding from time to time of the successes, and how pleasurable those successes are. Supervisors need to be aware of the kinds of problems that students might well be facing. They certainly need to take on board the recurrent finding that research students feel some degree of isolation. To some extent, as we have acknowledged, intellectual isolation is inherent in the role of the graduate student: the long-term pursuit of an individual research project for which – ultimately – the student has sole authority is, almost inevitably, a lonely and risky business. The student who is not aware of those risks and the consequent loneliness at some point in her or his career is probably insufficiently reflective. On the other hand, undue social isolation can be detrimental. Supervisors need to beware the research student who loses his or her way and starts to drift aimlessly, or whose work becomes such alienated labour that the savour of research fades. By the same token, the research student whose research is not 'working' for whatever reason is by no means rare. As we have seen, scientists' experiments do not always run smoothly; social science students may have difficulty obtaining access, or usable samples of respondents, or interpretable results; humanities students may find themselves adrift in a sea of texts or archives, and cannot see the wood for the trees. Whatever the reason, ennui and disillusionment are real dangers. Good supervisors look out for the signs, and try to work out with the student where the problems seem to lie, what kinds of solutions will be most fruitful and practical action plans to tackle them. Avoidance of these issues, through misplaced tact, embarrassment or guilt on either side, will only perpetuate and exacerbate them.

7

Contorted corkscrew: the getting and giving of judgement

accentuated by the presence, on the chest of drawers, of a curious statuette or three-dimensional diagram carried out in aluminium, which resembled a gigantic and contorted corkscrew, and was labelled upon its base: ASPIRATION.

(Sayers 1972: 12)

Introduction

When Dorothy Sayers wrote that paragraph she was contrasting an undergraduate's lack of aesthetic 'taste' with the sophisticated judgements of good and bad art made by the older woman looking at the statuette. The focus of this chapter is on how the supervisor can guide the student towards developing the academic equivalent of 'good taste' (Bourdieu and Passeron 1977, 1979). The research student has to develop the skill to judge when an experiment has worked and when it has not, when an analysis is 'correct', when a reading is plausible, when the null hypothesis has been falsified and so on.

Such judgement is a vital part of being a fully accredited professional. As the Nobel Laureate biochemist 'Spencer', in an interview with Gilbert and Mulkay (1984), makes clear: 'If you are an experimenter you know what is important and what is not important.' Similarly, a physicist interviewed by Gumport (1993: 265–6) said:

I try to teach them a set of skills. The biggest one is to know when you're right and when you're wrong. It's common for them to miss it when they're wrong. After a while they can see it. It's intuitive partially.

Some of these issues have been foreshadowed in Chapter 5, but we have returned to them here because judgement is such a crucial issue in doctoral supervision. Both parties have to develop judgement. The student has to learn, over the three years, to judge his or her own work by standards appropriate to fully independent research, rather than undergraduate student standards. The supervisor has to learn how to judge not only the student's current work, but also the potential for further improvement, while at the same time helping the student to develop his or her own skills.

This is a complex area, particularly because it deals with the indeterminate, tacit and implicit aspects of a particular academic discipline (see Atkinson *et al.* 1977 for a discussion of this terminology). It is much easier to teach technical, explicit things than indeterminate, implicit ones. This is very clear from the literature on occupational – especially professional – socialization, particularly that on medicine (Becker *et al.* 1961; Atkinson 1981, 1984, 1996), nurses (Olesen and Whittaker 1968), lawyers (Phillips 1982; Granfield 1992), schoolteachers (Atkinson and Delamont 1985) and even apprentice musicians (Kadushin 1969). However, we do not know very much either about how apprentice scholars learn the necessary discriminations in their discipline or sub-specialization, or about how established scholars exercise discrimination in their own work. The literature on academics (e.g. Lynch 1985; Latour and Woolgar 1986; Bourdieu 1988; Evans 1988, 1993; Becher 1989, 1990; Ashmore *et al.* 1994) has not produced an easily transferable 'model' of how academic judgement is exercised: because, of course, such a model is inconceivable. Experienced academics 'learn' how to judge research and publications in their field over the course of their career, without explicit instruction for the most part, as the physicist already quoted has stated.

In this chapter we discuss how to cultivate your judgement of the student's work, and how to help the students to develop their own 'taste' and discrimination. Before we move on into detailed discussion of how judgement and discrimination can be developed, two contrasting stories will make concrete the type of issue that is central to this chapter. Two of the respondents to the Eggleston and Delamont (1983) survey had had problems with deciding which statistical techniques were appropriate for their data.

> The analysis of data was not a problem until the thesis, submitted on the advice of the internal supervisor, and presented for examination, was returned on the grounds that the methods of analysis were not suitable. A new external tutor was appointed to take a fresh look at the data. Work has since progressed in a very satisfactory way but this problem has taken one academic year to resolve. It has also involved me in much extra expense.
>
> (Len Clement)

> A crucial problem arose in the statistical evaluation of my experimental data. Having completed a number of experiments I read a paper by an American Psychologist criticising the sort of statistics traditionally used in that type of experiment. I had succeeded in doing the original

statistics only through the guidance of Violet Willet and the convenient provision of a ready-made computer programme.

It took me a long time to realise that the criticisms actually applied to my statistics, and even longer to understand exactly what the objection was. For some reason I felt disinclined to broach this question with my supervisor until I could at least explain sensibly what the problem was. When I did raise the matter my supervisor (Prof. Burnaby) was so helpful and understanding about it I regretted not seeing him earlier. He immediately set to work helping me to find a method of re-analysing my data in response to the more rigorous requirements outlined by the American.

(Joseph Trevelyn)

In the case of Len Clement, the problem was not spotted by him or his supervisor until the external examiner referred the thesis. Len's recognition of the judgement came too late. One aim of this chapter is to help supervisors and students to avoid scenarios like Len's. The second respondent – Joseph Trevelyn – is a more positive example, because it is clear that he has learnt how to make his own professional judgement. Joseph's story, in which he read a paper, realized the criticisms applied to his own work and decided to reanalyse his own data, is an excellent example of a research student becoming a mature scholar exercising judgement.

Statistical techniques are only one possible area where judgement has to be exercised, but these two contrasting stories show one aspect of the wider issues we raise in this chapter. We have divided the argument into three major sections: on how supervisors can develop their judgement of work in progress; on how supervisors can train students so their judgement develops; and on examining, an issue we raise here before returning to it in Chapter 9. This area is largely absent from the literature on doctoral supervision (see Phillips 1994) and is addressed in an unsophisticated way in Phillips and Pugh (1993) and Cryer (1996). We regard it as a fundamental part of doctoral studies, during which successful students will become discriminating scholars as well as finishing their own theses.

Joseph Trevelyn had clearly learned a great deal about standards of statistical rigour in psychology, and had realized that he had learned it. Len Clement is less explicit, and it is not clear whether he accepted the judgement of his external examiner or not. The good supervisor wants the student to learn, before submission, as Joseph did.

Developing your judgement

New supervisors are frequently unsure about their own abilities to judge the work of supervisees during the registration period and, most crucially, when deciding if it is 'good enough' to be submitted for examination. One useful way to develop your judgement of doctoral work is to read some successful theses supervised by colleagues, and then talk to the colleagues who supervised and/or examined them.

It is especially difficult for younger academics to feel that they have sufficient confidence in their own judgement to advise advanced students appropriately. Given the nature of academic life, it is always hard to do something for the very first time, given the general lack of explicit instruction. It is now widespread practice for such scholars at the beginning of their career to undertake higher degree supervision jointly with a more experienced colleague. The gains from sharing the supervisory task are several. In particular, the more senior partner can be relied on to provide general advice and support concerning strategic planning, and to advise both the candidate and the fellow supervisor on general requirement, and that elusive but crucial aspect – the appropriate scope and standards expected of the research and the relevant degree aimed for. Likewise, younger supervisors can often gain the necessary experience through the supervision of part-requirement dissertations associated with taught masters degree schemes.

The critical issues that are valuable here are concerned with the development of informed confidence. We have been at pains to emphasize at various points that 'confidence' is of fundamental importance in the entire supervisory process. The supervisor needs to feel confident in the student, and the student needs to feel confident in the overall judgement of the supervisor. Such confidence has to be 'informed', not blind faith. To a considerable extent, confidence comes from experience. It comes, more crucially, from the supervisor's own research activity. For the reasons we shall explore below, the assured supervisor needs to be an active researcher who can provide and encourage a broad view of the discipline, and can help the candidate to keep a strategic perspective on the whole research enterprise. The confident supervisor can help to develop many of the indeterminate skills that the fledgling graduate student will need to acquire.

In addition to learning through joint supervision, learning from being an examiner is invaluable. It is now standard practice for higher degree theses to be examined by an internal examiner who has not been involved in the supervision, in addition to the external examiner. Acting as an internal examiner is an excellent way of gaining experience in judging theses; discussion with the external examiner and participation at the viva voce examination (if there is one) will provide excellent experience in evaluating the final product, and insight into how academic judgement is brought to bear. Equally, of course, the experience of external examining is directly transferable to that of supervising. It is extremely useful to see how other people's students have tackled things, and how they and their supervisors talk about the research process. It is usually reassuring to discover that other university departments do *not* have very different experiences, and that good theses from elsewhere have the same sort of strengths and weaknesses as your own.

Being an examiner, of course, forces you to read the thesis in question. By and large most of us read only those theses that we supervise or examine. But if you feel you lack confidence and experience as a supervisor, then reading other theses can be a very valuable experience. Indeed, this is a good way of acquainting oneself with some of the best and most recent work in your field – by borrowing some of the doctoral theses from good research groups, by young scholars who are making a mark in the field. In many disciplines – especially those in the humanities and social sciences – it will take a long while for the best doctoral work to appear and make its full impact: monographs appear years later, and journals often have long lead times. Reading the original thesis will have several advantages: you will read the whole thing long before the monograph appears; you will get a very good sense of the standard and overall style of doctoral work in your field; you will start to identify the good new researchers in your field (which may be useful in sponsoring them and in building your own research group).

There is also a danger of treating supervision as a largely private matter (even when conducted in pairs as a joint exercise). As a professional activity it is often much less visible than undergraduate teaching (given that lecture courses appear in timetables, undergraduate results are discussed at departmental examination boards and taught courses occupy the greater part of most academics' teaching loads). There is no reason why graduate students' work and progress should not be regarded as a collective, shared interest. Supervisors should feel free to discuss their graduate students' work, as a matter of their own professional commitment.

More generally, there is no reason why issues of graduate thesis supervision should not feature in a university-wide or departmental staff development programme. While the bases of judgement and 'good taste' are usually tacit, and are highly specific to particular disciplines, general discussion about how to approach the relationship between supervisor and supervised, and how to promote an appreciation of academic culture, norms and judgement, is beneficial to all parties.

In general, the getting of judgement by graduate students depends in large measure on how supervisors and their academic colleagues sponsor graduate students into the full range of the academic culture. One needs to remember that the majority of new graduate students will have a very limited exposure to academic life. Undergraduate degrees introduce one to a very restricted version of academic knowledge, and – understandably – inculcate 'textbook' knowledge (Fleck 1979). Even taught masters courses provide few opportunities for students to become incorporated into the complexities of academic life and work. They have relatively little insight into the *processes* of knowledge production, as opposed to consuming the products. It is important to help the students to gain insight into the diffuse, personal and practical issues and contingencies that permeate the academy. A recognition of those aspects of academic life will help the graduate students in various related ways: they will start to gain a mature perspective on their own work; they will start to see their own work in relation to that of others in the discipline; they will start to understand and to put into practice the everyday, local knowledge of the discipline; they will more readily become colleagues and members of the research group and/ or department, as we shall elaborate below.

Training the student's own judgement

There are two aspects to this: things you can (and should) do during their period as students, to show them, as explicitly as possible, how the scholarly community exercises its judgements, and the more implicit aspects of scholarly activity. Graduate students need to be introduced to the ways in which the academic community functions: how 'peer review' works in your discipline and your speciality. You also need to be able to set up contexts and occasions in which students can learn how to discriminate, without explicit instruction in the more mechanical procedures. The more the student is cue-deaf, the more explicit you need to be in teaching him or her about judgement.

This is an area of supervision where the more professional contexts the supervisor is active in, the better. If the supervisor is editing a journal, refereeing journal articles, refereeing conference proposals, writing book reviews, going to conferences and examining theses, then there are many opportunities for the supervisor to practise academic judgements, and to explain and share them with graduate students. The less the supervisor is active in the discipline, the less chance the student has to learn about judgement. So one important way to help your students is to be active yourself.

Let us take some concrete examples. When relevant visiting speakers come to the department or the university, you should attend yourself with your graduate students, encourage them to ask questions (if appropriate) and afterwards discuss with them what was good and bad about the session, and why. If you are unable to attend, get them to tell you about the talk and the discussion, drawing out the criticisms made. When a relevant conference comes along, this process can be repeated in an expanded form: discuss explicitly what you do at conferences and why, go to papers together and then discuss your responses and theirs. If they go to a conference alone, encourage them to debrief you about what you missed – and if you can compare their reports with those of colleagues, share those comparisons. This only works, of course, if they learn to respond honestly: if they are unimpressed by a great name, they need to learn to justify their criticisms.

A second way in which students can be helped to develop judgement is for them to read work in progress. You can encourage them to read each other's work, but it is even more helpful for them to see and comment on the work of established scholars. You can share your draft papers with them, encourage colleagues to do the same and discuss why you are preparing your work for publication in the way that you are. If you get a paper back from a journal with referees' comments, and can face sharing them with students, that is a priceless experience for them. It has value for the development of their own career (a theme we return to in Chapter 10) and for helping them to learn about how peer evaluation works.

If you are involved in refereeing other scholars' work (for a journal, a conference or an edited book) and you can allow your graduate students to help, this will show them peer review in action. This must be done within the ethical constraints of confidentiality, of course, and if the refereeing process is not being undertaken anonymously you will need to exercise discretion. But where work is read anonymously, it is often useful on both sides to solicit the advice of graduate students – especially if the subject matter falls within their specialist area. They may discover that they are more knowledgeable than you are!

It is easy for experienced academics to assume that aspects of academic work like peer review are self-evident. It is so pervasive in the approval of material for publication, the award of research grants and recognition exercises that we all become thoroughly involved in it, and – however irksome we find it on occasion – most of us participate in the general process. We get used to the fact that it is part of the general give-and-take of the profession, and how important these human judgements are in promoting academic disciplines, approving or rejecting scholarly work and so on. It is easy to overlook the fact that more junior students see little if anything of that process. We have occasionally been surprised to discover that in the course of classes for graduate students, they have welcomed the opportunity to discuss peer review and its implications – in particular how it will impinge on their work, and in more general terms its place in the exercise of academic decision-making.

In such contexts students can be introduced to a range of specific issues that will inform many, if not all, such decisions. The kinds of checklists that journal editors, commissioning editors and grant-awarding bodies often use can form the basis of a workshop discussion. The group will be able to see the range of criteria that are commonly brought to bear. Commercial publishers ask things like: Is the material clearly organized? Is it an important addition to the existing literature? Who will be the audience? Is the coverage comprehensive? Research Councils ask: Will this make a significant theoretical/methodological advance? Is the research timely? Is it original? How does it relate to prior work in the area? Will it make a significant contribution to the discipline? Will it have important policy implications? How does it relate to current research priorities? Is the research feasible? Are the research methods appropriate? Is the time-scale realistic? And so on. Journal editors need to know: Are the research methods described adequately? Is the research ethical? Is the analysis correct, using relevant methods? Is the discussion clear? Is knowledge of the relevant literature demonstrated adequately? It does graduate students no harm to be introduced to the constraints and opportunities of policy frameworks like the Technology Foresight Initiative, or European Union directives. These are intrinsically valuable aspects of academic socialization in general. Moreover, students can start to appreciate the range of criteria that are brought to bear on scholarly work, and how particular interests and audiences are implicated in the different kinds of decisions that are made. Some of the specific criteria are not directly relevant to their own thesis work, of course, and higher degree students are fortunate in having some degree of licence in pursuing curiosity-driven research. Nevertheless, they can start to think about their own research and that of others using the same kinds of interpretative frameworks.

However much graduate students are free to pursue 'blue skies' research, they still need to be aware of the fact that evaluative criteria will be brought to bear on their work. Immediately, of course, they need to think about their own project and the ultimate evaluation of their thesis. It does no harm to share with them the kinds of criteria that external examiners are asked to consider by universities. The actual lists differ from institution to institution, but judicious use of your own institution's criteria, and those from elsewhere, can help to develop an informed awareness of the assessment process. Of course, the application of those criteria is what is important. The requirement that doctoral research is an 'original' contribution is key – as in other contexts – but what 'counts' as originality is diffuse. Seminar or workshop discussion about degrees of originality, and how the notion is typically interpreted in the discipline, can help to illuminate general features of academic judgement, as well as helping students to become aware of how it might apply to their own work. Likewise, the criterion of whether aspects of the work are 'publishable' can help students to reflect on the significance of their work, and also their plans for publication in the short to medium term. A realistic appraisal of these and related issues can help students to formulate realistic reviews of their progress and aspirations. In the absence of such perspectives, graduate students can all too easily arrive at quite unrealistic views of themselves and their work.

If graduate students can start to gain an informed impression of these kinds of issues, then they can start to build their self-confidence. They will begin to appreciate how their own work compares with that of their peers and with more established members of the profession. It may help them to put their own work into scholarly frameworks and perspectives. By thinking critically and pragmatically about the research of others, they will be able to locate their own work. They will have the kinds of analytic tools to place their own contribution within the intellectual traditions of the discipline, and relate it to other research that is going on in an informed way. They will not start to handicap themselves by harbouring over-ambitious plans, and thinking they have to satisfy evaluative criteria that are unrealistically demanding. If they can begin to think reflectively about these kinds of issues, then they will start to gain a sense of many of the less tangible aspects of academic judgement. In recognizing that issues like 'originality' are not absolute criteria, and are not subject to formulaic prescription, they are in a better position to develop the kind of 'feel' for their own and others' work that comes with growing experience and confidence.

It is notoriously difficult to pin down the more tacit aspects of the culture. We aim to help graduate students to become 'reflective practitioners' who are able to internalize skills and criteria, in order to exercise judgement, and reflect on their own work in progress. The discussion of formal, explicit formalities and contexts can at least provide the kind of framework within which more personal, tacit knowledge can be gained and deployed. It is on the basis of such awareness that students can start to appreciate those intangible things that external examiners find themselves looking for. (We shall return to how external examiners express the issues themselves below.) Reading others' work, discussing formal and informal requirements together, supervisors and students can start to share a sense of the overall style and 'shape' of successful research. Depending on the discipline, they can start to appreciate the balance between data, findings, analysis and interpretation; how references to previous research can be woven into discussions of their own research; how to discuss and develop theoretical ideas; how to construct a thesis that 'hangs together' as a coherent piece of work; how to master the particular stylistic requirements of scholarly writing. They can thus be helped to grasp – often knowing at the same intuitive level as their more seasoned peers – the features of their work that will help to establish them as accomplished and self-assured practitioners of their craft.

Another source of coaching in judgement is the reading of PhD theses: as well as reading some good local ones, it can be useful for students to get, on inter-library loan, theses from other universities – perhaps including theses that you externalled, or that relevant colleagues examined, or that were supervised by potential external examiners of their own work. The student can then usefully read publications that came from those theses, to see how they differ and how the work has been developed for that purpose. Again, these tasks will work better if you can encourage explicit discussion.

If your students do undergraduate teaching, and especially if they mark work, this can also help them to develop a sense of discrimination and judgement. As they learn to tell first-class work from more run-of-the-mill student efforts, and start to gain experience in providing constructive feedback to more junior students about their work, so they can be encouraged to develop a more discriminating approach to their own work, and to respond to your own feedback on their working papers, draft chapters and so on. Supervision of laboratory practicals, if discussed with more experienced colleagues, can help graduates in laboratory subjects to think about good and bad experimental work.

The acquisition and exercise of academic judgement becomes pressing for postgraduate students when it comes to shaping their work into a thesis that is ready for submission. This needs them to be able to stand back from the detail of their work, and to learn to see the big picture as well. Too often, students cannot see the proverbial wood for the trees. Understandably enough, they become absorbed in the minutiae of their particular study, often becoming bogged down in them. They can become obsessive about small issues, and lose sight of the greater ones.

The supervisor's task is not always about resolving the details. It is often about helping the student to gain a sensible perspective on the overall project. A good deal of this work hinges on realistic aspirations for what a postgraduate thesis is meant to be. Too often, students become obsessed with impossible aspirations. The PhD is the highest earned degree that most people aspire to: the higher doctorate is awarded to relatively few academics, and only when they are very well established in their own right. The PhD is, in one sense, the pinnacle of academic training. In a sense, therefore, the PhD thesis is a 'masterpiece' of academic work. In saying that, however, it is useful to recall the original sense of 'masterpiece'. That is, a piece of work that confirmed the status of the 'master' craft worker, and the transition from apprenticehood. Too often, the notion of the 'masterpiece' dominates doctoral work in its more romantic sense – the great *chef d'oeuvre*. Many graduate students need to be disabused of the latter notion, and have their sights firmly set on the more realistic and more appropriate kind of aspiration. In many disciplines the implicit requirements for a doctoral thesis seemed to have grown, to the extent that experienced academics came to harbour unrealistic expectations for their own students, and to pass them on to succeeding generations. In recent years, there has been a trend towards more realistic goals. The external pressures on funding and completion rates, while not always welcome in themselves, have provided a useful impetus towards collective and individual appraisal of what is realistic. Students and supervisors need repeatedly to ask themselves: what can realistically be achieved in the registration period? They need to keep before them the appreciation that this thesis itself is not the be-all and end-all of the research enterprise, or of the graduate student's career. The thesis itself is just one of a number of outcomes of the research work. Depending on the discipline, the PhD project should result in a monograph or a series of journal articles, form the basis of further research and applications for external research funding for postdoctoral work and so on. If student and supervisor become obsessively focused on making the thesis alone the ultimate goal, then they can both all too easily lose sight of the more general issues of academic progress and achievement.

Losing sight of the overall goals can occur at any stage of the doctorate, but analysing the results of empirical work often provides this loss of vision. Many students pursuing empirical projects flag when faced with their own data. Many research students either are paralysed when faced with data, or become so engrossed in the technicalities of analysis that they lose track of time and 'drown'. Here we consider how the supervisor can help the students to master analytic techniques with confidence and prevent them drowning in technicalities. Many experienced supervisors will be familiar with the phenomenon that graduate students just collect 'too much' information. This is not always a major problem – if one recognizes that the thesis itself will not be the only outcome, then having more data than actually are used in it can provide a useful resource for future research activities, future publications and so on. The period of initial registration for full-time students will be a rare period in an academic career when research can be pursued with few other distractions, and can result in a 'camel's hump' of research material that can be used in the future. On the other hand, an over-enthusiasm for detailed work can prove a waste of time and effort. An example from sociology is given in Example 7.1.

Example 7.1: George Lomax

George Lomax was being supervised for a PhD by Prof. Lucien Bex. He moved smartly through data collection, doing a large survey of town planners. All the questionnaires were coded, and the data put into SPSS analyses. That is when George stuck. For four years he ran analyses of his data set, never reaching any conclusions or writing anything. Then he took a job in the USA and abandoned the higher degree and the data. Five years later, when we moved to another building, we threw away all his data, punch cards and print-outs. All wasted.

Such wasted time and effort reflect a lack of judgement. The supervisor's main task here is to help the student to recognize the overall purpose of the tasks of information-gathering. Students often recognize that they are in danger of becoming like George Lomax. As some respondents to the BERA survey wrote, when asked to describe a problem they faced:

With 40 per cent of the data collected, what to do with it. It includes transcripts of two rather different sets of interviews, and two different sets of pencil and paper exercises. There just seems to be so much of it. I must learn new methods of analysis and at the same time see each piece as a part of a whole.

(Gerald Wade)

One problem which was critical for my study was the use of a computer for the analysis of my results. I did not have any experience in the use of computing when I started my research work . . . After about six months of struggle I am now able to use the computer with some confidence.

(Bill Eversleigh)

Attempts to use factor analysis on the data – on this I spent quite a lot of time, and it was to no avail for it just seemed to complicate the picture. This should have been spotted at an earlier stage than was the case. It was a pity, for with different guidance I might have been able to make something of it; in the end it was abandoned.

(Ada Mason)

Analysis of over two years' data from classroom observation, teacher reports, case study notes and transcripts present a problem.

(Lawrence Redding)

The biggest problem I faced was a lack of knowledge of statistics. I was not prepared to solve this problem, never having studied this area, and having done no mathematics since O levels. This problem was solved by the fact that my second supervisor within the polytechnic was able to give me sufficient help to understand the use of SPSS [Statistical Package for the Social Sciences] and to help me in my initial problems in using the computer. I was able to pick up sufficient knowledge to cope with my own programmes. Following this my difficulties continued when I wrote up the chapter and my thesis dealing with the statistical findings, as I worried about the correct use of statistical terms. Both my supervisors guided me to useful references in the literature, and I was able to read around the subject.

(Nick Buckley)

There are several ways in which the supervisor can pre-structure the student's analytic work which might help prevent data handling becoming a problem. First, the supervisor needs to be ruthlessly honest about his or her own shortcomings. Analytic techniques may be moving faster than a supervisor has been able to keep up with, especially software packages for humanities and social science. It is vital that a supervisor with weaknesses explicitly sends the student elsewhere for expert help: to a colleague, a summer school, a special training course. All meetings of students produce stories of supervisors who have fallen behind in their field, but are too insecure, jealous or even ignorant to recognize that their students need help from someone more *au fait* with current analytic techniques.

Example 7.2: The outdated supervisor

In the late 1980s there was a seminar at Warwick University for graduate students and supervisors using qualitative methods in a variety of social science disciplines. In a discussion on how to keep supervisors up to date with a rapidly changing field, Paul mentioned the need for supervisors of qualitative work to keep abreast of the new developments in computer software for handling qualitative data. Professor Rupert Bateman, an active researcher, asked 'What software packages? I don't know of any such packages', revealing his own need for an 'update'.

Second, the supervisor needs to focus the students on the big picture – on the whole thesis – and keep them from drowning in analytic detail. Third, the supervisor can work on the analysis alongside the student, which gives the supervisor first-hand experience of the analytic technique, the students' competencies *and* any snags with the techniques in question.

Our last theme in this chapter is that of the 'final' judgement: the recognition of doctoral quality.

Recognizing doctoral quality

In the course of our own research on academic socialization we interviewed experienced supervisors about a range of issues, and included questions about their experience as external examiners of PhD theses. Their responses are illuminating, and may help to illustrate several of the issues we have raised in this chapter. It is, incidentally, worth noting that even among well established academics, the spread of experience is broad. Some have accumulated a good deal of relevant experience, others may have examined very few theses in the course of their career. This no doubt reflects various factors, including the nature of their particular specialism, and the character of their academic network. One should not assume, however, that there is a large cadre of experienced external examiners who are totally confident about what they are doing, and 'know' how to apply the right criteria in precise ways. The comments of these experienced academics show a range of responses.

These experienced academics all want to identify in successful doctoral theses work that 'makes a contribution'. This general description, in a number of variants, recurs throughout the interview data. There is some degree of consensus about how a 'contribution' is to be described and recognized and a view about 'competent work'. Professor Paget (town planning) described his extensive experience ('I've examined an awful lot of PhDs') in terms of topics, scope and competence:

> A whole variety of things. Substance again I think is important. I do think it needs to be a fairly meaty document. I don't mean tomes and tomes. I've had some two volume, eight hundred page jobs, and frankly I think they're nightmarish. So topic is important. The conduct of the thesis – an understanding of literature, of method and its limitations and strengths, an application of general research methods . . . The best PhD I've ever read: it was beautifully presented, rigorously argued, delightfully researched, the literature was bang on, theoretically very competent, methodologically very competent – in essence it seemed to me to be honest.

Here, then, is a fairly recognizable listing of elements of the successful PhD, expressed in terms of a range of competencies. As Professor Woodrose (development studies) expressed it, a contribution has to do with the candidate's grasp of the literature, the adequacy of the methodology, and the likely opportunities for publication:

> I guess there's a minimum level. At a minimum level I'm looking for a good understanding of the state of the literature. I'm looking for total confidence in the application of research methodology. And I'm looking for anything that allows me to say 'This is a contribution to knowledge.' I guess if I'm going beyond that I'm looking for the kind of PhD that one hopes produces papers or a book. I'd like to see something that looks original – a true contribution to knowledge. It's something about the scope of the exercise, that they've really bitten off something – either to apply a set of methods to a new country, or to a new sector, or that they've applied them in a rather distinctive way.

Some of the academics we interviewed expressed the criteria for success in terms of the achievement of 'objectives', such as Professor Portland (urban studies):

> Clear specification of objectives of research, careful design of research, good literature review – well structured, not rambling – fair amount of precision in thought, good strong use of theory, picking out appropriate propositions which are being tested . . . Good ability to manage data handling. Good writing style and good conclusions.

For the most part, however, merely meeting the objectives of the research is insufficient without additional value. As Professor Pethwick, a political scientist, told us:

> Fundamentally, whether the aims of the student, that they've set, have been accomplished. And whether the research is sufficiently original in terms of sourcing material, the ways it's been executed, the way it's written.

A number of supervisors emphasize that same sense of going beyond mere competence. Making a contribution means something more than satisfying the formal, mechanistic requirements. That extra something is, as Dr Ridgeway (urban studies) expressed it, 'something that grabs you':

> Looking for originality and excitement, critically . . . A PhD has to have something about it that's theoretically exciting, and original, without being world-shattering . . . But I think originality is the critical thing. And excitement. Something that grabs you. It's not just a competent pragmatic piece of work. There's something behind it that shows the person is engaged in the debates.

'Originality' is clearly a key issue in evaluating whether a PhD thesis has gone beyond the minimum basis of competence and starts to 'grab you':

> A coherent argument. I look to see what they are setting out to do. I look to see whether they've done it. I look for a decent chunk of empirical work which relates to the argument and supports it. And I look to see whether there's a spark of something original which makes something more of it than just putting together a literature review and empirical material – not something desperately new, but evidence of original thought. I weigh it as well. If it's more than eighty thousand words – brevity is something I look for, economy let's say not brevity – there isn't more there than there needs to be.
>
> (Dr Rowlandson, geography)

> First of all I'm looking for the originality of the work – is it just a very competent piece of work with clear presentation of ideas, or is it really going to be a new contribution to knowledge? And underlying all that is the rigorous approach of the candidate – the independent approach to the work and how testable that particular work is – so I know that what the person proposes is valid both theoretically and practically.
>
> (Dr Savanake, town planning)

Then, for some of the academics we interviewed, all this needs to be organized and presented with coherence and style, and needs to engage with theoretical development:

How clear is the analytical framework that is being used, and is it being used to illuminate a particular theme or thesis, or is the substantive area being investigated being used to test the robustness of the theory? I clearly feel more comfortable if I see theory testing going on and some contribution to theory . . . I'm very pleased when I find it.

(Prof. Borringer, urban studies)

In addition, a recognition of the limitations of the research may be looked for. Confidence should, from this perspective, be mingled with a proper degree of reticence:

I guess I look for, increasingly, a sense of intellectual modesty about the contribution of their particular research to knowledge. An understanding of the fragility of understanding anything through social science, and therefore a willingness to make tentative claims, to be very explicit about the way to approach different alternative answers, weaknesses with the data – that approach is more than any other thing what impresses me . . . I tend to look for fluency in writing, presentation and argument . . . definite linkage to an existing body of theory.

(Dr Huntingforest, geology)

I see the PhD as incorporating a number of skills. You've got your research skills, your analytical skills that are brought together, then you've got the pure administrative skills of actually writing, ensuring that the references are correct, making sure your section heads are appropriate – the actual putting together of the thesis itself . . . critical perspective . . . thoroughness . . . coherence – a picture being built up – a systematic progress through the thesis.

(Dr Wishart, development studies)

I guess coherence to start with . . . is there a definite topic, a defined problem, have they been able to cut that problem up into a set of hypotheses and have they been able to operationalize those hypotheses – are they testable? Have they been able to relate that to the literature on the field . . . Next, fieldwork . . . Have they been able to conduct fieldwork, have they used their methodology as planned, have they been able to cope with problems in the field which inevitably arise? Can they present the data clearly and can they tie their data into their actual hypotheses?

(Dr Wynyard, development studies)

In a PhD you are looking for a development of ideas, methods, concepts beyond the current literature, into a new area which excites the examiner and the supervisor and in which the student feels perfectly assured. Just that . . . if it extends me in some way. If there has been a good coverage of the previous literature, theoretical and substantive, and there has been some well-conducted fieldwork that further illuminates the theory, then if that is well done, written well, organized well – that for me is a PhD.

(Prof. Sherring, biochemistry)

This chapter has covered what is, in the great scheme of things, the heart of doctoral supervision: how to help students to become scholars who can exercise the judgements appropriate to their discipline. We move on to other topics: writing, the examination and career building. These are relatively straightforward for the supervisor whose students have developed appropriate judgement.

8

An emotional excitement: writing up the thesis

'Isn't the writing of good prose an emotional excitement?'
   'Yes of course it is. At least when you get the thing dead right and know it's dead right, there's no excitement like it. It's marvellous. It makes you feel like God on the Seventh Day – for a bit, anyhow.'

(Sayers 1972: 171)

Introduction

In Chapter 1 we outlined a typical supervisor's problem with student writing – the student who seems to have got blocked (Vignette A about Wendy Jackson, an environmental scientist). We have already referred to the need to get students writing from the earliest days of their registration – persuading them to 'write early and write often'. Students' attitudes to writing are highly variable, as are the skills they bring to the tasks involved. Sometimes, as in our vignette, the problem is writer's block, and a reluctance or inability to draft thesis material. Sometimes the problem is more about the structure and style of the writing that students do engage in. We saw from the remarks we quoted from experienced academics in Chapter 7 – talking about the criteria they use as external examiners – that the capacity to organize the material into a coherent text is crucial if the student is to succeed. Most, if not all, graduate students need advice about their writing, and such a need is not confined to students. All academics can benefit from a critical and reflective perspective on their writing, and many of the things we discuss in this chapter apply to one's own writing as well as students' efforts.

   This chapter is focused on how to help the research student to write. It is a mixture of data, of tips based on courses we have run, and some reflections on the nature of academic writing in the social sciences and the natural sciences. We start with a quote from a woman doing a PhD in geography, asked about her 'writing up': 'It has been a lonely process.

There are ups and downs. There are times when I'm sick and tired of reading my own prose, I don't want to do it any more' (Eunice Lester). Similar points were made by two respondents to the BERA survey:

The major problem was in getting used to the 'academic' style of writing expected. The nature of the project, whose leader is also my supervisor, has given me daily contact in working with and writing with him and another colleague. This has been invaluable, and I would, I suspect, have faced an almost insurmountable problem had I not had this advantage.

(Emily Trefusis)

The most critical problem in my view was that of actually getting down to writing. It is so much easier to keep collecting material from the primary sources, making notes, sorting them, filing them, reading them, re-reading them – anything rather than organizing the material into a coherent piece of writing. I have seen this happen to my daughter and my son-in-law, both of whom started working for PhDs but have not completed the projects. Both have mountains of notes etc. but only a few slender pages of their own written work. Now here I believe I was very fortunate because within a few months of my embarking on reading, my supervisor started asking for written work and refused to be put off by my pleas that I wasn't ready to write yet. So, just to satisfy him I started writing – a piece of work which in the end was only of limited use for my thesis but that didn't matter: I had passed the great psychological barrier of starting the writing and, from then onwards, I carried out my supervisor's recommendation to work at research and writing simultaneously even if it meant that some of the earlier pieces of writing had to be partially rewritten later.

My thesis is finished but at least two problems remain, and if anything are worse than before. One is the domestic problem of finding uninterrupted time in which to write and the other is the increasing sense of isolation, particularly as I no longer have contact with the university. This can only partly be offset by reading appropriate journals. Possibly later I may be able to attend conferences and join in the discussion groups with other people working in my field.

(Mary Pearson)

Many of the PhD students Odette Parry interviewed had problems with writing up their theses. Not only that, the supervisors interviewed were eloquent about how the students' writing successes and failures were central to the supervisory process. One very famous respondent even admitted that he was frequently tempted to draft the PhD thesis for the student. This man, Professor Brande (a social scientist at Hernchester), recognized that he was in danger of being too interventionist a supervisor. He told us:

I think also I'm too anxious to do the work for them or with them.
I can't bear to see them do something which I could do slightly better
... I tend to be too closely involved ... it gets to be my dissertation
rather than their dissertation and that's not fair on them. It's even
worse with word-processors because they bring in their text on a disk
and you sit at the keyboard together.

In this quote from Professor Brande he raises the whole topic of the
supervisor's appropriate role in the production of the text of the thesis,
which was a problem for many of our supervisor respondents. A social
scientist, Professor Woodrose of Latchendon, told us that 'You can't drive
them any faster than they can write – the papers, the literature reviews, the
definitional papers which take them on to the next stage.' Dr Godlee, from
Gossingham, was eloquent about the supervisor's role in text production.

you get a first draft which consists of probably some interesting sets
of ideas, but not very effectively linked together. And most students
I've supervised seem to have a lot of difficulty in establishing a clear
line of argument which runs through the thesis as a whole. My job as
a supervisor is to try to discuss with the student the different stories
that can be told with the material that has been assembled and then
to execute the option which is selected as professionally as possible.

The experienced supervisors we interviewed tackled the writing issues early.
As Dr Jelf says, 'I try to get them writing very early on. I insist on that. It's
essential. They don't solve half the problems they come across until they
try to write them down.'

This chapter is about helping students like Eunice Lester by offering
some strategies to them: strategies to avoid taking over their text, as Professor Brande reported, and fulfilling Dr Godlee's and Dr Jelf's aims. The
chapter makes some very concrete proposals, and then steps back with a
consideration of the ways in which it is possible to supervise the text.

Practical advice

Harry Wolcott (1990) advises researchers to plan the eventual text at the
very outset of the project. This is certainly an excellent piece of advice for
a PhD student, and so, at a very early stage, we recommend getting the
student to take step 1.

Step 1: The plan

At an early stage do a thesis plan, with the words divided up across the
chapters, and a timetable for writing them. For instance:

Figure 8.1: Specimen progress tracing chart

Chapter		Draft 1	Draft 2	Draft 3
Introduction				
Part 1	500	x		
Part 2	1,000	x		
Part 3	500	x	x	
Part 4	100	x		
Part 5	2,000	x	x	x
Literature review				
Introduction 500		x	x	x
Material up to 1970				
Key psychological studies				
Critique of key studies				
Methods				
Pilot study		x		
Questionnaire design				
Response rate				
Analytic strategies				
and so on				

Literature	5,000 words	August 1997 to October 1997
Methods	6,000 words	November 1997 to January 1998
Introduction	5,000 words	May 1999 to July 1999

Once this is done, and agreed with the supervisor, it can be pinned up above the desk, and also turned into a progress tracing chart, such as that in Figure 8.1.

It is useful to encourage students to break the task down into very small steps, and to mark their progress in small stages, so that the crosses march across the paper and they can see themselves making progress. A 'progress' chart on yellowing paper that only moves when 20,000 words are written will not help anyone. If there is a visible mark for each small piece of writing, the student can build in rewards (such as having an evening off) and also safeguards (such as backing up each piece and putting the disk somewhere secure). The precise form and content of such a chart needs to be devised so that it is informative and motivating for the student, and the supervisor can help to explore a form that works for each student. It may be sensible to have one chart for the whole thesis, and a much more detailed one for each chapter, so progress can be made on one chapter and traced, while the overall chart is not showing much movement. Getting students to do a thesis plan, timetable and progress tracing chart

early on is the first step in getting them to write. It not only sets the tone
– that the writing is part of the deal, can be done and will be done – it
also encourages students to start writing from day one.

Step 2: The two golden rules

These two rules are so important that it would be worth having them
on T-shirts or lapel badges. They are: (a) *write early and write often*; (b) *don't
get it right, get it written*. Students may not realize how vital these rules are,
or why you are advocating them. Offer the following explanations. Take
the two golden rules seriously. The 'write early and write often' rule works
because:

1 The more you write, the easier it gets.
2 If you write every day, it becomes a habit.
3 Tiny bits of writing add up to a lot of writing. Break the writing up into
  small bits. Write 100 words on X, 200 words on Y, and file them safely.
  It all mounts up.
4 The longer you leave it unwritten the worse the task becomes.

The 'don't get it right, get it written' rule works because

1 Until it is on paper no one can help you to get it right. Draft, show the
  draft to people, redraft.
2 Drafting is a vital stage in clarifying thought (see Torrance and Thomas
  1994).
3 Start writing the bit that is clearest in your head: *not* the Introduction,
  but Chapter 4, or the appendixes, or the conclusions, or the methods.
  As you draft, other bits become clear.
4 Drafting reveals the places where 'it' isn't right (yet) in ways that nothing else does.

Step 3: The safeguards

Students never believe that their work can get lost, stolen or destroyed.
Do say to them that it is not paranoid but sensible to have several copies
of what they have written. Hard disks crash, floppy disks get lost, laptops
are wiped by the airport X-ray and so on. So just as it is vital for them to
keep writing, it is especially vital to back up the disks, keep a spare set in
a safe place, keep a hard copy at their family home, put a set of disks in
a place a thief will not steal them. They need to keep back-up disks and
keep photocopies of any key bits of writing.

The best way to ram this message home is to steal the work of one of
the current cohort, but assuming you are too moral to do that, a dramatic
story is one way of getting the message across. The following are possibles.

1 Screen the episode of *Blackadder III* (the series in which he is butler to the Prince Regent) in which Dr Johnson's dictionary and Blackadder's bonkbuster novel are destroyed by Baldrick.
2 Tell the best 'lost manuscript' story in your discipline: in history, Carlyle's maid lighting the fire with the manuscript of Gibbon's *Decline and Fall*; in the social sciences, Franz Steiner's leaving the only copy of *Taboo* on the Underground.
3 Tell one of your own disasters with a disk or manuscript.
4 Tell your best 'lost manuscript' story about a fellow PhD student or one of your previous students. The three below are all true, but we have changed the names because all the postgraduates are still alive and well – and might even read this book.

Example 8.1: The clot

Paul Renauld was finalizing his PhD thesis in the days when most social science departments only had one daisywheel printer, so a graduate student had to stay up all night to print a copy of his manuscript. Paul did this, and then gave the only hard copy to his supervisor, Lucien Bex. Prof. Bex lost the typescript from the back of his bicycle.

   The moral of this story is that Paul should have remembered that Prof. Bex was *always* losing things, and taken a photocopy for him, not entrusted him with the original.

Example 8.2: The thief?

Françoise Arrichet was scheduled to have the final version of her thesis typed privately by a secretary, Prudence Crowley, during the Christmas vacation while the university was closed. She made all the final amendments and additions (many hand-written), put the papers in the secretary's pigeonhole late one afternoon and went home to her parents. In January she returned to the department to be greeted by, 'I thought you were going to leave your thesis for me to type over Christmas.' Prudence had gone to her pigeonhole the morning after Françoise left the thesis in it, and it was not there. Françoise had to dig out a much earlier draft, and do another two months' work on it, to recreate what had vanished.

   We *never* solved this mystery. The cleaners denied removing it, and several searches of the whole department failed to turn up any trace of it. Sara Delamont believes that either it was stolen out of malice by someone jealous of Françoise or, once it had been knocked out of the pigeonholes carelessly, it looked like rubbish and was dumped in a bin.

Example 8.3: 'The miracle'

Eustace Pedler had been destined for the Catholic priesthood, but had decided he lacked a true vocation, and was doing a PhD instead. He had, however, remained a communicant, and was, therefore, well known in the university's Catholic chaplaincy. One day he left an advanced draft of his thesis – in the days before microcomputers when the text was produced on a manual typewriter with carbon paper copies – in a telephone box in a suburb. It was in a folder which did not have his name and address on it, but did bear the telephone number of the Catholic chaplaincy. The next person to use the phone box dialled that number, and told the chaplain that he or she had 'found something that looks important'. The chaplain got on his motorbike and drove to the phone box to retrieve the folder, recognized that it was Eustace's work and was able to return it to him.

The moral of this story is that God clearly forgave Eustace for not becoming a priest, but most students cannot rely on God, a Good Samaritan or a chaplain with a motorbike.

Once you have alerted students to the need to write regularly from the earliest days of their enrolment, and convinced them to keep back-up disks and keep them safe, you have helped your students more than most of us older academics were ever helped. However, there are several other ways in which the supervisor can encourage students to see writing as an integral part of the whole doctoral process, and even learn to enjoy it. When Paul and Sara were doctoral students, Liam Hudson offered us a set of guidelines which we have shared with graduate students ever after, modified in the light of our experience. We have reproduced it here as Figure 8.2.

A set of guidelines like this can be quickly produced for any discipline. Despite the supervisor and the golden rules, many PhD students need help to make the transition from undergraduate to professional writing. The supervisor can lead them to sources of help, and create a climate in which students realize that writing is a technical skill that can be learned, not a 'natural' talent given only to a few. Some students are helped by reading books on writing, and we discuss these later in this chapter. Others are helped by practical activities, and others by making the process collegial; for instance, by writing circles. The most important role for the supervisor is to force the students to discover what will help them, and then cajole them into using that help.

Dispelling the myths

Probably the biggest favour a supervisor can do for PhD students is stop them developing a belief that 'writing' is a separate kind of activity that

Figure 8.2: Some practical suggestions for thesis writing

Technical writing does not come easily – as the contents of the university library testify. There is no recipe for success, but there are rules of thumb:

1 Allow yourself time. No one will believe in advance how long analysis, writing-up and checking take.
2 Set yourself deadlines, and hit them with zeal. (And beware the typist who lets you down at the last moment.)
3 Give shape to what you write. There are all sorts of usable models: the hypthetico-deductive (theory, prediction, verification); the ritualistic (introduction, review of literature, method, results, discussion); the 'auto-biographic' narrative and so on. The choice is largely a matter of taste. Pick the one that gives the least sense of artificiality.
4 Use sub-headings, at the side and/or in the centre of the page, to structure your text, and include lots of sentences that tell readers where they have been and where they are going next.
5 Method: just say what you did, in words that a child would understand. Keep your discussion of methodology, the pros and cons of the various possible methods, to a minimum. Don't feel compelled to report in detail everything you do.
6 Avoid clichés. 'Situation', 'at this moment in time', 'in this regard' and anything else said frequently on television should be avoided.
7 Decide which of your results are the important ones, and give them prominent place.
8 Don't allow technicalities to clog up the main text. Put them in appendices.
9 Expect to suffer over the presentation of statistics. Raw data belong at the back, next to the references. The right way of summarizing them in the main text may only come to you after weeks of trial and error.
10 Tables should speak for themselves. Don't force your reader to grope around in the main text to discover what your tables mean.
11 Don't pad out your references with works you haven't read.
12 Hack and hack at your own prose. Sentence by sentence, the simplest form is usually the best. At the level of paragraphs and chapters, aim for the sequence which gives the smoothest flow.
13 Most examiners dislike the first person singular, so use it sparingly.
14 Don't circumlocute: 'It will be seen that the above tables are not without significance . . .'
15 Re-examine any piece of jargon. As often as not you will find that it disguises sloppiness. Bear in mind, too, that the educational sciences are interdisciplinary. What you write should make sense to any intelligent person, irrespective of his or her particular technical skills.
16 Proof-reading your typed version is essential. Ideally work with a partner and read it aloud, punctuation and all.

can or should be left until 'the end', an activity that is somehow different from everyday life as a researcher and teacher. Nothing is more inimical to productive writing than the romantic image of the lone author, searching for inspiration and struggling for expression. Writing is not a special kind of experience, and – as we have emphasized already – it is not a natural talent. While it seems to be true that some people find it easier than others, it does not come naturally to anyone. It is something that all authors have to work at. Books, theses, journal articles and all the other 'products' of academic life do not 'just happen'. Students need to be encouraged to recognize that their scholarly writing is simply a part – albeit it a very important part – of their everyday work. They need to lose any idea they might have had previously that 'writing up' is something they can always leave until the end of everything else, or that it can be done at the last minute.

This is, indeed, one area in which the transition from successful undergraduate student, or even masters student, to research student may prove tricky. Even very good undergraduates may be able to manage their university career by treating writing as a relatively unproblematic activity. Many essays and projects are written in a short time span, and any experienced internal or external examiner will recognize that much work is submitted in more-or-less first draft. Students carry forward such behaviour into research work at their peril. Many have come to grief – or at least have come to a grinding halt – when they recognize that writing the equivalent of a complete book cannot safely be left to the last minute.

Inappropriate expectations and patterns of behaviour about writing need to be tackled if students are to develop sound and productive work habits. Many academics suffer from myths about writing and supervisors themselves need to reflect on whether they may inadvertently encourage them in their students. Experienced academics sometimes cling to the myth of 'getting down to it during the summer'. This is an extension of the understandable desire to devote coherent stretches of time to writing tasks – such as drafting the next book or writing up the current research project. It is perfectly reasonable, and the rationale for relatively short undergraduate terms is to release academic time for scholarly tasks. On the other hand, the long summer 'vacation' often is not all that long, sandwiched between assessment periods at each end, and with many other academic tasks to complete. If any real holiday is to be taken, and family or other social obligations are to be fulfilled, then the summer suddenly seems very pressured. The mirage of the empty summer can prevent busy academics from looking for ways to fit their writing commitments into regular schedules. A similar, equally handicapping, myth is to wait until 'the desk is clear'. Again, this is based on the desire to write only when other pressing commitments have been got out of the way. The problem with this belief is that an empty desk is a very rare privilege. Again, the solution is to schedule writing as a regular commitment like any other. A third mistake arises from the desire to delay writing until 'all the data are collected and finally analysed', or the equivalent. As we have suggested already, leaving writing to the end, and treating it as a final 'big bang', is a risky attitude. It can leave a huge new task to be tackled after a great many other activities have been completed. While some people can cope successfully with this strategy, a good many find it daunting, and paralysingly so. Such 'myths', then, are based on a need to see writing as a separate and special activity; needing different time and concentration from routine activity. This is damaging for most people: summer is very short, desks are *never* clear, the data are never all collected and finally analysed. Established academics need to review their own work habits, and think whether they base their own work on unhelpful assumptions. They also need to consider whether they may inadvertently promote such behaviours in their graduate students.

If writing the thesis is not seen as a separate kind of activity, then it is not necessary to harbour these sustaining myths. So the wise person does not rely on periods of time totally free of other commitments to 'write up'. Even if the student does have a clear desk or a period of leave, it is *not* a good idea to wait for such things to do a thesis: it may be useful to finish and revise the thesis but not to start it from cold. In addition, we have to recognize that major writing undertakings may need commitment of time and effort over and above nine-to-five working hours. There is no great need, in our experience, to work all the hours or to forgo everything else. Most of Paul Atkinson's productive writing is done in the evening – usually between about 8.30 and 10.00 p.m. Some people manage to get an hour in early in the day. Since Paul does not function particularly well in the morning, that does not work for him. So, part of the task seems to involve the *management* of time and effort as well as freeing oneself from myths that actually hinder productivity. The other side of the equation would seem to be the management of the task. We need to free ourselves from any disabling myths about theses as process or product. Theses are only a type of routine, craft work like any other. They are divisible into entirely manageable sets of small tasks.

Students should be encouraged to think about writing projects, including the entire thesis, in terms of sensible and manageable chunks of effort, time and other resources. Sensible planning and regular work habits can help to transform writing into perfectly manageable everyday activities. The agreed thesis plan should exist – and there is no point in writing without one – then the synopsis or outline will already have been constructed and will already define the structure. While plans and structures should always be subject to review, and should not be a straitjacket, provided they are realistic, students should always be able to write productively on identifiable aspects of the thesis. This in turn means that students need encouragement to break the tasks down into bite-sized chunks. Whole theses and whole chapters are major undertakings: sensible, robust structures and plans will help the student and his or her supervisor to identify manageable stretches of writing.

Equally, one needs to work flexibly within the thesis plan. Students often need to be encouraged *not* to think they have to 'start at the beginning', or turn the thesis plan into a temporal work plan. Starting at page 1 is rarely a sensible approach. Students should be encouraged to feel able to write what they feel like writing at the time. There should always be something about which they feel relatively confident, or about which they have ideas that need drafting out, or where they feel they have a 'finding', or a significant story to tell. If so, why not encourage them to write about *that* aspect of the work? In other words, students should not be not tied to their structure, but encouraged to use it as a framework to keep control over the emerging whole.

Advice on writing, then, needs to concentrate on helping the graduate students to approach their work pragmatically. It is not a huge task to write a PhD thesis, provided they do not *make* it look that way. We encourage our own students, as we have said, to try to write as part of their normal academic work, and to mingle writing with other research activities. Equally, therefore, we urge them never to approach writing 'cold'. Sitting down at the desk, with a blank computer screen or a blank sheet of paper, can be paralysing. It is all too easy to suck the pen or fiddle with the mouse without getting words down. Students should be helped to recognize how helpful it can be to have some ideas about what to write and how to start before they begin the mechanical work. Thinking about how to start, an apposite quote to get them going, a striking bit of data, a concrete instance, a striking analogy: all these things can be thought about creatively before actually settling down to 'write'; on the way to and from work, in the shower, or wherever. They do not need to have everything mapped out beforehand – just a starting point.

In the same vein, one needs repeatedly to counsel most graduate students against yet another paralysing belief: that they have to know exactly what they think before they dare start to write. Many experienced academics know that what they think emerges partly out of the acts of writing. Waiting until everything is perfectly understood and perfectly planned out is a sure recipe for yet another displacement activity. Students need to be encouraged to realize that early drafts are just that. Supervisors therefore need to establish the kind of trust that allows students to share with them preliminary draft material. The supervisory relationship needs to give students 'permission' to produce material in a preliminary form, in the knowledge that they will be redrafting. Equally, supervisors need to be able to comment constructively on draft writing without undermining the student's confidence by being unduly critical of early efforts. As with so many aspects of that working relationship, this is based on the establishment of mutual trust and confidence.

Research students may also be encouraged by the thought that, in many ways, writing a thesis is more liberating than trying to produce the equivalent output in terms of research reports and journal articles. A thesis is much less restrictive in terms of formats, style, internal structure and length than articles or research reports: the author of a thesis can be more idiosyncratic, can set the agenda, can control the process much more. While there are many requirements and obligations in terms of structure and content, the author of a research thesis is able to exert more individual control than he or she will be able to in many other academic contexts. Not only is the research the student's own, original work, the thesis is something he or she can 'own'. For that reason, writing a thesis should be exhilarating, not a crushing obligation.

Many graduate students need to be reminded that reading is the thief of writing. It can easily become another kind of displacement activity, that rivals waiting for the uninterrupted period free of other tasks. Graduate students have to read, of course, and they must make sure that they are 'up' with the research literature. But obsessive reading can severely interfere with getting the work written. Since 'the literature' can be virtually infinite, the belief that one should *read first* can put the thesis off indefinitely. Likewise, students can put off writing intermediate and final drafts by persuading themselves that they cannot embark on those tasks until they have tracked down and read yet one more vital text, or chased further elusive references. One does not produce manageable draft writing out of the activity of reading and taking notes from sources. Students need to be encouraged not to confuse reading and writing (it is obvious, but a lot of people in fact do so). Indeed, they often need to be persuaded to *stop* reading the work of others, in order to step back from other people's writing, and their own information, and to start marshalling their own work into their own texts.

Help with writing

Apart from establishing early on that students should write regularly right from the beginning of their higher degree, a supportive supervisor will want to provide a context in which learning how to write, and seeking help with writing problems, is part of the PhD experience. We will discuss a number of ideas here, starting with building a library of books on writing, and then writing circles, writing clinics, dealing with writer's block; then we briefly address students' word-processing needs.

One of the ways in which the life of a PhD student or young scholar
has improved in the past decade is the explosion of helpful books on
academic writing and publication. We have separated three kinds of books
on writing. First there are style manuals – to help people write clearly and/
or in the style of a particular journal, such as the American Psychological
Association's style manual. This category would include old favourites,
such as Turabian, *A Manual for Writers of Theses* (1937, 1982, 1995), Gowers,
The Complete Plain Words (1986) and Fowler, *A Dictionary of Modern English
Usage* (1994). However, there are many more recent books in this category, such as Dummett, *Grammar and Style* (1993). We have provided a list
of such books in the Further Reading chapter. The second category of
books contains advice provided for people in one discipline, or a group
of closely allied disciplines. Social scientists are particularly lucky in that
there are three outstanding books for them about how to settle down and
actually produce something. They are: Becker, *Writing for Social Scientists*
(1980), which is marvellous, helpful *and* funny; Wolcott, *Writing up Qualitative Research*, which is similar, though less funny; and Richardson, *Writing
Strategies* (1990), which demonstrates how to redraft the same material for
different types of audience, such as for a thesis and for an article in the
Guardian. This last text is especially good, in that it helps students to think
about how to present their ideas to particular types of reader. Such books
for sciences and humanities students are less common. Supervisors might
find that their students could benefit from them anyway, and they might
even help a science student to think about the contrast between the conventions of natural science and other disciplines. For scientists there is Day,
How to Write and Publish a Scientific Paper (1995), which covers all aspects
of scientific publication, not just journal papers. There is a useful section
on thesis writing, as well as on preparing for all forms of public presentation,
oral and written. Pechenik and Lamb, *How to Write about Biology* (1995),
lacks jokes, or any sense of excitement and buzz, but has good biological
examples. For humanities students, Barzun, *On Writing, Editing and Publishing*
(1986), remains a classic. We have again provided a list of such subject
specific books in the Further Reading chapter. Third, there is a large
literature analysing the appropriate rhetorical styles of different disciplines,
to which Paul Atkinson (1990, 1992, 1996) has contributed. We have put
a select list of titles on the rhetoric of inquiry into the appendix: further
reading.

What unites these three types of book is the belief that writing is a
technical, or craft, skill which can be improved with self-conscious practice. Books of advice like this are invaluable resources. Students should be
encouraged to think positively about them – that there is nothing intrinsically stigmatizing or 'naff' about using them, and thinking in a critical
way about one's writing. It will often help if students can recognize that
their supervisors also need to think carefully about their writing: that it

does not come naturally to them either; that it is hard work for everyone; that everyone needs to work at writing in order to improve.

Books of advice are, as we have suggested, an invaluable resource. Students and supervisors alike need to build up a systematic acquaintance with such resources, and get into the habit of consulting them and using them. But one cannot learn and improve only from the use of handbooks. There is a great deal to be said for running some collegial seminars and workshops on writing. (This, incidentally, is where Becker's *Writing for Social Scientists* is especially valuable, even for colleagues in other disciplines, as it reports on experiences of such a seminar group on writing.) Such occasions can be part of a training programme for graduate students in the faculty or department; they can also become part of a regular 'writing circle' that draws together graduate students, research workers and more experienced academics.

However the membership is drawn together for such groups, there is always need for mutual trust. We all know that having our writing evaluated by critics, however sympathetic, can be traumatic. It is difficult to distance oneself from one's writing, and anything that smacks of adverse criticism can hurt. Participants have to commit themselves to work constructively with one another, to agree to share equally in the group's activities and to maintain mutual respect. Sometimes it may help things along to have a shared writing exercise. This helps everyone to focus on the same task, and is an easier introduction to sharing processes, problems and products that are more personal.

One set of classes we have run in Cardiff is based on the strategy outlined in Chapter 12 of Spradley's two parallel books, *The Ethnographic Interview* (1979) and *Participant Observation* (1980). Spradley breaks writing down into nine steps, as follows:

1 Select an audience.
2 Select your major argument/theme/thesis.
3 Make a list of topics and create an outline.
4 Write a rough draft of each section.
5 Revise the outline and create sub-headings.
6 Edit the rough draft.
7 Write the introduction and conclusion.
8 Reread the manuscript to check that there are enough examples.
9 Write the final draft.

We had a group of eight or nine higher degree candidates and colleagues, and we all worked together through Spradley's early steps, in a weekly class. After the first meeting of the group, everyone agreed to carry out the first two steps: choosing an audience, and stating the main argument. Each member of the group wrote a paragraph or two about her or his current work under these two headings, and handed it in a day before the next class. We photocopied all the examples and in class circulated and discussed them. We have included here the contributions as tabled by two of the authors of this book and one MPhil student who was a regular member of the circle.

Examples of Spradley's first two steps

Sara Delamont: a chapter on sex/gender in middle/secondary schools

1 *Audience*: educational researchers, with some teachers.
2 *Thesis*: that pupils' taken-for-granted gender roles are reinforced, rather than challenged, by teachers in everyday interaction, by curriculum content and by the organization of the school.

Chris Stevens: an MSc Econ thesis on gay women

1 *Audience*: external examiner.
2 *Thesis*: to show how some gay women – especially those 'off the scene' – manage their homosexual identity. In particular, what the identity 'homo-sexual' means to them, how they came to identify as such, how far they see it as important in explaining their behaviour and affecting their daily lives, and the social areas where being 'homosexual' is thought relevant. A consideration of what this may reveal about the taken-for-granted notions about sex and gender.

Odette Parry: an MSc Econ thesis on naturists

1 *Audience*: external examiner, whom I will assume for my own convenience to be an audience not unsimilar to that of my supervisor, Sara (because the substance of the material is naturism, I will be presuming that my audience will be largely in the dark concerning the basics of the activity).
2 *Thesis*: naturists are often reticent about declaring their activities because of expected social reprisal. Because information about naturist clubs is far less available than information about other social clubs, views of naturism tend to be limited only by the polite or otherwise imaginations of the non-naturist public. This paper looks at the ways in which naturists present themselves in a club environment in accordance with naturist beliefs about what constitutes proper and respectable nudist behaviour.

Spradley also argues that there are *levels* of writing, and that good writing comes from combining statements at the different levels. We have tried out these 'levels' on our own students. While they may appear to impose a somewhat mechanistic framework on the work of authoring, they can be invaluable in helping participants to concentrate on issues of audience and style. Spradley gives examples from his ethnographic monograph, *The Cocktail Waitress* (Spradley and Mann 1975). Here we have used a mixture of examples from Spradley and Mann and from Cardiff theses to illustrate work produced in the group.

Examples of Spradley's levels of writing

1 Every society takes the biological difference between female and male to create a special kind of reality: feminine and masculine identities.
2 Cross-cultural descriptive statements, e.g. 'In Boston schools for five year olds are ... In Goa schools for young children ...'
3 General statements about a society or cultural group, e.g. 'Police stations in Wales are places in which ...'
4 General statements about a specific cultural scene, e.g. 'Teachers in Goan schools experience high levels of stress when ...'
5 Specific statements about a cultural domain, e.g. 'Many doctors in the Sudan have to treat infectious diseases. These include ...'
6 Specific examples of incidents, e.g. 'In a French lesson on a wet Tuesday Miss Phillips was explaining tense to 2C when ...'

Colin Rees

1 *Universal statements.* Records are a general feature of many people processing organizations.
2 *Cross-cultural statements.* Records made by social workers may contain more personal statements by the writer than those made by medical staff. Patient records tend to contain entries which appear to have been made by 'any doctor'.
3 *General statements about a society or cultural group.* Ward routine on the paediatric ward was punctuated by the use of the medical record.
4 *General statements about a specific cultural scene.* When it comes to the 'dirty work' of looking after records on ward rounds it is usually the house officer who takes the appropriate record out of the trolley and is delegated the job of recording the consultant's 'pearls of wisdom'.
5 Although the house officer makes almost daily entries in the notes, an examination of those comments reveals that they say very little about the patient. 'No change' says little about the patient but it does tell the reader that the patient was seen by house officer X on that day.
6 We came to a cot of one child and the consultant said, 'What's she got?' David, the house officer, already had the notes in his hand and said, 'Diarrhoea and vomiting. It says here she'd had it for 12 hours before coming in.' The consultant took the notes and flicked through the pages himself.

Sara Delamont

1 All human societies have a division of labour of sex, and therefore a sex-role or gender-role system.
2 Whereas in many tribal societies there is consensus about the gender-role system to be inculcated in children, modern Britain is divided about 'correct' sex-role socialization.

3 Schools are places where sex/gender-role socialization takes place, but generally as a by-product of other activities.
4 Pupils' own sex-role stereotypes were reinforced by many aspects of their school lives.
5 Schools officially separate boys and girls in many ways. For example, all six schools list boys and girls separately on the registers, have separate lavatories and changing rooms, and teach them different sports and games.
6 In the woodwork room at Melin Court School (on 4 September 1978) the new pupils are being allocated places at the benches, in alphabetical order, with boys first. When Mr Beech found he had 23 in the group it was girls left without bench places – about three girls were left to work where someone was absent (i.e. changing seats every week or starting each lesson trying to find a space).

Our Cardiff group used Spradley's (1979) ideas on writing to provide a syllabus for its work for an eight-week period. Fox (1985) contains an autobiographical account of how a writing circle helped some young American scholars to become productive authors, which can be recommended for emulation by graduate students.

Writing clinics, in which the participants become self-conscious about their writing practices, and experiment with other ways of writing, can be beneficial for doctoral students. It may be helpful to get an 'outside expert' in to run such a clinic, but a trusted friendly member of staff from the department may be equally able to run it. Torrance and Thomas (1994) report on three different ways of running such clinics, all of which were found to be helpful by doctoral students. Torrance and Thomas argue that, at doctoral level, it is particularly important to focus on the production of text in the clinics (not on strategies for planning text) and to allow for individual variations in approach. Torrance and Thomas are also convinced, on the basis of extensive empirical research on academic writing, that PhD students should be encouraged to abandon the 'think then write' or 'plan then draft' approach, and replace it with a model of 'as I draft I clarify my thinking' or 'I draft therefore I think'.

Part-time students with full-time jobs may genuinely find it hard to clear time to write. For such students, 'little but often' is a vital rule: they need to learn to write small bits whenever they can. For part-timers particularly, encourage them to recognize that the 'patchwork quilt' principle applies to theses. If they break up the task up into small chunks – five hundred words on this, a thousand on that, two hundred on the other – then they can write the two hundred on Monday, half the five hundred on Tuesday, the rest on Thursday, do the thousand on Friday and so on. Encourage them to realize that *it mounts up*.

Encourage students to travel by train, and never to get on the train without a task that can be done on it. They can learn to write on the train (using a laptop or a dictating machine), or make notes while the train is moving, summarizing at stations. The literature review can be completed on train journeys if the student reads and writes on trains in a cold-blooded and disciplined way. For *Fieldwork in Educational Settings* (Delamont 1992), Sara needed to 'gut' journal articles: it was done on trains. The student can read and re-read the piece that he or she is criticizing and make the notes to write from.

If the graduate student is teaching others, it may be possible to organize that teaching so that bits of the thesis are coming from his or her lecture or tutorial preparation. As the classes have to be given, chunks of thesis-relevant work will have to get written. Fixing up a course on a topic forces all of us to prepare coherent ideas on it. However, students on the course may pester graduates for help and take too much of their time.

Finally, the most important thing is to ensure that your PhD students learn to engage in tough-minded self-examination. Could they get up an hour earlier each day for a year? Could they establish office hours and stick to them. If they are routinely disturbed by undergraduates coming to the postgraduate room or asking for help with experiments, can they establish clearly specified and limited office hours for such consultations? Could they stay home one day a week and not do the housework? Do they *need* a new computer, a new printer, a dictaphone, new folders and pens, a new desk, a decent working chair? Train them to examine where they can write, when they can write and how they can write (on their lap, in bed, in the bath, in the pub?), and then to go there, at that time, with the tools, and do it.

In general, encouraging and helping students to write is one of the most rewarding aspects of the supervisor's role. Writing is a set of craft skills, and once a graduate student has begun to learn and apply them, he or she will be able to write for the rest of his or her academic or professional career. Seeing the draft material take shape, and pile up over the weeks and months, is as gratifying for the supervisor as it is for the student. When they have worked collaboratively on writing as an activity, they can share the pleasure equally.

Dealing with 'writer's block'

If the worst comes to the worst, and despite your best efforts the student does get blocked with writing, you need to act quickly. It is easy to miss the onset of a writing block because students may avoid supervision appointments and/or fail to mention the problem. Once you realize that there is a difficulty, you need to act. We have already suggested ways to remotivate a demoralized candidate in Chapter 6, and all these ploys can help with writer's block. There are some other strategies that you can try specifically to jolt the student into producing draft text. First, you may have to change your role from 'good cop' to 'bad cop'. We have advocated throughout this book an approach based on supportive cajoling, but it is always worth thinking about a tactical change. It may be time to get tough: to set a series of deadlines quite close together and demand small bits of text before each. If the student fails to produce, then the pair of you need to examine very closely and seriously what is holding the student up – a fear of failure, a misguided perfectionism, unhelpful working habits, apprehension about your response to the work or whatever it may turn out to be. In some cases, you may judge that getting tough will work. In all cases, positive reinforcement will be in order. If you can coax some text out of a blocked student, then a display of enthusiasm may lead to further writing. Your response to the draft material will need careful handling. Students who are anxious about their writing can easily be discouraged. They can easily interpret an enthusiasiastic and energetic engagement with their draft (lots of marginal comments, questions, lots of red ink) as damningly critical, and lose all confidence. If you do have a great deal to say and write about draft material, then you do need to persuade students that you are doing so because you believe in them and the work. The occasional treat and reward may work too – a drink or a shared meal, a book or some similar token.

Apart from emotional work, the supervisor may need to engage in writing *with* the blocked student. You and your student can try sitting side by side at the desk or at the PC, drafting or redrafting in concert. Get the student to decide what needs to be in a paragraph and start working on it. With luck, the student will start out by dictating to you, and you can let him or her take over. If not, then you may need to meet the student regularly and frequently to help get through the block with such joint sessions – until the student does take off on her or his own, or until you decide that the tactic is not paying off.

It may be helpful to get the student to try drafting by dictating on to tape rather than writing (although dictating needs its own skills). Sometimes it may help to tape a supervision, during which you get the student to talk through the issues he or she is struggling to express. A transcript of the discussion may be a surrogate first draft. More prosaically, a deadline for a seminar paper in the department, or a conference paper, may exert external pressure, and produce useful material. (Again, the presentation itself can always be taped and form the basis of a written version.)

Sometimes the problem is less drastic than a complete block, and the student can leave a particular chapter on one side and work on some other part of the thesis. Occasionally the problem may arise because the student is trying to write the 'wrong' section anyway. Some students seem to be convinced that they must start at the beginning of the introduction, or get their literature review sorted out first, or describe the methods before they can write about their results. A temporary block can often be overcome by persuading a student to write something that comes more easily, rather than getting stuck at one particular point.

If a student is blocked in a slightly different sense – with a chapter or section that the supervisor thinks unacceptably weak and that the student cannot seem to improve – we would recommend putting that section aside and writing something else. The student is less likely to become demoralized, the supervisor can take a rest and the student may learn how to rework the weak part while pushing on with another. At least the student will have a break, and may be able to see the weaknesses in the work when he or she revisits it. This certainly happened to Annabel Pierce.

Example 8.3: Annabel Pierce

Annabel Pierce had done a masters degree, which included a 20,000 word thesis, supervised by Sara. She then registered at Lymstock University to do a PhD, supervised by Megan Hunter. Eighteen months into the PhD, Megan told Sara that Annabel was having enormous difficulty producing an acceptable 'theory' chapter. That same week, Sara met Annabel at Sainsbury's and Annabel told Sara the same sad story. Sara suggested to both parties, separately and without disclosing it to the other, that it was perfectly sensible to put the unsatisfactory draft aside, and to push on with a draft of the rest of the thesis. This would restore Annabel's confidence, give Megan a respite and get the rest of the thesis drafted. Six months later, when Sara next met Annabel, she was much more optimistic about finishing: she had realized how weak her original theory chapter was in comparison with the more sophisticated material she had succeeded in writing since.

In general, we have found that getting a first draft of the whole thesis, and then redrafting it, moves the student on faster than trying to get each chapter 'right' in isolation. The refrain of the *Star Trek* song about 'always going forward' is a good motto for writing a thesis.

Word-processing

It is very easy to assume that all today's graduate students are computer literate and skilled at using word-processors, spreadsheets, graphics packages and so on. Such assumptions are not usually made about overseas students from developing countries, or mature students (unless they have been office workers in a previous career). But it is all too easy to make such an assumption about graduate students in their twenties. Equally, one may well assume that the sort of research training that is now available in most departments will ensure that students acquire the relevant skills.

The wise supervisor will not, however, take such skills for granted. Research on doctoral students in pharmaceutics in schools of pharmacy in 1994 (Whittlesea 1995) revealed that many of them were hampered by a lack of word-processing skills. These respondents were all first-language English speakers with a recent UK degree in pharmacy. However, many of them reported that the word-processing skills that they had 'picked up' as undergraduates were inadequate for doctoral work. Many needed formal courses, or tuition packages, or extensive personal help. The supervisor needs to ask students how good their skills are, steer them towards relevant courses or ensure that they use the tuition software that the university has available. In doing so, one should be aware that not all students are able to diagnose their needs and abilities accurately, or to gauge what range of skills and software they will need. Rudestam and Newton (1992: Chapter 10) is an excellent discussion of how graduate students can learn to maximize their information technology skills.

Part of the supervisor's task is to ensure that students learn to word-process well enough to be able to prepare drafts of their work. They should discuss with their students the initial and final word-processing of the thesis itself. There are some key questions that need to be addressed. When the student is full-time, access to an adequate workstation should be routine. For part-time students it may not be straightforward. One cannot take access to a machine for granted. It is important to establish in the early stages of the part-timer's research how he or she is to maintain access to the necessary computers – at work, at home or in the university's facilities in the evenings and at weekends. If part-timers are dependent on home or work, then it is important for them to ensure that they keep up to date with changing software, and remain adequately compatible with the university department. (A well resourced university or department can alleviate these problems by lending or hiring out laptop computers to graduate students who cannot otherwise be guaranteed access.) The cases of Harriet and Linnet set out in Example 8.4 occurred in the 1980s, but equivalent problems can still hit part-time students who do not live near the university.

Example 8.4: Harriet and Linnet

Harriet Laverton and Linnet Doyle were part-time MPhil students who lived over fifty miles from Cardiff. Harriet, who worked at another university, began her thesis drafting on an elderly Amstrad, using Locoscript. Linnet was working on a PC at work. Harriet realized that if she was going to get a professional typist to prepare the final version of her thesis for submission, or produce a high-quality product herself, she would have to convert the files. Her own university proved unable to do so, as did several commercial agencies. A colleague of Sara's finally solved the problem for her, but the process had delayed her by several weeks. Linnet was made redundant by local government reorganization and lost access to her machine, just as she was too broke to buy her own or pay a typist. She lived too far away to make convenient use of the university's PC facilities. She was lucky enough to borrow a machine from her flatmate's boyfriend while he spent three months in the USA, but for a while it looked as if she would be unable to submit because she had no access to a computer.

It is useful to discuss with the student from early on how much of the final thesis text he or she will prepare. Students may decide to prepare their own drafts, but pay a professional to complete the final editing, formatting and printing; or they may elect to do the whole thing themselves. If they want to do the whole thing, you can discuss with them where they can get access to a good quality printer. The student needs to cultivate the skills of a careful proofreader, as well as learning to use a spellchecker. He or she will also need to learn how to format the page correctly, in accordance with the university's regulations, lay out tables, prepare graphics and so on. Software for the management of references and bibliographies is almost always useful for graduate students, and rarely introduced as part of basic word-processing courses. Training and practice need to be planned: it is a bad idea to try to do all these things in a rush at the end of the research.

Access to word-processing can handicap some students because they keep fiddling with their texts in a way that was never possible in the days of typescript. Likewise, they can waste precious weeks perfecting the appearance of the thesis, as if it were an exercise in desktop publishing. Others, on the other hand, are liberated by writing and editing directly with the word-processor. Here again, an explicit discussion of how word-processing has affected academic writing, and how the particular student prefers to work, can be beneficial. Like many academics, our colleague Barbara Adam waxes lyrical about how composing at the keyboard 'takes the dread out of rewriting' and 'turns editing into a pleasure'. Discussion of the intersection between the medium and the process is usually helpful for students.

Lastly, the supervisor may also need to help the student to *stop* writing. The most able of students can sometimes find it hard to let the thesis go. Writing and rewriting can sometimes become almost obsessional. The cultivation of a certain perfectionism in polishing the text can become a kind of displacement activity. Supervisors can find themselves in a kind of double bind. Having encouraged the able graduate student to draft, redraft and respond to critical appraisal of their work, they can finally find themselves telling a student *not* to write any more: not to add that further chapter; not to incorporate yet more recent or obscure literature; not to be influenced by yet another fashionable theorist. But to call it a day. To recognize that it really is done. Again, this depends to a considerable extent on mutual trust between student and supervisor. The student needs to have sufficient faith in the supervisor's own academic judgement, and ultimately in her or his own, to recognize that the writing has reached its end – at least as far as the thesis is concerned.

Once the thesis draft is advancing towards completion, the supervisor can focus on preparing the student for the examination, which is the subject of our next chapter.

9

A lack of genuine interest: choosing the right external, and preparing the student for the examination

Fundamental mistakes arise out of lack of genuine interest.
(Sayers 1972: 171)

Introduction

A good supervisor does not lose interest in the student when the thesis is written up. The student needs continued help until the viva is over, and that help has to be grounded in a genuine interest in the choice of examiner, the preparations for the examination and the final presentation of the text.

In some universities the supervisor is not empowered to choose the internal or external examiners, and may not be involved in the viva voce examination in any way. This can lead a supervisor to forget his or her most important task: that is, preparing the students for their submission, examination and viva. This chapter is written for supervisors who have some role in choosing the external(s), some role in the viva voce and, most importantly, a major role in preparing the student for the examination. The chapter deals with choice of external, preparing the thesis for submission, preparing the student for examination, the conduct of viva voce sessions and the role(s) of examiners. We hope that it will be useful for lecturers who have not yet examined a thesis themselves, as well as those with students coming up for submission. We start by recommending that you read the fictional viva voce from Cross (1970). This is a viva in the Graduate School of English Literature at Columbia, taking place at the height of the anti-Vietnam War movement, during a year of campus unrest. The heroine, Professor Kate Fansler, is presenting Mr Cornford for a PhD, and his thesis is on W. H. Auden. American universities do not use external examiners, but make up panels with professors from other departments in the same university. Cross's account takes eight pages, and is *extremely* funny: among other problems, the panel is supposed to include Professor Chang from the Department of Asian Civilization (because Auden had been to China and had written about it), but in fact another Professor Chang, an expert in limestone landscapes from the School of Engineering, is there instead. This Chang opens up his contribution to the viva by asking, ' "Tell me please", Professor Chang said, turning courteously in his chair, "in China your Mr Auden found limestone landscapes? And what, please, is dildo?"' Although there are a great many campus novels (see Carter 1990), there are very few doctoral vivas depicted in them, and this is certainly the funniest. But no one would want his or her own students to be exposed to anything like it.

Preparing for the examination of the thesis

Background work

Few students realize why there are external and internal examiners, and what they are supposed to do. Nor are they aware who is eligible to be an external or internal, how the external and internal get chosen, who appoints the external and internal examiners or how long the whole process from submission to viva may take. Supervisors have a duty to explain the procedures that operate in their institution – first ensuring that they actually understand them themselves.

One of the first things to find out about is submission dates and how these relate to degree ceremonies, funding council deadlines, local rules about continuation fees and other timetabling constraints that may affect students. Many lecturers do not need to have such dates in their heads, and most students are blissfully unaware of how bureaucracies work. It is a shame if a good relationship and the processing of a sound thesis are spoiled by discord over the technicalities of submission, examination and graduation. That happened to us in the case of Guy Pagett, a lecturer in the School of Modern Languages, who, it transpired, had never been involved with any higher degree submissions and did not know the timetable governing submission and degree day at Cardiff.

Example 9.1: Mrs Pagett's hat

Guy Pagett was a lecturer in the Department of Russian, who was registered for his PhD in sociology. Sara was director of graduate studies. In Cardiff, staff have to have two external examiners, and no internal. We had some trouble finding two appropriate externals free on the same day to viva Guy. One of our original choices was in Canada on sabbatical, and we only got the panel fixed up as Guy was getting his thesis bound. Guy handed in his thesis in May, thinking he could graduate at the 10 July ceremony, for which his mother had already bought a new hat. In fact, in the University of Wales, 15 April is the last date on which a thesis can be submitted if the candidate is to graduate in July, and the viva has to happen before 15 June so that the paperwork can be completed. Sara took it for granted that Guy knew these things because he was a lecturer and they were all in the university *Calendar*. She had not explained to Guy that as he had missed 15 April *and* as his panel had been problematic he would not be able to graduate at a ceremony that year. She fixed the viva for 3 July, it took place and Guy passed. He was then hurt and angry to find he could not graduate for 12 months, and his mother was mortified. What should have been an unalloyed pleasure for Guy – the thesis had been a long time coming to fruition and he received lots of praise from his examiners – was soured by this lapse of Sara's.

It is always wise to spell out to students how the institution works and what consequences that will have. Students also need to understand how the pressure on institutions to improve their completion rates, and the impact of the Reynolds Report (CVCP 1985) on examination procedures, have changed the pattern of submission and examination respectively over the past decade. The paragraphs we issue at Cardiff read:

> Since the Reynolds Report (prepared for the CVCP in the 1980s) there have been changes in the way theses are examined. For Masters degrees by thesis (MPhil) and PhDs, there will be an external examiner (from outside the University of Wales) and an internal examiner (from UWCC – but not your supervisor). The head of the department is legally responsible for choosing the external – but the supervisor's suggestions are normally followed. The external examiner should be interested in the topic, an expert on it, and an established scholar. For PhDs a Professor is ideal – but there may not be a suitable Professor around.

Such a paragraph begins the education of the graduate student. It is usually illuminating for graduate students to talk through the criteria used in the department to choose an external and the internal. Among the points to discuss will probably be: how poorly paid examining is, the motivation of examiners, the balancing of specialist knowledge and 'fairness', and the longer-term consequences of the choice. We discuss all these briefly below.

Students are very unlikely to know what sort of fee external examiners get (and that internal examiners are not paid at all). It is illuminating to explain that being the external examiner of a thesis pays considerably below the hourly rate envisaged in any post-Maastricht proposals for a national minimum wage. (The actual hourly rate depends on how good or bad the thesis actually is, and therefore how much effort must be put into reading and annotating.) This reason for choosing an external with an intrinsic interest in the topic is probably hidden from candidates. It helps to explain to them that there are no worthwhile extrinsic rewards for being an external examiner. Rather, the intrinsic interest is the 'bait' we all dangle to persuade colleagues to act. While we are on this topic, it is useful to mention that externalling a thesis can be stressful for the examiner too: candidates are rarely good enough at 'taking the role of the other' to realize that until they become an examiner themselves. Paul always warns his students – undergraduate as well as graduate – that they might as well assume that their examiner for any examination or piece of course work is tired, over-committed and stressed. They should therefore write with a view to seizing his or her attention, making their work as clear and accessible as possible. If they can do that, then they can make their work accessible and memorable for other readers as well, now or in the future.

The question usually arises: why does anyone agree to be an external? Among the reasons that motivate externals we know are altruism and 'duty': it is part of the generalized reciprocity all academics owe to the continuation of the system and their particular disciplines. That explains the general predisposition and willingness to serve. As far as agreeing to act for specific candidates, the main motivations are probably interest in the topic, friendship or reciprocity with the supervisor or head of department, level of work commitments at the time of year, including other externalling tasks, and perhaps some personal reasons. This last category can include combining the viva with a visit to family, friends or collaborators, the proximity of a sporting venue or access to some other treat. Among possible externals we have used in Cardiff, Tim Allerton's in-laws live in a nearby town and he and his wife are always pleased to have a long weekend staying there. Coming to Cardiff from Tim's university involves passing through a town with a bus museum Tim loves to visit, as the curator is an old friend. Consequently we can always persuade Tim to come and external for us. Another colleague, Guido Richetti, comes from a South Wales Italian family and is always pleased to come 'home' to see his mother. Similarly, Sara has family in Brighton and will always accept invitations to external at Sussex or Brighton Universities.

There is one other extreme reason for agreeing to be an external, which is a principal reason for agreeing to be an internal examiner, and that is gaining the experience. Like many tasks, the more often one has examined a thesis the more confident one becomes, and therefore the easier both supervision and examination are. The more examining you have done, the better supervisor you may be.

From the supervisor's viewpoint, the choice of external involves judging how far the potential external should be *the* specialist expert on the topic, how far a generalist in the area, and how far that expertise has to be balanced against her or his reputation as a fair, judicious, rational examiner. An expert on the topic who is horrendously severe on students or obsessively 'picky' is probably a bad choice; a more generalist, less specialized, external who is fair and makes balanced judgements will be better. The supervisor needs to decide whether or not to discuss that judgement call (but not, of course, discussing specific individuals) with students. However, we all have a duty to protect our candidates from externals who behave unfairly, and that means, brutally, 'gossip'. If you and your close colleagues do not know how Professor X behaves as an external, then it is necessary to ask around and find out.

Students often ask if they can have someone 'soft' or 'easy' as their external (though often not in so many words). That is a good enquiry because it allows you to discuss explicitly the importance of having the right external, not just for the viva, but for their longer-term future. The animal welfare slogan about pets and Christmas can be modified as: 'An external isn't just for the examination – he or she can be a patron, referee and gatekeeper for life.' You know that it is important to have an external who is not just about to retire but will be active for a decade or so, so that he or she can write references, open opportunities and make recommendations for the candidate for years to come. See the case of Bartholemew Strange in Chapter 4, for instance (Example 4.4). Examples 9.2 and 9.3 set out some pitfalls surrounding the choice of external. Example 9.2 reflects successful choices, while Example 9.3 was a disaster.

Example 9.2: Long-term benefits for Margaret Rushbridger

When Margaret Rushbridger finished her thesis we chose Professor William Purvis. We had rejected using the leading theorist at the centre of Margaret's argument, because we felt he would find it difficult to judge objectively a thesis which was very largely critical of his work. Prof. Purvis liked the thesis and Margaret's work. The PhD was awarded and praise bestowed liberally. Prof. Purvis subsequently sponsored Margaret's career so that she got a trip to Australia and became reviews editor of Purvis's journal, and he commissioned from her two chapters for edited collections. The leading theorist only read the ideas once they were published, by which time he could debate with Margaret as an equal. We were pleased with our choice.

It is a good idea to find out both what the formal rules are in your own institution and what the local/departmental customs are. The rule book may very well say that the head of department or dean of the graduate school chooses the examiners, but you probably need to find out what advice they take. If the decisions do not formally include the supervisor, it may be normal for someone to take 'soundings' from him or her. There may be many informal ways to influence the choices: by having good ideas, by squashing bad ones, by asking colleagues to drop hints and so on.

There is also the thorny question of the candidate's own views on the prospective external(s) and internal. Many places have rules against the student being consulted, but it is very hard, and can be very risky, not to have at least a general discussion about the issue. Whoever makes the final choice, he or she needs to know whether the potential examiners have any pre-existing links with the candidate, formal or informal, licit or illicit, good or bad. It would be very easy, if the student were not at least consulted in general terms, to appoint a candidate's godmother, aunt by marriage, discarded or current lover, former landlord or squash partner. More realistically, and less facetiously, it is necessary to ensure that sensible choices of external examiner are made, in order to avoid unnecessary disputes about fundamental disagreements over research philosophy, methodology and the like. There are appropriate arenas for vigorous disputes to be conducted among academic equals. They have their own entertainment value for spectators and their own rules of engagement. The exchange of vituperative recriminations through correspondence pages of academic journals or the public press is good blood sport, perhaps, and the academy would not be the same environment without it. But a graduate student's examination is not the right place to practise the academic equivalent of the martial arts.

Students often think that they need to know who their external is before they finalize their text, so they can include positive citations and/ or remove negative ones. That is, of course, not necessary in itself, but if an external is relevant enough to the thesis to examine it, then his or her work should probably be cited somewhere in any case. Students need to be reminded that they need to think, if at all, not so much about who their external will be (as an individual) as about what he or she will be (in terms of interests, experience, skills and interests). Preparing for a more generalized audience than just the one ideal external – who may not be available, and may not be appointed anyway – is a more productive way of approaching things, and is a more fruitful way of constructing an 'implied reader' for the thesis anyway. Discussing a small shortlist of examiners may well be a tactic to force a student to check the comprehensiveness of his or her coverage of the field. The crucial issue is whether the external examiner is going to be an *appropriate* one. As we have implied already, there are various ways in which one might usefully think about what appropriateness means in this context. A supervisor, or a director or dean of graduate studies, will normally do well to think constructively about at least some of those criteria when proposing or approving the nomination of an external for a particular student.

This brings us to the academic criteria that should be used in choosing external and internal examiners. There are several criteria to be borne in mind. First, does the potential examiner suffer from the 'drawbridge' mentality? This is a common disease. The examiner, having achieved a higher degree, believes that he or she should be the last person to enter the ivory tower before the drawbridge is raised, and unworthy unwashed multitudes lay siege to the castle. In practice, that means that all attempts by higher degree candidates to join the elite are repulsed as below standard.

The second issue relates to broadmindedness or matching. The good examiner needs either to be a user of the same broad theory and methods of data collection and analysis as the candidate, and have an interest in the empirical subject matter, *or* to be broadminded enough to appreciate the merits of approaches other than his or her own. It is reasonable to expect students to have a reasoned defence of their theories, methods and topic choices, both in the thesis and orally in the viva. However, it is not reasonable to ask the student to defend a school of thought against blind prejudice. If the external examiner is implacably and irrationally hostile to a position, she or he will in all likelihood not prove a fair examiner.

Example 9.3: The wrong external, circa 1976

Virginia Revel was a friend of Sara's who had had three different supervisors for her thesis on women in Brazil. The first two had left the university for posts elsewhere. Her third supervisor knew nothing about Latin America, and appointed an external who had been chosen by the second supervisor, who had returned to New Zealand. The external was an old-fashioned Marxist who believed passionately that men built revolutions and women should be barefoot, pregnant and ignored by social science. Virginia's thesis was a piece of socialist feminist analysis, focused on the role of women in Brazilian trade unions. The external hated it, because, at root, he did not believe that Brazilian women should have any role in trade unions. He found a great many typing mistakes and grammatical errors, a good deal of missing literature and some problems in the way the data were presented, but, at bottom, he loathed the whole idea of the thesis.

Virginia came to see Sara and her flatmate, another social science lecturer, with the external's written comments. The three of us rewrote the thesis, correcting the typing mistakes and making it grammatically perfect, incorporating the missing literature, re-presenting the data and, most vitally, explaining, expanding and defending the central assumptions and arguments, using quotes from leading male scholars who worked on Latin America to justify studying women in Brazilian trade unions, so that it became a more blatantly mainstream thesis. Meanwhile, the original examiner withdrew because he had been offered a chair in the USA, and Virginia used her network to do research on alternatives. She persuaded her supervisor to appoint a person more sympathetic to feminist ideas. Virginia passed her resubmission, which was an infinitely *better* thesis: better typed, more grammatical, better grounded in the literature, much more coherently argued and with infinitely improved data presentation. The final thesis became a book.

However, this all took a year. The supervisor only realized at the first viva that she or he had *not* done enough research on the examiner, who was, it transpired, notoriously hostile to feminism, research on women, women candidates and anyone who challenged the ideas of his 'school'.

The examiner's reputation in the discipline may be very relevant. If the student is at all likely to have an academic career, then it is wise to find an examiner who can help with that career: someone whose sponsorship will be seen as a bonus. The examples of Rosalie Otterbourne and Luke Fitzwilliam illustrate this.

Example 9.4: Rosalie Otterbourne and Luke Fitzwilliam

Sara was Rosalie Otterbourne's external examiner, Anthony Cade was Luke Fitzwilliam's. Sara became one of Rosalie's referees and was able to recommend her to Anthony Cade when he needed a research assistant. In turn Anthony, who had been impressed by Luke's PhD, recommended Luke to Sara as a strong candidate for tutoring at a summer school Sara was running. Rosalie and Luke both got their careers boosted by recommendations from their externals.

Sometimes the choice of an academically appropriate external can have social consequences. For example, the best external may involve the candidate travelling to the external, or possibly chaperonage, as in the following example.

Example 9.5: The chaperoned viva

Norman Gale had supervised Fatima Ibn Battuta for a PhD on women and rural development in northern Nigeria. The best external we could think of was in a city in the north of England, was willing to act, but was not well enough to travel to Cardiff. It was agreed that the viva should take place in 'North City', and Norman prepared to drive there with Fatima. At this point her husband, another PhD student, said he could not allow his wife to be alone in a car with Norman for two long car journeys. He insisted that a male cousin, doing a degree at Swansea, travelled to North City with Norman and Fatima so that her honour was seen to be protected. Because the external was a woman, he did not insist that the cousin attend the actual viva.

By contrast to the bad experiences of examinations and inappropriate selection of external examiners, one must emphasize that when an external examiner is the right sort of person, and when things are handled well, the entire process can be a thoroughly rewarding one for all concerned. When a thesis is a competent one or better, and when it satisfies the normal criterion – that it is an original contribution to knowledge in the candidate's field – then reading it and examining it should be interesting and, indeed, pleasurable for the examiner(s). Likewise, when there is little or no chance of the degree being withheld, the viva voce examination itself may prove to be a worthwhile experience. Under such circumstances, the occasion becomes much more collegial than might otherwise be the case. The candidate can talk about her or his plans for future research, plans for publication, ideas for further research funding and so on. On such occasions, the external examiner can prove to be a genuine advisor, and help can often be promised for the future. The occasion of the examination becomes a two-way exchange of views and ideas. When the thesis is sound and the external examiner is the right person, the 'examination' becomes something altogether more egalitarian and less confrontational than that term normally conveys.

On the receiving end

The higher degree student may well fear and dread the examination. Even when the student is outstandingly competent, and however excellent the thesis itself may be, the process of examination can be a stressful one. Given that the assessment of the thesis is indeed an examination, conducted primarily by one or more examiners not well known to the candidate, one can argue that the process is necessarily so. We know from a survey of higher degree students (Eggleston and Delamont 1983) that most feel worried by the indeterminacy of thesis examination, and that inexperienced supervisors are common.

Consider the account of an examination by Dr Nancy Enright, who was regarded by Kingford as one of their most successful alumna, and is now a lecturer at Latchendon University. Her story of her viva was not a recollection of a happy experience:

> I had the most horrible viva anybody could ever have, I think. I did the most deplorable thing, I got upset and burst into tears, and that was awful, so I have a very bad memory of my viva. Looking back at the one I assisted with, I realized that with mine it was a question of human rights. It was appallingly badly examined. It was probably partly my fault, because you're not meant to know who your external is going to be, but usually there's an unofficial discussion about it.

And I was not entirely happy about my external ... I was examined by a historian from Reddingdale. There were things like he didn't know the conventions for the bibliography in anthropology – we have a convention where you don't capitalize every single word in a book title – and I had a twenty-five page bibliography and he went through and put a circle through every single letter he thought should have been capitalized. There were a lot of typing errors, but I got the cheapest typist I could, who typed a lot of things wrong, so that he said things like, 'This sentence hasn't got a verb in it.' And the examiner missed the train, so I was waiting for two hours with the other examiner and the supervisor, so in terms of nervous stress it was awful ... And they didn't say, 'Well done' or anything, it was just, 'We want the typing mistakes corrected in three weeks.'

Supervisors can, and should, reduce the fear and the pain. A great deal can be done to reduce anxiety, both by demystifying the processes and by helping the student to reduce the likelihood of a referral by impeccable presentation. In preparing our own students, and in the attempt to dispel some of their anxieties, we include sessions on the viva examination in our series of graduate classes. We have a handout on some of the procedures, and then we provide two types of mock viva. These are introduced in the next section.

Reducing the fear

In Scandinavia, the Netherlands and Belgium, the doctoral viva is a public event, so a candidate can watch other people defending their theses. In the UK, vivas are private, so the supervisor and departments need to think about ways of simulating the viva. There are two ways to do this: an individual mock viva and a public mock viva. Each has its merits. Students can also be helped by handouts and classes about what happens in a typical viva, and about the criteria that externals use to evaluate theses. We have reproduced here, as Figure 9.1, our handout on external examiners' criteria, and then – in Figure 9.2 – our handout on what happens in a typical viva and how students should present themselves. We then discuss how to simulate vivas.

The individual mock viva is particularly useful for students whose first language is not English. The ideal format is to have a couple of staff who are relative strangers to the student, who have read the thesis abstract, introduction and conclusion. They should take about forty minutes, and grill the student in a shortened version of a real viva. Ideally this should be taped, or even videotaped, so that the student can be taken through his or her performance by the supervisor, and helped to think about how to frame answers to questions and defend the thesis.

Figure 9.1: What does an external do?

The following are important things that an external examiner will think about – but not necessarily in this order:

1 Typing/word-processing. Are there lots of mistakes? Does it need to be referred for retyping, or can it be hand corrected?
2 Is the bibliography complete? (Is every reference in the text listed at the back?)
3 Is the bibliography correctly prepared?
4 Is the literature review comprehensive and up to date? If not, how much more work does the student need to do?
5 What sort of thesis is it? If it is empirical, the following questions arise.

    (a) Is the problem worth studying?
    (b) Were the right (or at least relevant) methods chosen?
    (c) Were the methods used properly?
    (d) And are the relevant methods textbooks cited?
    (e) Was the sample big enough? Chosen well?
    (f) Are the data presented clearly?
    (g) Has the author a realistic understanding of where his or her data fit into the literature?
    (h) Does the discussion illuminate the results?
    (i) Do the conclusions follow from the results?

If you want to read about examining, pages 141–6 in G. Brown and M. Atkins (1988) *Effective Teaching in Higher Education*, are about being an examiner.

Figure 9.2: What happens in a viva

Be prepared
The viva will take at least one hour, and can last for four to five hours. Make sure that you are wearing clothes that enable you to sit comfortably, and that you won't need to go out to the lavatory too often. Don't have garlic, curry or alcohol for lunch!
Don't wear a *strong* cologne, perfume or after shave: vivas are hot sweaty occasions.

You should have with you:

(a) a copy of your thesis
(b) a pencil, a pen with *black* ink, a note pad
(c) a clean handkerchief
(d) a list of typing mistakes you've already spotted in your own thesis since you handed it in!

Figure 9.2: (*Cont'd*)

What will probably happen
Your external, internal, chairperson and supervisor will probably have had lunch together. (Most vivas happen at 2.00 or 2.15 p.m.). They will certainly have met, and discussed what they think of your work and how to organize the viva. So they will have prepared questions, statements etc.

You will be invited in, and you should be introduced to the external (and the internal if a stranger). The chair will tell you what's going to happen. 'Dr X will start the questioning . . .' or 'Both Professor Z and Dr P have some questions, but I'd like to start by asking . . .'

Sometimes the panel tell you at the beginning that you have passed. If that happens, fine. If it doesn't, *don't panic.* Some externals prefer to examine you before they judge your work.

You can expect to be asked – and should prepare to answer:

(a) Why did you choose this topic, this method, this sample?
(b) What would you do differently if you were starting this work now?   *answer needed.*
(c) Summarize your main/the most important findings.
(d) What problems did you face? How did you overcome them?

If the examiner says 'On page 69 you say' – don't look surprised. She or he should have read it that carefully. Just turn to page 69 and take time to re-read what you *did* say! However idiotic the question, be polite.

If you didn't understand the question, *say so.* Ask politely to hear it again.

If you are nervous, say so: 'Sorry, I'm very nervous. Could you ask that again, I'm not concentrating very well.'

Sound modest, but not grovellingly wet.

Try not to waffle. Answer concisely, with reference to the thesis.

Defend your work firmly but calmly: 'Yes, that is a good criticism. At the time I didn't realize X so I did Y. There are benefits from doing Y – as I show in Chapter 7.' 'I'm afraid I don't agree. Atkinson's work is interesting – but it really isn't relevant to my argument in Chapter 7, as I explained on page 10.'

If you are asked to leave the room and wait, don't panic, and don't vanish. If you have to go and phone someone, tell the secretary where you've gone and be quick.

The public mock viva is a parallel way to demystify the viva. We have organized at least one every year since 1987. This is how we do it. First, a staff member who has a PhD 'volunteers' to be the candidate. She chooses a published article, held in the university library, and it is designated as 'the thesis'. Other staff are chosen to act as external examiner, internal examiner, supervisor and chair. A date is set, invitations are issued to postgraduates and posters are put up; for example, the one shown in Figure 9.3.

Figure 9.3: Poster for a mock viva

MOCK VIVA 1997

This year's mock viva will be held on
Tuesday 4 March
at 5.30
in Room 1.19 Humanities Building

The Candidate:	Dr Sara Delamont, SOCAS
The External:	Prof. Richard Whipp, Cardiff Business School
The Internal:	Dr Jane Salisbury, School of Education
The Supervisor:	Dr Andrew Pithouse, SOCAS
The Chair:	Prof. Derek Blackman, School of Psychology

The thesis: Graham Goode and Sara Delamont's paper: 'Opportunity denied', in S. Betts (ed.) *Our Daughter's Land*, Cardiff: University of Wales Press, 1996, pp. 97–115. (Copies available from Room G2 in the department.)

On the appointed day, the cast assembles in the lecture room, and the chairperson explains what is going to happen. The 'candidate' waits outside the room, while the chair introduces the panel to the audience, explaining their roles. Then the viva begins. The chair reminds the panel of their duties – quoting the university's rules – and then asks to have the candidate brought in. We then have a viva, lasting forty minutes or so, with the candidate trying to answer the panel's questions as well as possible, and the panel asking supportive questions. That is, the first performance is a successful viva: the thesis is a pass and the candidate is trying hard to be a 'good' student.

After the first enactment of a viva, we stop and send the candidate out. The lecturer alters his or her appearance – swapping the smart suit for a t-shirt and jeans – and is again brought in. This time the candidate acts bad student, and the panel are forced to fail the thesis. Different staff play 'bad' student in different styles – weeping, monosyllabic, depressed, aggressive, drunk, elaborately flippant. One year, Dr Ian Shaw played 'bad' student as an increasingly depressed person, who shrank into a foetal curl, and developed a maddening sniff. Paul Atkinson has played it as a sixties communard, accusing the panel of middle-class prejudice against working-class candidates whenever he did not like a criticism.

We get an audience of 50–75 doctoral students, with a few staff who are about to be an internal or external examiner for the first time. The audience watch the successful performance with interest, but when the student is 'failing' they become completely absorbed in the drama. They groan, squirm with embarrassment, wince and giggle nervously as the lecturer messes up her or his chances of getting a PhD. When a question is mishandled, the audience reaction is clearly audible. A few people find the mock viva frightening, but most respond that it is both entertaining and informative. It takes a good deal of organizing, but the benefits are worth it. The event is demystified.

The supervisor can choose the examiners carefully, and set up all the mock vivas in the world, but it is also important to ensure that the student has done all the basic presentational work on the thesis properly, so that the ideas are examined, not the typing.

Preparing the student for submission

Students rarely appreciate how long it takes to proof-read a text, especially if they have typed it themselves. They need to be told, repeatedly, that they must find a friend and read the whole thing *aloud*, punctuation and all, especially checking all the tables, figures and data against the original lab books, computer print-out or hand-drawn versions. It is helpful if the supervisor can pay the student to proof-read something the supervisor has written early on in the registration period, so the student learns how to do it professionally. Postgraduates can, and should, be encouraged to work together, helping each other to proof-read each other's theses. The story of Jimmy McGrath, coupled with that of the worst case from your own expereince, should encourage your students to aim for an immaculate presentation.

Example 9.6: Jimmy McGrath

Jimmy McGrath was Paul's PhD student. He completed his text, and Paul had approved its content for submission. However, despite warnings about the large number of typing errors in the last draft, the submitted text was riddled with errors: two or three on every page. The external, Anthony Cade, referred the thesis because the presentation was so bad, demanding that it be retyped, and commenting 'Why didn't you pay Prudence Crowley to do it? Other work from Cardiff that I've seen has been immaculate, and has acknowledged Mrs Crowley — I'd use her.'

Students may need advice on whether to submit in temporary or permanent binding (depending on the university's regulations), help with the paperwork required by the university (such as notification of intention to submit, if such a procedure exists) and/or a loan to pay the immediate costs of submission (if required). They may be shy about asking for help. Again, do not underestimate the extent to which some students are 'cue-deaf' and fail to register what other students take for granted. One student we heard about submitted his thesis on bright blue paper, having failed to read the university's rules.

Once the thesis is handed in, and the candidate is waiting for the viva, the supervisor can do little more, except 'rehearse' him or her for the event. However, one way to help candidates to prepare for their submission and examination is to encourage them to work through the relevant chapters of Cryer (1996) and Phillips and Pugh (1994). They have a number of good ideas for how students can usefully occupy the time. But supervisors should be very wary about recommending them all uncritically. Phillips and Pugh, for instance, advise students to compile a detailed (obsesssively detailed) condensation of their thesis by way of revision and preparation. For many theses that would be inappropriate, while for some students such an exercise would provoke anxiety and do little or nothing to improve their performance. On the other hand, all students can probably benefit from thinking of a few good questions to ask the examiners – advice about publication being a recurrent topic for such enquiries. Likewise, some general homework about the external examiner may be useful. Equally, however, one should not make a fetish of it, or expect the candidate to come over as fawning by focusing too much on the external's interests and achievements.

Finally, it is vital to ensure that the student realizes that submission leads to an examination. Your role is to decide the thesis is ready to be submitted and examined, not to guarantee that it passes. Irrespective of whether they have followed your advice to the letter or not, candidates do need to take responsibility for their own work. It is they who will be awarded the degree if they are successful, not their supervisor.

The examination and its outcomes

Before your student actually walks into the viva, there are three tasks you need to have performed. First, you need to be aware of the regulations governing the degree the student is being examined for, and especially what the possible outcomes of the viva can be. These are different in different universities, and are subject to change, so it is easy to think one knows the ropes when in fact one's knowledge is out of date. Second, it is useful to know what happens in vivas in your department or institution: who attends and what roles they have (some, for instance, have a chairperson, others do not). In particular, you need to be clear about whether you are expected to attend or not, and if you are, what role you are supposed to play. (In some universities the supervisor is clearly expected to be present, although not as an examiner; in others the presence of the supervisor is explicitly proscribed.) Third, you need to ensure that your student is clear on these points. The candidate especially needs to know whether you will be present or not, and if so in what capacity: one cannot assume that he or she fully understands the niceties of having a supervisor present, but not as a full participant in the examining process, for instance.

In Cardiff there are the following outcomes from a PhD examination. We use them here as the basis for a brief consideration of what the supervisor can do once the verdict is arrived at and announced to the candidate. Examining boards in the University of Wales may recommend one of the following outcomes:

1 That the thesis be approved for the degree of PhD. (An Examining Board may require a candidate ... to make typographical or minor corrections in a thesis which has been approved for the degree of PhD, before deposit in the library.)
2 That the candidate be not approved for the degree of PhD but that, the thesis being satisfactory in substance but defective in presentation or in detail, the candidate be allowed to modify the thesis and re-submit it on one further occasion, not later than two years from the date of the official communication to him [*sic*] of his result by the University Registry, for the degree of PhD on payment of a reduced fee.
3 That the candidate be not approved for the degree of PhD but be allowed to modify his thesis and re-submit it on one further occasion, not later than two years from the date of the official communication to him of his result by the University Registry, for the degree of PhD on payment of a re-presentation fee.
4 That the candidate be not approved for the degree of PhD.
5 That the candidate be not approved for the degree of PhD, but be approved for the degree of MPhil.
6 That the candidate be not approved for the degree of PhD, but be allowed to modify the thesis and re-submit it on one further occasion, not later than two years from the date of the official communication to him of his result by the University Registry, for the degree of MPhil, on payment of an examination fee.

Universities have different regulations and wordings: supervisors and students must make absolutely sure they know and understand the regulations that apply to them. Looking at the University of Wales rules we have just reproduced, you can see that the possible outcomes of a PhD examination are varied. They are not perfectly straightforward either. It sometimes takes judgement on the part of the examiners and the chair of the board to determine precisely which category to apply. The differences between outcome 2 and outcome 3 are not clear-cut, for instance. It is, therefore, important that the examiners and the chair know and understand the categories and their normal interpretation. External examiners cannot be expected to have a feel for all different universities' practices. It is therefore especially important that the chair of the exam board, or the director of graduate studies (or whoever is responsible), ensures that the external examiner does understand what decisions the examiners are empowered to come to.

If the version is either of the first two, then the supervisor's role is to join in the celebrations, and after the excitement has settled down, to get on with helping the newly elevated Dr So-and-so progress her or his career still further. (We discuss this in the next chapter.) If the thesis is referred for revisions, then the supervisor can usefully do several things. The first is to discuss with the director of graduate studies, the head of department or whoever is responsible, and the candidate, whether a different staff member could better oversee the revisions. Often a fresh perspective helps everyone. Second, the supervisor can ensure that the examiners have provided a clear rationale for the referral, so that he or she *and the student* understand the reasons for the outcome, and that clear guidance has been provided as to what revisions are being required. If the supervisor is to retain responsibility for the candidate, and is charged with supervising the revision process, then it is imperative that he or she should understand thoroughly what is being asked of the student, the time frame within which the revisions may (and must) be completed and the regulations governing resubmission and examination. Supervisors can be very disappointed by any outcome that is not an outright pass and award of the degree. A referral for a moderate amount of revision is not a disgrace for a student or the supervisor, however. If everyone passed first time, then it would not be much of an examination – and it certainly would not carry the cachet that a PhD does. That does not preclude some degree of self-examination on the supervisor's part. It is worth reviewing whether the weaknesses in the thesis could and should have been spotted and corrected at an earlier stage; whether one's advice was always for the best; indeed, whether the student has followed advice adequately. One can always learn something from the examination of one's own students' work, whether they pass or are referred, and in the latter case one does need to think whether there are lessons for the future. Of course, you may feel that the examiners were purblind idiots to refer your student. But if they both had the same problems with the thesis, then perhaps you and your student need to accept the fact that the argument was not quite as convincing as you thought, or the evidence not quite as strong, or the conclusions not quite as self-evident.

Outright failure is uncommon, but not unknown. We shall not go into lengthy discussion of that outcome here. It rarely comes as a shock to supervisors and internal examiners. It normally reflects a major weakness or problem that will be known to you already. Unless something is sadly amiss, it often reflects a student's failure to perform tasks that the supervisor has proposed and agreed, a failure to accept advice, an omission of major parts of the research literature to which the supervisor has directed him or her. In these cases, it is especially important to ensure that your role is properly understood and documented. If it comes to complaints and appeals at a later stage, you do not want to stand accused of incompetent supervision because the student has not followed it. The actual process of appeal is very different in different universities and we do not need to dwell on it here. But if you have had problems with a weak or lazy or headstrong student, and the thesis is failed as a result, you do need to be prepared. It needs to be clearly understood, as we have said already, that in supervising the work you are not implicitly guaranteeing that the thesis will be successful.

Sometimes the student who has written a reasonable text can behave foolishly in the viva, as in the case of Dulcie Caterham. Such cases are mercifully rare.

Example 9.8: Poor viva performance

Dulcie Caterham had been supervised by a colleague who had retired, so Paul oversaw the final writing up and submission. The external was a leading scholar who asked very reasonable questions. Dulcie snapped out monosyllables that were – frankly – rude. The chairperson and external decided she was nervous and awarded the PhD, but Dulcie nearly talked herself out of her higher degree: not because she was being impolite, but because she appeared not to be addressing the examiner's questions properly. Paul decided afterwards that he had not spent enough time impressing on her how important it was for candidates to treat the examination process appropriately.

Once the examination or re-examination is over, the supervisor has one remaining responsibility to discharge: launching the student's career. This is the focus of the next chapter.

10

The brave pretence at confidence: launching the student's career

The brave pretence at confidence had been given up ... They were no longer angry and suspicious. They were afraid.

(Sayers 1972: 248)

Introduction

Sayers was describing a group of women threatened by anonymous letters and malicious damage. Many graduate students who want to stay in academic research and teaching are equally suspicious, afraid and even angry with the scholarly world. Many supervisors may feel that their job ends at the viva, and what happens thereafter is none of their business: it is the PhD student's career, let her or him build up a CV and find a post. We do not take that position, and believe instead that a good supervisor should help doctoral candidates to build good strong foundations for their careers.

We believe that supervisors should see the doctoral period as an important part of the career, and help the student to develop the beginnings of a well rounded CV, a list of useful contacts and a set of strategies for advancement. Once the viva is over, the former student can usefully be helped into single-handed publication and a first job. This chapter is divided into three main sections: career building while a PhD student is still a student; job-seeking after the viva; and publication matters. Clearly, much of this chapter applies primarily to the full-time student who wants an 'academic' or research job, rather than the person who is heading for a career in commerce or industry, or the part-time student who enjoys his or her current career.

For both stages of career building, the supervisor may find it helpful to consult the literature. There is a series of slim volumes, 'Survival Skills for Scholars', published by Sage, which has reached title number ten. Whicker *et al.* (1993) cover 'getting tenure', Smelser (1993) writes on 'effective committee service', and Weiner (1993) on 'improving teaching'. Working through relevant titles can be salutary for the experienced university academic as well as the novice. The series is written by American authors. The non-American reader can learn much, both directly and indirectly, by comparing and contrasting his or her own experience with the American university. The cultural and organizational differences between university systems can help to throw into relief one's own assumptions and practices, provide alternative perspectives and suggest strategic responses to challenges and problems.

There is good evidence that students are not knowledgeable about the job market, and it is clear that understanding of the workings of academic careers is not great in the student body (e.g. Startup 1979). The most recent research also suggests strongly that recent graduates are ill-prepared for the contemporary labour market. Brown and Scase's (1994) study is a case in point. Their empirical material at the heart of that volume is drawn from a questionnaire issued in 1990 to students in three English universities – 'Inner City' (a former polytechnic), 'Home Counties' and 'Oxbridge' – and 120 interviews with students at the same three universities done in 1991 and 1992. These data were supplemented with employer interviews: 30 'graduate recruiters' (p. 50) from 16 organizations; and with second interviews with 20 of their students a year into employment.

The authors were investigating 'the changing relationship between higher education and the intergenerational reproduction of class inequalities' (p. 165) in England. They wanted to use data to test the two competing theories which explain the relationships between occupational stratification and educational stratification. The first of these, social exclusion theory, emphasizes how elite groups were offered differentiated credentials to exclude certain social groups from top jobs, and is associated with Randall Collins's conflict theory. The second theory, a technocratic one, associated with Burton Clark, sees mass higher education as a necessary correlate of an increasingly complex post-industrial society in which the credentials are used to sort qualified people into specialized jobs.

Brown and Scase (1994: 173) conclude that in Britain:

> the recent increase in graduate numbers will simply mean that differences between the institutions of higher learning will increase . . . and the labour market for graduates will become polarised between the 'fast-track' leading to senior managerial positions, and a mass of other jobs which offer little in the way of career prospects.

They are pessimistic about the prospects of talent-led economic innovation in Britain because 'traditional processes of cultural and social reproduction are able to sustain themselves' (p. 175). Brown and Scase found that the twenty graduates they re-interviewed were disillusioned 'with the realities of working life' (p. 147), partly because they were 'unprepared for the realities of life in the 1990s: namely the more uncertain career prospects of the adaptive organisation' (p. 147). The middle-class, and Oxbridge, educated graduates were 'better-prepared for the transition to work' (p. 147). This was related to the findings from the employer/ recruiter interviews, which led Brown and Scase to conclude that 'the demand placed on employers to ensure a personal fit between existing employees and new recruits led to a search for "safe bets"' (p. 144).

There is no reason to believe that the PhD student will be any better prepared for career building than these respondents of Brown and Scase's. While few doctoral candidates today come out of their period as a research student as naive about, for example, publishing as many of their supervisors were in the past, it is easy to overestimate their sophistication. Sara Delamont (1984: 18) produced this account of the natural history of her failure to publish her PhD thesis:

> The data on St. Luke's lie, relatively unknown, in the Edinburgh University Library. This is not because I was ashamed of my work, but the result of a series of accidents. I submitted the thesis in August 1973 and started work at Leicester in September. I had asked Routledge, who had published Roy Nash's PhD in 1973, if they wanted to see mine, and despatched it as I left for Leicester. Some 6–9 months later, having heard nothing, I wrote to ask for my manuscript back. Routledge replied that they had lost it, would pay for a Xerox, and wished to have a photocopy so that they could consider it for publication. The second submission reached an academic referee (Brian Davies) who recommended that a revised manuscript be published. Routledge rejected this advice, pleading the economic climate, and so I was back at Square One. However, by this time John Eggleston had asked me to write *Interaction in the Classroom* (1976a), so the thesis was put aside. Thus apart from 4 papers (Delamont, 1976b, 1976c, 1984; Atkinson and Delamont, 1977) the research is only known from *Interaction in the Classroom.*

It is hard to believe how little advice and support our generation received in both the practicalities and the politics of publishing and other crucial aspects of career building. In the next section we address ways in which tomorrow's students can be prepared better.

Career building during the PhD registration

In this section we focus on using the doctoral registration period to set the foundations of a career in place. We start with teaching the courtesies, and move on to building a well rounded CV, networking, conferences and becoming aware of fund-raising. Publication issues are covered in the third section of the chapter.

Teaching the courtesies

One of the important tasks that might fall to the supervisor is training the student in academic courtesies. This can begin very early in the registration period. Some students do not seem to realize why academic work includes acknowledgements, and need to be trained to thank the funding body, their mentors, technical, secretarial and library staff, the head of the department or research group and their supervisor. In the early days a supervisor can discuss why there is an acknowledgements page in the thesis, and suggest the student opens a file, or keeps a notebook in which the names of helpful individuals are recorded so they get remembered. If it is possible to acknowledge students in a publication of yours, this will be motivating for them and a part of their training. Much later on, checking the acknowledgements section of the thesis, and ideally the footnote in which they put their acknowledgements in their early publications, enables you to train them so they do not offend others for much of their lives. Students may need to be told that readers will check their acknowledgements to see where they 'fit' into the discipline, that sponsors and funding bodies *require* acknowledgement and that a nice acknowledgement creates loyalty and renewed enthusiasm in clerical, technical and library staff. It may be necessary to explain explicitly that scholars who do not acknowledge help are likely to lose out in career opportunities, as in the case of Roger Ackroyd.

Example 10.1: Ungrateful Roger

Roger Ackroyd was a very successful PhD student, whose thesis produced several publications. However, he *never* acknowledged his supervisor Rufus van Aldin in any of them. Consequently Rufus never puts opportunities Roger's way: if looking for contributors to a conference or project he will not ask Roger, whom he perceives as 'ungrateful'.

Building the curriculum vitae

The successful graduate student will need to think about a bit more than just completing the research and submitting the thesis (though for much of the time even that may seem quite demanding enough). It is worth thinking more broadly about career development. The ambitious student may want to think constructively and strategically about how to acquire useful skills and experience that will give him or her an edge in the career stakes. They include: the acquisition of teaching skills and experience; the projection of future research; identifying funding sources and research sites. The precise mix of experience will depend on the discipline and on practical circumstances, but some broad issues will be generic.

Most graduate students and research assistants are permitted to undertake specified amounts of teaching. Indeed, some varieties of institutionally funded studentships and tutorial posts specifically require a commitment to teaching as well as to doctoral research. Research council studentships explicitly permit a small number of hours per week. If the department has a teaching programme (and in exclusively research centres and institutes things are different) then graduate students should be encouraged to acquire teaching experience. This is normally acquired through the provision of tutorials/seminars and, in the laboratory sciences, demonstration (supervising practical classes). Teaching experience is valuable in its own right. Many academics find that the necessity of preparing their thoughts in order to teach undergraduates helps them to organize their material in a way they otherwise would not. Teaching – even if only demonstrating and conducting tutorials – thus has intrinsic value for the younger academic. The ability to organize one's thoughts in order to help the average undergraduate may also help to articulate hitherto implicit ideas. Equally, and even more importantly for the longer term, the would-be academic needs to be thinking about how to build some teaching experience into the curriculum vitae. Few academic departments these days can afford to overlook the potential contribution to a teaching programme when making appointments to their regular staff.

The role of the research supervisor may be fairly remote from the allocation of basic teaching duties in the department. Her or his relationship with the graduate student, on the other hand, means that input on general career planning may be appropriate – possibly in discussion with the director of graduate studies, the dean of the graduate school or whoever has overall responsibility. Even though graduate students' teaching is not a major part of their commitment, they should not be used as 'dogsbodies' without having their efforts recognized, and without proper supervision and training. It is increasingly recognized that some initial training and mentoring in introductory teaching should be provided as part of the staff development offered to graduate students, research assistants and the like. They should not be thrown in at the deep end, with no guidance, backup or advice. The overview taken by the supervisor might well include general advice on how to manage the allocation of time between research, teaching and other activities. Equally, it should probably involve supervisory discussions on what skills and experiences the candidate wants to accumulate for career-building purposes. If there is access to a certificate in teaching, which many places now offer part-time to postgraduate tutors and demonstrators, then it is worth discussing with the postgraduate student whether she or he can and should obtain the credential. The benefits of teacher training for chemistry postgraduates was made clear in the evaluation of an experimental PhD/PGCE programme conducted by Galton and Delamont (1976). Students, supervisors and the heads of chemistry departments all saw benefits for the chemistry PhD stemming from the PGCE element.

As well as formal credentials, students need to build networks.

Networking in general and conferences in particular

Academic life is dependent on networking: keeping up with the field, judging the merits of others' work and one's own, discovering the status of journals, looking for externals, finding publication outlets, hearing about conferences, jobs and gossip, and making life tolerable are all vital parts of academic life that rely on networking. Students have to learn this, and the best way to help them into networks is via yours. Some students seem 'naturally' to be able to develop their own networks, both with people of their own generation and with more senior colleagues. Others need to be encouraged and sponsored, and some may even need to have the significance of networking pointed out to them explicitly. Students may not realize that they need to build up a network of contacts in their discipline, and that it is never too soon to start. Summer schools attended by graduate students from a number of universities are a good start, followed up by conferences.

Academic conferences are, of course, one mechanism for promoting students' professional networks. If you enjoy going to conferences, then it is straightforward to encourage your doctoral students to come with you, so that you can introduce them to your friends, enemies and the publishers' representatives. The main obstacle is money, and it is important to find out what funds are available for them in the department, the university and beyond, and encourage them to apply for financial support. Some students may be unwilling to go to the professional meetings, and if so you need to find out the source of their reluctance.

If their reluctance is due to ignorance of the importance of conferences, or to shyness or feelings of inferiority about mixing with 'big names', then the supervisor needs to explain why serious scholars have to overcome those barriers. If the problems are financial or domestic (children who cannot be left overnight, or a sick spouse who needs nursing), then a long-term plan to find solutions to the problems will be necessary – to help to enable the student to get away.

If there do not seem to be any opportunities for your graduate students to attend conferences elsewhere, it may be necessary for you to organize one, or help your students to do so in your own university. Involving graduate students in conference organization is excellent professional training for them: there is nothing like discovering than an FRS cannot complete a simple form indicating whether he wants a vegetarian meal or not to prepare the novice for university life. More importantly, the practical experience of conference organization – especially gained in the relative security of one's home department – represents a set of transferable skills that can be deployed most usefully in later years. Conference organization, together with conference attendance, is part of the network-building strategy that many younger academics will need to start cultivating.

It is also important for students to start presenting their results at the right conferences. Again, the precise range of opportunities varies from discipline to discipline, and our general observations must remain general. Some professional associations have regional conferences intended specifically for postgraduate students and other junior staff to present the results of research in progress. These are very useful occasions for one's students to learn the basics of conference presentation, as well as presenting their materials before a wider professional audience.

Larger national and international conferences may also offer the opportunity for graduate students to present their work. In many disciplines, the poster presentation is an appropriate method for graduate students to get their results out to a professional audience. There may also be opportunities for research students to participate in roundtables, symposia and the like. The major international conference is rather like 'The Season' of a former era. You can 'bring out' your graduate students, your research assistants and other junior colleagues. Successful presentations can have a significant impact on research students' reputations, and can also have a very positive effect on that of the department and the research group.

If conference presentations are to be successful, then preparation and training will be in order. Enough of our readers will have suffered the excruciating pain of sitting through conference papers that have been prepared inadequately – that typically overrun the allotted time, are delivered inaudibly, have illegible overheads and so on – to appreciate the value of preparation. The conference presentation is an unnatural mode of communication. There are very severe constraints on time and format. Members of the audience may not be especially interested. Supervisors and members of the graduate committee or school should ensure that research students and others have every opportunity to practise their presentation skills.

At Cardiff we have a regular programme of 'research days'. These are mixed events, and regularly include presentations by our graduate students of their current research. We expect their fellow students and members of the academic staff to turn out and make an audience. We allot the students exactly twenty minutes, and allow them to choose what aspect of the work to present. Full-time students are required to make such a research presentation each year. We explain to them that while twenty minutes may sound like a niggardly allocation, that is the longest time they will get at a major conference, and in many cases they will get less.

We also explain that we are an audience of friends and colleagues, and therefore students should get used to presenting their work to us before they venture on to the conference circuit. While we comment on the content of the students' presentations, we also offer advice on 'artistic impression'. We comment on how to get the key ideas over to the audience, for instance: experience shows that too many presenters (of all ages and statuses) take too much time going over inessential preliminaries rather than getting to the heart of their work immediately. We encourage students to have punchy papers, with a small number of bullet points to get over. We can also help them to avoid the dreadful pitfalls of the poor presenter – such as reading the paper without looking at the audience! Doing handouts and using the OHP are encouraged, and the chair behaves very strictly, stopping the presentation dead on time.

It is often a good idea to ensure that new students do not go to conferences alone. Experienced academics can sometimes forget that academic conferences can be quite daunting and lonely occasions. A group of students and younger researchers can be a valuable source of mutual support. Sponsoring and mentoring does not necessarily end with helping a student to get an abstract or poster accepted. If a student is to get out of a conference all that she or he might, then the supervisor or other senior colleague should be alert for opportunities to effect introductions to useful contacts and give advice as to which sessions will be worth attending (if any!). Since our own discipline is heavily dependent on books, we believe that it is an important function of conferences that our students and colleagues get to meet the publishers and their representatives at the publishers' exhibition. They will not necessarily start to negotiate with the publishers when they first meet them, but it may be valuable in the medium term to establish friendly professional relationships with representatives of key publishing houses. In some disciplines, meeting the equipment sales staff may be just as important. Students should learn to do what politically astute professors and lecturers do at conferences.

Before your students are launched into the conference scene they might enjoy, and learn from, reading some of the novels in which wise and foolish academic conference behaviour is featured. David Lodge's *Small World* (1984) is the most famous, but there are many others. Emma Lathen's *Green Grow the Dollars* (1982) features an American plant science meeting, while Jones's *Murder at the MLA* (1993), set at the Modern Language Association, compares and contrasts different people's trajectories through the meeting. Taking a few minutes to discuss the novel(s) with the student is, of course, necessary if the message is going to be understood.

General networking can be extremely valuable for the graduate student's immediate and mid-term career. The typical career trajectory differs from discipline to discipline. But personal knowledge and professional relationships are almost invariably important. Career development in the laboratory sciences is often dependent not just on the research degree itself, but on postdoctoral positions and postdoctoral research development. Sometimes that can be pursued in the same department, sometimes the research student can move to another lab for a period of postdoctoral work. The supervisor and student will need to discuss and think about how to manage such career contingencies, recognizing that the PhD is not the be-all and end-all: it is an important stepping stone towards a more general career. The development of professional networks can be a significant part of career planning – helping to identify laboratories and research groups in which further research can be pursued.

Postdoctoral reseach in the laboratory sciences reflects the funding and relative stability of successful research groups. Labs and groups that are able to attract external research funding at a sufficient level expect to maintain a population of postdocs. They often take on day-to-day tasks of supervising and looking after the graduate students. They are crucial to the continued well-being of the research group, and postdoctoral research in a laboratory with the right kind of reputation can be a most valuable credential on a young scientist's career. Networks and collaborations that are established at this stage can have significance for the rest of one's career.

In other disciplines, external funding may not provide a regular supply of postdoctoral positions. That does not preclude planning for future research after the completion of the thesis. Supervisors and their students can always think constructively about obtaining external funding to develop good research through a new project, and in order to secure a short-term continuation of the student's career. This is possible in disciplines in which external research funding is possible. It is hit-and-miss career planning, in that the odds are usually against any particular proposal actually being funded by a research council, charity or other agency. Nevertheless, a joint research proposal between a supervisor and research student can be a useful avenue to explore. Indeed, drafting a plausible and fundable research proposal is a research skill that can be included in any programme of research student training and academic staff development. Involving students in discussions about how to raise funds, for an archaeological dig, for a foreign trip, for equipment, for CD-ROM resources or for whatever, should figure in their development.

Publication is one aspect of career-building during the registration period that needs attention. We have, however, devoted a separate section to that topic, after the next section, which deals with job seeking.

The job seeker's dilemmas

In this section we deal mainly with references, where the role of the supervisor is crucial for the student's future career.

References and referees

The working relationship between the graduate student and the supervisor may well continue for years after the thesis is submitted and the degree awarded. The supervisor can often be a useful sponsor in the years ahead. The external examiner can come to fulfil a similar function, which is one reason for thinking strategically about the choice of external, as we stressed in Chapter 9. Here we concentrate on some of the continuing obligations of the supervisor.

The supervisor can expect to be a professional referee for his or her graduate students. The provision of references – mainly for academic and other posts – is an important and recurrent duty for virtually all academics. Like refereeing journal articles and grant applications, writing book reviews and the like, it is a task that contributes directly to the reproduction of the discipline. Like those other tasks too, it impinges directly on the career prospects and interests of individuals. We all have a dual set of obligations. We have an obligation to our colleagues, to ensure that the right things get published, the right research gets funded and the right people get appointed. Equally, we have an obligation to our students and former students to ensure that we help them in making the best of themselves, and have reasonable career prospects.

Academic references are an interesting genre in their own right, and one could easily devote a small volume about the conventions of writing and reading them. We shall not do so here. Suffice it to say that inexperienced academics would do well to seek and take advice on how to support their own students in this way. There are many ways of expressing positive support and enthusiasm, and there are many ways of expressing reservations. Referees often damn candidates with faint praise rather than with outright criticism, for instance. An inexperienced referee might well benefit from showing a draft to a more experienced colleague, in order to see if she or he is achieving the desired effect. If a reference is too tentative and low-key, for instance, it may come across as an unsupportive one, even if the author really intends it to be positive. Equally, one needs to get some sense of the appropriate style for the expression of enthusiasm. There are undoubtedly cultural differences in this regard. Referees in the USA seem to be expected to be positive in a way that British academics might regard as 'over the top'. Academics from the USA seem much more inclined than their UK counterparts to claim that a particular candidate is the most outstanding graduate student they have ever taught; UK academics may be less overtly enthusiastic. Indeed, too many superlatives in a reference for a British appointing committee may do the candidate a disservice. (Equally, of course, a reference written for an American institution may need to comply with their cultural conventions and expectations.)

The novice academic needs to learn something of the genre of references, if her or his former students are to get the best possible career opportunities. It is a good idea to ask a more experienced colleague for pointers. For instance, readers normally assume that the failure to mention some particular attribute or aspect of work is a deliberate omission, and is to be read as such. Readers of references are accustomed to 'read between the lines', and to decode the reference. The writer and would-be sponsor therefore need to understand the code's conventions. Omission of something as a consequence of oversight, or because it is thought unimportant, may inadvertently disadvantage the candidate. Equally, careless references can be damaging. It is a good idea to read the further particulars of the post being applied for: a reference that makes no reference to teaching competence when the candidate is to be interviewed for a lectureship may not cut enough ice. Equally, failure to stress the originality of someone's research and the importance of its contribution to the discipline may be damaging.

The supervisor will not just be a referee for the candidate's first job. The obligation may continue for many years. There is often a continuing relationship, changing subtly from that of student/supervisor, to junior colleague/senior sponsor, to a collegial relationship between equals. The successful supervisor of successful graduate students may have to provide suitable references throughout their careers, up to consideration for readerships, chairs and fellowships. It is important for successful supervisors to be aware of the various demands and conventions that are brought to bear on such documents, and to respond accordingly. It is equally important for graduate students to be taught to understand the process involved, encouraged to keep their supervisors and other senior staff up to date with their plans, current curriculum vitae and so on. Students may need explicit statements from you about whether, for example, you will always routinely do references or wish to be asked afresh each time an application is made. Whatever you decide, it is important to ensure that you have accurate, up-to-date information on the student or former student before you provide a reference, that you have some idea of why the student wants the job, so that you can angle the reference accordingly, and that you know how it will be used in the future.

There is also an issue about providing open or closed references. This is a matter of personal choice, but if you do show the reference to the student you should tell the potential employer you have done so. And, of course, you and the subject of the reference must recognize that it may be disregarded if the candidate has seen it. There may also be times when you can, and should, decline to be a referee, or warn the student that if he or she uses you, then you will not be able to be positive. If a student applies for an inappropriate post with a department that will value your opinion, you have to refuse to be a referee or write a negative reference:

the damage to your reputation if you lie will carry over to future candidates for other jobs, and might even harm you.

There is no doubt at all that career development for aspiring young academics should include advice on referees and potential sponsors. It is not necessary to encourage Uriah Heap like behaviour, but you should encourage graduate students and postdocs to think constructively about who they will be using in that capacity, and how to ensure that they are fully acquainted with their work, and have a favourable view of them as potential researchers or lecturers.

Job seeking

Research students may need your help if they want to stay in academic life. If they want a job outside universities, the careers service may be able to provide what they need, although careers in private sector firms with whom there is research collaboration may also depend on the supervisor and other members of the research group. If you and your colleagues routinely hear from postgraduate students that the careers service is 'not much help', then it may be sensible to talk constructively to the relevant staff there, and explain what your postgraduates might need – and see how the careers service and the department can cooperate on it.

As far as academic jobs are concerned, students may need help in discovering where opportunities are advertised – in specialist journals, general weeklies such as *The Times Higher Education Supplement, The Economist* or *New Scientist,* newsletters produced by learned societies, newspapers or on the World Wide Web. Point out that with the financial constraints on universities, posts may be advertised in only one national newspaper, so students may have to scan several. If you have been settled in your own job for several years, you may be out of date, and need to work with students to rediscover where the opportunities are to be found advertised.

Graduate students may well want careers counselling in various ways – or at least to talk over with you various options. While the academic labour market is very tight in many disciplines, and becoming increasingly so in the wake of renewed financial constraint, jobs do arise with a fair degree of regularity in most general disciplines, and graduate students are sometimes faced with choices. The answers to their dilemmas cannot be reduced to simple formulae, and must depend on a host of individual considerations. But students need to be aware of, and be able to talk over, the relative merits of different kinds of appointment (such as a lectureship versus a postdoctoral fellowship) in different kinds of institution ('old' versus 'new' universities). Preferences will not always be straightforward: a permanent lectureship in a decent, but not outstanding, university as against a fixed-term appointment in a highly regarded department is not an easy choice to make. Personal choices may depend on a host of circumstances, such as relative geographical mobility, family commitments, tolerance of insecurity and so on. It is, however, an important part of a supervisor's general mentoring role to be able to provide students with the kind of general advice they need in order to make informed choices. They may rarely have the luxury of choosing between job offers, of course, but they may avoid making inappropriate applications, and wasting their own and others' valuable time. For graduate students attempting to enter the job market, dummy selection interviews may be a useful preparation. It is easy to forget that students may have very little experience of being interviewed or of other aspects of job selection – such as the requirement to make a brief presentation about their research and career plans. For some students, practice in a familiar environment, with a small number of academic staff role-playing a selection committee, may prove a valuable investment of time and effort.

In order to come to sensible career-building and job-seeking strategies, therefore, students need to gain a sensible understanding of the job market at any given time, and a realistic appreciation of their own strengths and weaknesses. They may need – especially towards the end of their initial registration period – the equivalent of 'appraisal' interviews when they assess the kinds of skills and areas of competence they have to offer. Throughout their graduate student career, they will need to consider the kinds of experience they can amass with a view to their future employability. The narrow areas of specialization encouraged by research degrees will often be supplemented by summer schools on specific research methods and techniques, staff development sessions, areas of teaching and demonstrating experience and so on. In other words, the specific focus on one's own research can usefully be complemented by a broader portfolio of competences, with a view to enhanced employability in the academy or elsewhere.

Employability is, of course, enhanced through publication, and it is never too early to be thinking about that aspect of academic career development.

Publication

Graduate students and their supervisors have joint interests and responsibilities towards publication in the promotion of the research itself and sponsorship of the student.

Sponsoring publication

One of the key areas in which the supervisor and the graduate student can work together in sponsoring and mentoring that student – often to mutual advantage – is in the general area of publication. For the purposes of general career development, graduates, especially those with aspirations to academic and research careers, need to recognize that the thesis is not the only product of the research, and certainly not the end-point of the process. The thesis is an important part of the work, and energies and intelligence must be focused on it. But career development will be furthered by publication as well as by a higher degree. It appears to be the case that graduate students who think about themselves and their work professionally in general will develop a professional attitude to publication in particular. Long-term success is likely to be based on attitudes and work practices that are established early in the academic career: the period of time spent as a graduate student is certainly not too soon to learn important lessons. For those reasons, the work of the successful supervisor or graduate committee is likely to involve some element of sponsorship in publication.

One area where graduate students benefit from a supervisor who is an active researcher is that of publication. A supervisor who is writing, publishing, refereeing for journals, vetting manuscripts for publishers and editing the work of fellow scholars will be more able to offer informed practical help to graduate students, and will be better placed to hear about opportunities for students to start publishing.

The actual practices of publication and the associated expectations differ markedly from discipline to discipline, and within disciplines there are differences in emphasis between different departments or centres. In our own discipline, we have worked with younger colleagues who have come from one highly regarded department in which graduate students are not specifically encouraged to publish: the view they internalize is that they should definitely finish the thesis first, before thinking specifically about publication. Our own view, which we try to instil in our students, is that while the thesis is their first priority, its prime importance does not preclude constructive thought about publication on the way. In some experimental sciences, publication of results of key experiments may be almost taken for granted – especially if the graduate student's work is part of a larger ongoing research programme, generating a more or less constant stream of research publications. In such research groups, joint publication of results is a collective undertaking, and an integral part of the research culture. In other disciplines, most notably in the humanities, early publication is less common, as is joint publication.

Notwithstanding the fact that cultural differences are marked, and very important, between the different academic disciplines (Becher 1989, 1990), we believe that it is no bad thing for students to be encouraged to begin publishing as soon as it is practical for them to do so, given their subject matter, the disciplinary and local intellectual traditions and the practical constraints within which they are working. The discussion of a publication strategy may, therefore, be a useful basis for aspects of general career development and socialization into an academic culture or subculture.

There are, for instance, background issues that novices can usefully learn about the processes of academic publication. All experienced academics are familiar with the hierachies of esteem that are attached to different kinds of output (refereed journals, conference proceedings, edited collections, textbooks, monographs etc.). Equally, they will be aware of the finer discriminations that may be drawn within those categories. The research active academic (and no one should be doing this if he or she is not active) will be well versed in the fine gradations that can be used to distinguish journals: to be able to identify the 'blue chip' or 'diamond' list of international journals, for instance, and the solidly respectable journals in the second rank, and separate them from the low-status, meretricious or local. Likewise, in disciplines that progress by means of monographs, they will be able to rank publishers – distinguishing among and between the university presses, the commercial publishers and others. These discriminations are part of the intellectual stock-in-trade of the successful academic. Judgements based on such criteria are brought to bear on individuals, when their CVs are scrutinized for appointment or promotion, on research groups and on entire departments. The recurrent pressures of Research Assessment Exercises lend ever greater urgency to an informed awareness of these niceties. It is therefore important to ensure that graduate students begin to understand the nature and consequences of these issues.

The correct response to such awareness is necessarily variable. But in our experience, and the experience of others, one should certainly not assume that graduate students, however successful and well motivated, will necessarily be aware of the issues involved. It is all too easy to take for granted how these judgements and processes operate, to let them remain at an implicit level and to find that students go all the way through their careers muddled or in the dark. A lack of awareness is, one suspects, most likely in disciplines where solitary publication is the norm, and students are not being socialized into research groups that routinely and frequently publish their results.

Students need not only to be aware, for example, of the personal and collective value of publishing. They also need to be given the kind of information that will allow them to make sensible decisions and construct feasible plans. Our own graduate students need not only to know, for instance, what are the most highly esteemed journals, but also to have a broad sense of their rejection rates, the likely length of time it takes to get reviewed and the typical delay between acceptance and publication in them. Graduate students can turn out to have rather vague understandings of the whole process of academic publishing, with little or no awareness of how academic journals operate, the responsibilities of editors, editorial boards, reviewers and the like. While it might be thought that novices and junior members of the profession do not need to have detailed understandings of these and similar areas, if they are going to commit their career prospects to the vagaries of academic publication, then we are in no doubt that they need systematic introduction to the general issues concerned. Graduate students cannot be told exactly what to publish, or exactly when to publish it. For any individual student there is always a potential tension between pressing ahead with the thesis and publishing aspects of the research as she or he goes along, and general prescriptions cannot cover all the contingencies of research timetables, time and other resources. Students do need to have the right kind of background information to make informed decisions, however: whether to concentrate on conference papers and conference proceedings, whether to go for 'research notes' and letters, whether to attempt to get into the top journals or try to place their papers with slightly less glittering outlets with lower rejection rates. They need to be helped to think strategically and pragmatically about what is publishable, and when to do it.

The issue of joint publication with a supervisor or a larger number of collaborators in a research group is, as we have indicated, very largely coloured by the conventions and traditions of particular disciplines. Beyond those, and especially in disciplines where collaborative publication is not necessarily the norm, graduate students and their supervisors need to establish some basic expectations and working agreements. Even in the humanities and social sciences, joint publication between student and supervisor may be a productive and beneficial strategy. There are always worries about the intellectual and moral exploitation of the junior partner in this process. Some academics and students in the humanities harbour stereotyped views of natural sciences, in which professors and research directors have their names on research papers solely by virtue of their position, and with no regard for any actual work that has gone into the research and the ensuing paper. By contrast, they assume that any joint output must necessarily reflect the asymmetrical power relationship, must be exploitative and oppressive, and that the practice of joint publication is to be avoided in most cases. Such views are based on culture-specific views of authorship and publication, and on specific views of collaboration. Experimental scientists are likely to have quite different views about what authorship and co-authorship actually signify, and the nature of the 'collaboration' that justifies such patterns of co-publication. Equally, one must acknowledge that there are always grains of truth in myths and stereotypes, and some graduate students and junior researchers do feel themselves exploited in the common patterns of collaboration and co-authorship. The point of our discussion here is not to attempt to adjudicate on these issues for individual students and supervisors. Everything we have said hitherto would render general precepts unrealistic. Rather, we advocate that supervisors, and/or those responsible for more general mentoring and training of graduate students, should pay attention to explicating these and other considerations that relate to publishing plans and procedures. The emerging scholar should be able to think clearly about what to publish, when to publish, how to publish, with whom to publish, as part of the growing cultural competence of becoming a productive academic.

We have already suggested in Chapter 2 that exploring the conventions of citation is one way of opening the research student's eyes to the politics of publishing. This should be followed up in a graduate class, or in individual supervisions, with a clear account of the stages through which a potential article moves from the author's word-processor to the editor, out to referees, back to the editor and back to the author with a verdict. It can be extremely useful to set up a 'dummy' exercise where a group of students practise refereeing an article for an 'editor'. Such exercises go along with the tasks we have proposed to improve judgement in Chapter 7.

We move on now to some specific guidance that can be given to graduate students on how to prepare their work for publication. In Figure 10.1 we provide an outline for possible handouts or advice for graduate students on the process and obligations of getting into print.

Figure 10.1: Advice on getting published

There are two main ways of publishing your research: as a monograph (i.e. a book), or as journal articles. Not all theses make books, but every successful thesis ought to have at least one journal article in it. If you want the world to know about your research, then try to publish it. Theses themselves are read by very few people and lie forgotten on library shelves.

Just as you have used your intelligence to do your academic research, so too you should research possible outlets. If you have spent a lot of time and effort collecting data and writing them up, then spend a bit more time and effort preparing the ground for publication.

That advice applies to journals and to book publishers, and means that you should think about the following:

1 Who publishes your area of specialization? Do any publishers have special lists or series in your area? Have any publishers already published similar studies? What specialized journals exist for your area? What more general journals are there that might welcome your sort of approach?
2 What sort of audience are you trying to reach? Fellow academic social scientists? Practitioners? The lay public? There will obviously be different outlets for different readerships, which will call for different styles of writing.
3 Are there any special or new outlets? Sometimes new journals appear, which put out calls for papers: they may be less heavily subscribed with papers than old established journals. Sometimes journals announce special issues and call for papers: if your topic fits, then you may have a better chance of publishing than in general competition.

Figure 10.1: (Cont'd)

Journals

Once you have done your basic research and identified possible journals, then you will need to prepare your paper(s). There are no guarantees of success, but the following will help:

1 Get the format right. Journals have 'notes for contributors', at least once a year, which specify basic requirements for submissions. Check them and make sure your paper complies with them.
2 Get the length right. Many journal submissions fail because they are far too long. Check the guidelines, look at the run of issues and get your own word-count right.
3 Write each paper about a clearly defined topic or issue. Many submissions fail because they are ill-focused, diffuse and incoherent. Do not write a paper which has several different papers struggling to get out.
4 Get the editor and the referees on your side by submitting a clear, readable, double-spaced typescript. Scruffy typescripts and faint Xeroxes do not add up to successful self-presentation.
5 If the journal has such a section, you may have a chance of getting a small, modest piece published as a 'research note' – especially if you are reporting empirical findings.
6 Do not send the same article to more than one journal at a time. Most journals have a policy of refusing to consider papers submitted to more than one editor simultaneously, and multiple submissions are almost always detected.
7 However, if you do get rejected by one journal, don't give up: try another one.

Books

Once you have identified possible publishers, you will need to have something to send them. The editor will *not* want to be sent a copy of your precious thesis. She or he will not give you a contract without detailed review of what you've got to offer. So prepare a prospectus which incorporates all the information an editor will want to know. If you follow these guidelines, you will look very professional and will get off on the right foot.

1 Working title.
2 Author's name and mailing address.
3 Brief synopsis of the book: background, aims, content.
4 Market. Who is the book aimed at? Students? Practitioners? What level? A level? Postgraduates?
5 Style. What degree of difficulty is the text to represent? What level of readership, in other words?
6 Will the book be designed for specific courses or types of course? For example, does every student in the country doing this subject have to do a course in your area?
7 Competitors. Are there any other books on the market with which you will be competing? If so, you will probably need to persuade the editor that

Figure 10.1: (*Cont'd*)

yours is different and better (after all, he or she will have to persuade other people of that).

8 Chapter outline. You need to present the chapter-by-chapter outline. You need to indicate the chapter sections and contents briefly. If you can't work that out yet, then you are not yet ready to plan and write the book.

9 Length. You should indicate the approximate length of each chapter, and the total length overall (expressed as thousands of words). This is important, as it will have a direct bearing on the marketability and pricing of the final product.

10 Indicate if there will be any special typesetting requirements (figures, tables, photographic plates). They are expensive and should be kept to a minimum. In our line of work they are rarely needed.

11 Biographical details: brief outline of who and what you are. Nationality is important (for copyright reasons).

12 Timetable: you should indicate a realistic date for the completion of the script. A publisher will be more impressed by realism than over-optimism.

13 Specimen chapter(s). You should have some specimen material ready – and indicate that it can be supplied. It is probably unnecessary to send it with the initial proposal, however.

In general, make sure the proposal is clearly presented, well typed and attractive. If you can't get the typescript or the proposal right, what chance is there for a book-length manuscript?

Be prepared to be rejected. It is very hard to get published. Theses are not popular material with commissioning editors. You will have to do a fair amount of work to transform a successful thesis into an acceptable book.

If you plan to publish a specialized monograph, then you may need to look to less commercial publishers and imprints. Major commercial publishers are not normally enamoured of detailed empirical research reports.

Do you need a literary agent? No. It is not necessary for this sort of book. You are unlikely to get involved in delicate negotiations for the film rights; if you're doing this for the money, forget it. In any case, as an unpublished academic you may have more trouble finding a decent agent than finding a publisher.

The most useful listing of publishers' postal addresses is given in the *Writers' and Artists' Yearbook*, published annually by A & C Black. It contains lots of other useful information as well.

Information of the kind packed into Figure 10.1 may seem dry and abstract to students, so we also use a set of vignettes to stimulate discussion among our graduates about publishing. These are shown in Figure 10.2. While ours are very specific to our kind of social science, they can easily be adapted for other disciplines.

Figure 10.2: Publication case studies: vignettes for group discussion

1 Harriet Vane has finished her MPhil thesis on primary teachers' ideas about sex education. She used a questionnaire to 123 teachers, then did interviews with 22 women who were practising members of the Church in Wales. Her supervisor suggests there are two papers in her thesis. What might those be? How could she find out about journals?
2 Mary Stokes has just started her MPhil. While reviewing the literature, she has found a gap. No one has ever studied fat ladies in circuses – all the circus literature is about the glamorous jobs (trapeze artists, lion tamers), not the 'freaks'. What could Mary do?
3 Dorothy Collins is two years into her MPhil. Her pilot study, of ten people with HIV positive status, went down well at a conference. Her main study, of 73 HIV positive women, is analysed and her supervisor suggests she publish an article while she finishes off the thesis. Is this a good idea? If yes, how do you decide where to send it?
4 Betty Armstrong had sent an article to *Sociology*. It has come back with a letter four sides long from the editor, and comments from three referees. The letter says the paper 'can't be accepted in its present form' and the three referees seem to disagree. Betty feels sick. You're her best friend in the department – what do *you* do?
5 Richard Tucker wants to get a paper into an American journal. It wants eight copies, a handling fee of 20 dollars, American spelling, and has an unfamiliar house style – but it is *the* journal on mental handicap. Richard's boss is hassling him to publish quickly – and his friend at the medical school edits a local, regional journal which wants two copies, no handling fee, and is in a style Richard regularly uses. What would you do?
6 Jim Winterlake was at a conference. His supervisor introduced him to Phoebe de Vine, who works for Peabody and Brodribb, a major publisher in social policy. Phoebe talked to him about his research, and said 'let me see a proposal – we might fit that into our ageing series'. What should Jim do next?

Conclusions

We have outlined in this chapter a variety of ways in which a supervisor can help a graduate to build an academic career. This is satisfying for the supervisor, and career-enhancing too, because one's own reputation grows if one's postgraduates are competent and successful. In the next, and final, chapter, we deal with the supervisor's enlightened self-interest and the development of a productive graduate culture.

11

A rather unpromising consignment: selecting successful students and building a research culture

His eye roving over a group of Shrewsburians a-sprawl under the beeches, like that of a young Sultan inspecting a rather unpromising consignment of Circassian slaves.

(Sayers 1972: 342)

Introduction

Hitherto in this book we have written implicitly as if the process and outcomes of higher degree supervision were solely matters of individual students and their individual supervisors. While many of the problems and their solutions that arise in day-to-day academic work are as we have described in the preceding chapters, it would be wrong to ignore some of the wider and more collective aspects of supervision and the sponsorship of graduate students. In this concluding chapter it is not our intention to recapitulate all of the contemporary policy and organizational issues that confront the contemporary institution of higher education. To do so would require another book, and would take us well beyond the specific remit of supervisors and their work. None the less, one must pay some attention to more general issues, as a supervisor, and as a member of a department, a research group or centre. Those issues include several, all related, that are concerned with the maintenance and betterment of a research culture, and the promotion of graduate studies. Here we shall deal with: the selection of students; the promotion of a graduate student culture; collective responsibility for the training of research students. All relate to how a department or centre is going to set about building and supporting a 'graduate division' or 'graduate school' – and how therefore it will reproduce itself. When we refer here to the promotion of a 'graduate school', we do not necessarily mean a university- or faculty-wide organization with its own physical space, staffing and so on. Of course, some institutions have such arrangements, and they can be very successful. But the kinds of things we want to raise are not entirely predicated on such formal arrangements, whatever their strengths and weaknesses. Rather, we mean to convey the institutional and individual interest in building and fostering a collective responsibility for research student training, and a collective identity on the part of the graduate students. Such a graduate student culture will help to maintain the flow of research problems and interests from one generation to the next, to promote coherent research orientations, to overcome the feelings of personal and intellectual isolation that so often assail the graduate student.

Selecting students

Selecting successful PhD students is the first problem facing any university department and any individual supervisor. When a department and the individual supervisor get selection right, everyone wins. The department gets a completed thesis, the supervisor has a satisfying three-year supervisory relationship, a junior colleague and a friend for life. The student has a happy three years and the platform for a career.

When the wrong students are selected, the results are serious for all parties. Nothing is more frustrating than pouring time into a research student who fails to respond, to settle to work, to cope with the poverty and isolation, to gather data, to analyse them, to write them up, to submit the thesis. The time, intellectual energy, emotional commitment and general all-round effort that has to be put into a PhD student is awesome. To pour all that into a person who drops out, especially two, three or four years into the doctorate, is one of the most miserable things that can happen to an academic. There are few other things which can take an hour or two nearly every week of the year and ultimately produce *nothing*. A department wants higher degree students who will complete as a group, the individual needs individual students who will fit in to his or her own style.

There is very little research available on selection, and none on whether the changing policy context has altered the selection criteria used by funding bodies and departments, or, indeed, by individual supervisors. Certainly, for much of the century the only criterion for acceptance as a PhD candidate was possession of a first-class degree. One of our social science informants, Professor Hakapopoulos, drew a vivid caricature of the British PhD in the past in order to contrast it with prevailing arrangements at Gossingham at the time we interviewed him:

> one still has the vague idea that this chap got a first in whatever field
> he's in, he has an intellectually orientated mind, he has an interest
> ing idea that he wants to pursue, he can sit down in the library and

occasionally chat to members of the senior common room and lo! a thesis will appear.

Here Professor Hakapopoulos identifies an important dimension of contrast. The point of reference is an image of the PhD which is from time to time offered as having been dominant in the past: something based on the personal qualities of individuals, with little or no structure, highly dependent on implicit criteria. In Professor Hakapopoulos's account it carries overtones of a leisured and privileged past. Today, all universities, all departments and most supervisors are keen to provide a much more structured context, in which the student proceeds smoothly through the stages of the higher degree. If it becomes normal for students to do a taught masters with a short thesis before embarking on the PhD, then selection processes will become easier for departments.

Hudson (1977) offers a vividly written argument about how to select PhD students who will finish their higher degrees, which is based on Paul Atkinson and Sara Delamont's cohort of fellow higher degree students at Edinburgh in the 1968–73 era. Hudson argues that the most important characteristic of those students who submit higher degree theses is self-confidence and an academic variety of 'killer instinct': the same kind of quality soccer managers want to have in strikers. While this may be true, it does not help the supervisor to select the students: first, because these are hard to define and identify; second, because characteristics that may exist in the undergraduate context vanish like smoked salmon on a buffet table when the doctoral blues set in.

The most important thing for a selector to do is to think carefully about the skills and abilities a student needs to produce a PhD in that department, and then separate which of these can be taught during the PhD. So if a student needs to be particularly deft and not clumsy at the laboratory bench, it is important to decide whether this can be taught and learned, or not. If not, then you need to ask applicants to carry out an experiment while you are interviewing them, and/or explicitly ask their referees about their dexterity and bench skills. If the student needs good IT skills, then you need to decide whether you can provide teaching in IT, or need a candidate who already has the skills. If a student needs palaeographic flair, then you must choose someone who has done well in a specialist palaeographic training, or provide such training, or look for evidence of relevant abilities in the references. In other words, when you ask for references, be explicit about the specific qualities you are looking for, so that you can get information on what you need to know.

Second, we do believe that doctoral students need to be highly motivated, and not just drifting into higher degree work. To complete a PhD a person needs to be passionate about the discipline and want to advance knowledge in it. The student also needs to be able to stick at tasks. If the student's CV shows many false starts and abandoned courses, then the selector needs to be very wary.

Third, PhD students need to be able to work independently: the CV and references need to be scrutinized for evidence of autonomous work. If the student's first degree included a dissertation or project, or if she or he has done a masters degree, then the selector should explore how much the student enjoyed the dissertation or project element, and especially how he or she approached the independent work involved.

Fourth, successful PhD students need to have intellectual creativity, or at least some ideas of their own. Testing this will be very discipline-specific, but it should be possible to invite applicants to display their ideas about where a particular line of research might go next.

Fifth, doctoral students need to be able to write. Again, it is important to ask students about their experiences with writing and their feelings about those experiences, and to ask the referees about students' writing abilities. Evidence may usefully be gathered from relevant examples of students' own written work – a report, a dissertation, a masters thesis or whatever is appropriate to the discipline, and is available. Many departments will ask for a research proposal as part of the application process, and much can be learned from that: not just about the candidate's specific ideas, but (probably more importantly) about her or his ability to express them cogently. In the absence of other evidence, it may be useful to ask some candidates to write a brief paper for the selectors.

Sixth, students who are going to be able to do doctoral work need to be critical of previous work, so it is worth exploring with candidates – through written work, through an oral presentation or at interview – if they can provide reasoned, critical commentary on key work in the discipline. One is not looking for a gratuitously negative view of existing theory, or of received wisdom in the research field, but the ability to use a critical faculty, and the willingness to offer an independent perspective.

In summary, therefore, we recommend that prospective PhD students should have the specific skills to carry out the proposed research project, or be clearly able to benefit from research training, be highly motivated and able to persevere with academic tasks, be able to work independently, be able to write and be able to exercise critical judgement. These are the individual qualities we recommend searching for in applicants, and the ideal applicant would have all of them. However, we are rarely able to select ideal applicants. For the most part, we find ourselves balancing strengths and weaknesses – as we do in most contexts. It is, however, clear that clever undergraduates who get good degree results do not automatically become good doctoral students without some of the personal and intellectual qualities we have just discussed.

There are two distinct aspects to the selection of PhD students: selecting them for the department and selecting them for one's own personal supervision. Both may be beyond your control: you may work in a place where others choose the students and then assign them to you, and be unhappy with the students you get. If you suffer from that problem, it is probably wise to argue for a departmental review of advertising, applications and admissions policies and practicalities, and a thorough discussion of sources of support for student funding, using the rationale that a review could lead to increasing the total numbers. Most departments need *more* PhD students, particularly overseas candidates and research council funded people: a departmental working group or discussion ostensibly focused on how to increase the total number may well be a wedge to open up discussion about who is doing the selecting, why, how and on what criteria. Most people can persuade colleagues that a review designed to increase the quality and/or quantity of doctoral students is a good idea.

Dissatisfaction with the allocation of particular individuals to you is a rather different problem and may need careful diagnosis and then even more tactful resolution. The causes of the problem are likely to be different in science departments and non-science ones. In many science and engineering departments the allocation of studentships to research groups and to particular supervisors may be based on money, the status and power of professors and group leaders, rather than issues of 'choice'. In an arts or social science department it may be impossible to contemplate supervising any student unless one has volunteered to do so because of the topic, except when someone else has left, died, gone off sick, gone on sabbatical or quarrelled irreconcilably with the candidate.

If you are in a department where other research groups, or the senior staff in your own group, seize the 'best' candidates and/or allocate to you people you find hard to supervise, you have to learn how the department works, what the power structures are, and seek advice on how to change them. The most productive strategy is probably to raise your own funds, and publish a good deal, so that your reputation rises and you can attract students to your specialism. In an arts or social science department, if you are not getting any doctoral students to work on topics you really care about, you probably need to be more proactive among the best undergraduates: are your lectures and seminars suffused with your excitement about the frontiers of your research area? It is also worth exploring whether your department's recruiting policies stress your specialism enough, and make it sound exciting. If the difficulty is getting ESRC funds to support the bright students, then two investigations are needed. First, ask someone in your field, ideally someone who has vetted such applications, to go through one of your potential applicant's forms with you, and help you to *sharpen* the presentation. Second, ask yourself if you are currently being 'research-active' in the area. If not, then you need to get research funds and ongoing publications in your own right, so that you are contributing to the field yourself. The current policy consensus is that doctoral students are best placed with staff who have research funds, and are actively building their disciplines. Therefore, if you are not being allocated, or are not attracting, the type of doctoral student you want, it is probably because you are not active enough in research yourself. In an arts or social science discipline you may be able to attract self-funding part-time students to supervise, and it is clearly better to have active supervision of part-timers than no doctoral students at all.

If you are allocated students to supervise whom you have not chosen, you need to see if you can work with them. If you cannot, they need to be placed elsewhere, for their own sake. There are two kinds of student who can be a problem: those who you do not feel able to supervise because they lack some fundamental quality(ies) or because of their topic, method or theoretical position, and those you just do not like. It is hard to imagine seeing someone everyday in your lab or for about an hour every week for four years if you actively dislike them, are afraid of them or find them maddening.

It is important to know and recognize some characteristics of potential students that will make them hard, or even impossible, for you to supervise. Here, the qualities of the individual which may make supervision hard are dealt with first, and then the issues around academic matters, such as topic, method and theoretical position.

Example 11.1: Frances Derwent, the whisperer

Frances Derwent is a whisperer. She is one of those women who speaks so quietly that you constantly have to request her to repeat things. She enters a room, crouches in a distant chair and then whispers as if she has no right to your time or attention. Such behaviour turns Sara into a bully. While Sara normally tries hard to be a *supportive* supervisor, she hears herself getting edgy at such apparent terror and self-effacement. When Frances decided to do a PhD in our department, Sara steered her to someone else, to avoid destroying her academic promise because of a distaste for her self-presentation.

One of the issues that can come between a supervisor and student is gender. Scholarly relationships between males and females are not necessarily easy, as the research on women in science (see Gornick 1990; Zuckerman *et al.* 1991) and on gender roles in higher education generally (e.g. Aisenberg and Harrington 1988; Delamont 1989c; Carter 1990; Lie *et al.* 1994) reveals. It is important to recognize a whole set of issues around this issue, which we can gloss as 'chaperonage'. Many male scientists and engineers have never had a woman PhD student or colleague; many women in arts and social science have never had a male PhD student. Coeducational higher education is a relatively new phenomenon, and one we are not all used to in everyday life, where some staff groups and some research groups are still entirely male in composition.

When we read accounts of the first women to be students or staff in universities, they seem antique and quaint. The period described seems much further into the past than 50 or 100 years (see Delamont 1989c; Dyhouse 1994). In some cases, women *are* relative newcomers. Women were only admitted to the University College of Lampeter in 1961 – the account of the decision (Price 1990) reads like an extract from Trollope's era, not C. P. Snow's. When many of today's senior male academics were students or junior faculty, not only were they undergraduates in single sex colleges or halls, they experienced 'male-only' social spaces such as 'men's unions' or, as at Kings College London when Crick and Watson visited Maurice Wilkins in the 1950s, *men's* senior common rooms (see Delamont 1989c). The relations between the sexes in the white middle classes in Britain have changed so much in the past 50 years, and the sexes are now so routinely 'mixed' together, that many people in higher education can be ignorant of, outraged by or discourteous to other cultures when they find people who want to segregate the sexes or practise chaperonage. This can be found in three quite separate ways, two 'traditional', one 'modern'.

Class extremities in the UK. The British upper class, and much of the working class in the UK, adheres to segregated sex roles more strictly than the liberal middle class. Students from upper-class homes, especially men from public schools, or working-class homes where a strong division of labour by sex operated, may be less comfortable with egalitarian relations between the sexes than those from liberal middle-class, dual-career, homes. Women supervisors may find that male students from such homes are uncomfortable with the prospect of a woman in authority over them, with accepting females as academically serious and with the day-to-day relationships of supervision. If you are a man who grew up in either of those class milieux, you may find it harder to work with women students. In either case, the shrewd supervisor recognizes the potential tensions and either brings them out for discussion and resolution, or passes the student to a more compatible colleague.

'Other' cultures. Both inside the UK and in many countries which send students to the UK to do higher degrees, particularly those with strong Islamic influences, sex segregation is much stricter than many supervisors are used to. Men doing PhDs may be genuinely appalled at the prospect of a woman supervisor, and vice versa. It may be impossible for women students from some cultures to have unchaperoned supervisions with a male supervisor. Handling these problems needs sensitivity: it may be that the latter problem (female student, male supervisor) can be resolved by agreeing to keep the door open, having a female secretary or technician in earshot or supervising students in pairs.

In contrast to the 'traditional' groups described above, there is a new kind of student around, the woman who is a separatist feminist.

Separatist feminists. There are women in higher education who are only interested in working on a feminist research agenda with a woman supervisor. Most of these will choose a woman's studies programme, but it is important to be sensitive to such perspectives.

Gender is not the only personal quality of students that can impede the establishment of a working relationship. People with strong prejudices and antipathies, whatever their targets and origins, are unlikely to get the best out of higher degree students they find it hard to get along with. There is no excuse for prejudices against women or ethnic minorities, or indeed against particular intellectual styles and interests. The most important thing to do if you know that you harbour any such biases is to do something about your own attitudes and values. Likewise, if you have a colleague who is disadvantaging applicants or students, then you, the director of graduate studies or the head of the department need to do something about it. In the interim, it may be best to avoid direct clashes of styles, personalities and attitudes through the careful allocation of students to supervisors. It is, of course, a particular benefit of having supervisory panels, rather than reliance on the lone supervisor, that direct personal confrontations and differences may be less stark. Apart from characteristics of the student, such as sex, religion or sexual orientation, there can also be people who are personally compatible, but whose topic, method or theoretical position is a cause of disagreement. Potential disagreements about thesis topic, method or theoretical position may not be apparent at the selection stage, and it is probably best to choose good candidates and ensure that there are clearly specified procedures for students to change supervisor within the department, and that all students are aware of them. If your department does not have any such procedures, then getting some agreed is a sensible step. Many personality conflicts can be resolved by a change of supervisor, as can disputes over the ways that projects are developing. The case of Margaret Rushbridger is an example of this.

Example 11.2: Margaret Rushbridger

Margaret had been supervised by Oliver Manders for two years, but they appeared to have come to the end of the road. Margaret was not writing, and Oliver seemed unable to help her. Margaret changed to Paul, who was much less in tune with her theoretical interests, but was able to re-enthuse her. He did little to affect her actual research, but was personally able to give her back some lost self-confidence.

While this book is designed for supervisors, it is important to recognize that students have a range of motivations to do postgraduate work, and may end up registered for a higher degree in places they did not choose, working on topics in which they have little interest. Before we turn to building up a research culture, we present some material on how candidates end up on doctoral programmes, in order to show how a range of different factors influence their 'choices'.

The view from the candidates

We know relatively little about what motivates students to do a higher degree, or how they decide where to apply and which supervisor(s) to approach. Our geography PhD students offered us mixed motives. Most had chosen to carry on and do a PhD in their undergraduate specialism because of their enthusiasm for the subject. Nineteen of the geography respondents specifically mentioned a love of geography, and this was the commonest motivation. Rick Moliner was typical when he said, 'It sounds a bit daft really. I've just got a thing about geography. I love the subject.' Jason Ingersoll, also at Boarbridge, expressed the same view:

> I've always loved geography since school, and I've always wanted to carry it on, go as far as I can with it. I can't think of anything I enjoy more than geography, I just love all sorts of geography.

Students from other places were equally enthusiastic about the discipline. For example, Sam Verney, at Tolleshurst, said he had 'discovered geography was the thing I really wanted to do', and that led him to do a PhD. Vicky McQuaid, at Ottercombe, said: 'I've always loved the subject I was doing, I was completely fascinated by it, really enjoyed it and wanted to do something more with it.' Eric Severance, at Hernchester, talked in the same way:

> I've always been interested in geography, I've always liked writing, and I was interested in economics, people, industry, that sort of thing, travel – and I thought it would be a nice thing to study.

Other motivations mentioned were, in descending order, that the person did not feel ready to enter the labour market and/or wished to stay a student, that the challenge of the PhD was appealing, that the respondent wanted a job in research or higher education which required a doctorate and that none of the alternatives appealed except a doctorate.

Once the student had decided to seek a place and funding to do a doctorate, he or she had to find a department, money and a supervisor. At the time of our fieldwork, the ESRC and NERC policy of blacklisting departments with poor completion rates was in force. Most of our sampled departments had been blacklisted by the NERC and ESRC for some part of the preceding five years and so could not offer government grants for doctoral study. Bill Staley, a physical geographer at Hernchester, described his 'choice' of that university. He had done his undergraduate degree at Tolleshurst:

> I did second and third year options with Prof. Cassands on physical hazards. I enjoyed Prof. Cassands work and the kind of fieldwork involved in doing his courses . . . When I decided I wanted to do a PhD . . . Prof. Cassands gave me four names – of people he thought it would be interesting to study under . . . I was interested in three of them – Luftkin in London, Prof. Lisle-Chevreuse at Reddingdale and Prof. Barsington at Hernchester . . . Reddingdale was blacklisted, so I couldn't get any money, and Luftkin retired. So therefore I was only left with Prof. Barsington . . . I came to the interview and liked the look of it here.

The availability of an ESRC or NERC studentship was the most powerful 'pull' factor reported by our respondents. Julian Perini had graduated from Tolleshurst, did an MA, abroad, and then came back to the UK.

> I went to the geography department at Tolleshurst, and I was talking to one of my old teachers, and he suggested I apply here [Hernchester] for various reasons. They weren't blacklisted for a start, they'd just got off the blacklist.

Elvira Tilley, at Boarbridge, answered our question, 'Why did you choose Boarbridge?'

> It was blackmail really. I came here for an interview and it was a competition award, the ESRC one, I was trying to get money to go to either Southersham or Tolleshurst. Here the ESRC award goes with the place. I got the place. I couldn't say no to this one at the time because I didn't have the guarantee of anything else.

Other students had been offered studentships funded by the institution or attached to specific projects, which had determined their 'choice'. Patsy Shroeder had hoped to go to another Scottish university, but Wellferry offered her a bursary, so she returned to the place where she had done her undergraduate degree.

Theo Karras, a physicist at Ottercombe, told us he had applied for 'numerous' PhD grants and places, then took 'the only one' he was offered. Yves Bisson had remained at Ottercombe because 'I like it here, it is a friendly department . . . they seemed keen to keep me if they could have the money, and in the end they offered me funding.'

Although departmental interests were obviously important to them, geography respondents highlighted funding as the most crucial determining factor in their choice of department. Sheridan Ireland, at Hernchester:

> I did my undergraduate degree at Ebbfield ... Why Hernchester? The supervisor of my choice was here, it's got a good reputation, the facilities are good, you get a lot of support, it's a big department. There are also social reasons – it's a good location. Hernchester and the department got a good UGC rating. Also I saw the advertisement, NERC funded: Hernchester had the funding, other places didn't.

Given such data – and there is no reason to believe that students in other disciplines are very different from geographers – it is important to try to select the best candidates, and to mould the students you do get into membership of a research group and participation in a shared research culture.

Building a research group

The opportunity to recruit successful students in a particular specialism, and to make them part of a collective research group, differs widely between the academic disciplines. In the natural sciences it is commonplace for research to be conducted in groupings, and for there to be a regular allocation of doctoral students to such groups. The doctoral students work on projects that fall within the scope of the existing research programme – often on topics prescribed by the senior members of the group – and are part of a substantial grouping that includes postdoctoral researchers as well as tenured members of the academic staff. In the humanities, by contrast, research students and studentships may be much thinner on the ground. They may be few and far between for any given supervisor, and group-building may be a much less natural kind of activity in such contexts. The long-standing tradition of individual scholarship in the humanities militates against a collective view of the graduate enterprise. While the traditions and resources are different between different departments and different disciplines, however, there is – as we have seen – ample evidence to suggest that social and intellectual isolation is a recurrent phenomenon for many graduate students, and that some degree of collective culture and orientation can be a valuable part of the postgraduate experience.

In the contemporary UK department there are external factors that push the individual supervisor and the department towards a more strategic and collective view of the matter. In the first place, as we have mentioned earlier, the 'graduate division' or 'school' is regarded as an indicator of esteem and success in its own right. As UK academics have become more and more attuned to the requirements and pressures of external review, they have also become more aware of graduate students, and the health of recruitment, as a performance indicator. For those kinds of reasons, the majority now recognize that the recruitment and training of research students, the provision of adequate facilities for them, monitoring of their progress and the promotion of their intellectual well-being are central functions of the academic department or research centre as a whole. They cannot be left to individualistic interest and sponsorship alone.

Some people believe that if they have shared social events with graduate students, the research culture will build 'naturally' and spontaneously. If the graduate students are homogeneous – usually all young, child-free, British men – and the supervisors match the students socially too, then this may well be true. Whatever the student body is like, social events, spontaneous ones like going for a drink after a seminar, or pre-arranged things such as a theatre trip, a pre-planned walk or the Christmas Dinner, can be useful in building social solidarity. However, certain categories of student, such as those with small children, or those (like Muslims) who do not drink, may be unable or unwilling to come to some such events, or unable to participate. Staff need to be sensitive to the dynamics of such events, and try to ensure that vital matters are not exclusively dealt with at such social events, excluding (unintentionally) those who cannot attend them, or feel uncomfortable at them. The autobiographical writings of women and ethnic minority graduate students frequently report feelings of exclusion from the group culture caused by well meaning but insensitive behaviour. To ensure that everyone is involved in building a research culture, it is necessary for it to have some more formal and planned characteristics.

Our suggestions on this score are in two parts: first, ideas to make the work of the research students a matter of general concern in the department; second, strategies to weld the research students into a coherent group. Both are desirable in building a research culture. In a very big department, with fifty or more lecturing staff, the strategies we outline below will probably be better implemented at a section level: in an engineering department with 100 academic staff, for instance, it may be sensible to build one research subculture around the graduate students in civil engineering, another in mechanical engineering and another in electronics. At the other extreme, in a department of history with fifteen staff, the whole department will need to cooperate in building one research culture.

There is a variety of ways in which a lecturer can encourage a *generalized* concern for the welfare and performance of the research students. First, it is important that the recruitment, progress and achievements of the research students are public, and are routinely discussed. This means having regular reports at the staff meeting and the more specialist sub-committees, such as the research committee or the teaching-and-learning committee. Ghettoizing graduate affairs in a graduate committee can allow some staff to ignore the research students. If there is a post of 'graduate coordinator', or equivalent, the person holding that post needs to report regularly in a way that interests the rest of the staff. Spreading the concern about research students among staff, so that people care about all the research students and not just their own supervisees, can be done by having a sub-committee to look at the graduate students' annual or termly reports (and if your university does not require such reports from research students and their supervisors, then you should institute them at the departmental level). The upgrading from MPhil to PhD can be a useful occasion to involve a range of staff beyond the individual supervisor. The internal examiner system can also spread the general concern about the graduate students. A staff discussion about recently examined theses, led by the internal examiners, can be a useful forum for the review of collective achievements, standards, criteria for success and so on.

Regular training for supervisors, and regular training for examining, are ways of spreading the culture of 'graduate school' activities. If the university has a published set of guidelines for supervisors, then discussion of them every 18 months or so is useful. If the university does not have such a list, then developing some for the department or faculty is a good way of focusing colleagues' minds on the work of research students.

It can be helpful for staff to have a list of what research students are registered in the department, what their topics are and who is supervising them. Such information – regularly updated – can be included in departments' internal newsletters, on their Web homepages and in other sources of information. The dissemination of such information can be especially helpful if there are many part-time students who are not regularly visible in the department. It can also help graduate students to find out about each other, while making research supervision a more visible part of the department's work.

Research students should be giving seminar papers regularly to the research group closest to their project (the mediaevalists, the French history group, the cliometricians, the feminist history seminar) and to the whole department. However good this is for them, it will not spread the culture of the research group unless staff and other students are encouraged, or even required, to attend.

To build camaraderie among the students we suggest the following. First, the department should provide the best facilities it can afford, ensure that all the research students are aware of them and encourage them to use them. Second, it should have clear policies on supervision, ensure that these are known to students and monitor them. Third, it should provide training and development opportunities for the research students throughout their registration period: apart from any formal courses required in the first year of registration, it is helpful to arrange classes on teaching (perhaps even the opportunity to do a diploma or certificate in teaching), classes on career-building (on getting published, giving conference papers, preparing the CV, job searching, raising research funds) and updating of skills (library skills, IT skills, writing, changes in the university or higher education policy). The mock viva (see Chapter 10) can be a useful developmental and social event: we find that students choose to attend all three or four of the 'performances' that take place while they are enrolled.

As well as encouraging or requiring graduate students' attendance at departmental seminars given by staff, fellow students and visiting speakers, it is particularly good to allow and encourage the graduates to choose some of the outside speakers (and even have a budget to invite some speakers to come and address them without staff involvement). When visitors are in the department, it is important to ensure that graduate students meet them, and are not just passive members of the audience, left to slip away unobtrusively at the end of the seminar.

All these activities will only work if the people organizing them make it clear why they are important and that the benefits are general. If a department has postdocs and other research associates and assistants, then they too should be included in these events. Their contribution to the overall promotion of a departmental research culture is invaluable. Experienced research workers can do a great deal to provide day-to-day advice to graduate students, while also helping to inculcate research awareness and research values among the group.

Conclusion

In this chapter we have widened our focus from the intensive relationship with the individual student to the departmental level. We finalized this book while the debate about the Harris Report (1996) on graduate education was taking place, and while evidence was being presented to the Dearing Committee on Higher Education. The dynamics of individual supervision will not be changed substantially by these official reports and any subsequent policy changes, but some of the strategies proposed in this chapter may be made redundant. However, the satisfaction that one feels when a former higher degree student publishes a good paper, delivers an excellent conference presentation, is appointed to a post he or she wants or gets promoted will never fade.

Appendix: Further reading

This list is in two parts: first, we have listed a few other sources on 'how to supervise', and, second, we have listed useful books for students on writing.

Other works on supervision

There are three types of literature on supervision: guidelines produced by specific learned societies dealing with appropriate behaviour for supervisors in that discipline; general guidelines; and reports of social science research on supervision. We have not listed examples of the first type of literature, but we strongly advise supervisors to find out if their learned society produces such guidelines, and if it does, to get hold of them and publicize them in their department.

General guidelines

In the UK, the research councils produce guidelines on good supervisory practice, available from each separate research council's Swindon offices. The National Postgraduate Committee (1995) also produces *Guidelines for Codes of Practice for Postgraduate Research*.

In your own university, there are probably some guidelines available, at institutional, faculty or departmental level, which you should get hold of. If the higher education funding bodies in the UK implement the Harris Report (1996), public money will only support higher degree students in institutions with a written code of practice governing supervision.

Australia has produced two useful sets of guidelines for supervision by Connell (1985) and Moses (1985). From the UK, there is helpful advice in Chapter 6 of Brown and Atkins (1988), and it is salutary to read the chapters on supervisors in the advice books for students by Cryer (1996) and Phillips and Pugh (1993). The collection on quality in postgraduate education edited by Zuber-Skerritt and Ryan (1994) is also worth consulting.

Research studies

Empirical evidence on postgraduate research students and their supervision has been accumulating rapidly in the past decade. The research on France, Germany, Japan, the UK and the USA can be traced from Clark (1993). The American scene can also be explored from Bowen and Rudenstine (1992). The British research can be found in Becher *et al.* (1994), Burgess (1994) and the evidence volume of Harris (1996). The Australian research can be traced in Zuber-Skerritt and Ryan (1994).

Books to help students with writing

In Chapter 8 we divided these into three broad categories: technical manuals, books on how to write and reflexive books on how texts are produced and received in academic disciplines.

Technical manuals
E. P. Bailey and P. A. Powell, *Writing Research Papers* (1987), is an American book for advanced undergraduates and people on taught masters courses. The UK equivalent is Cuba and Cocking (1994).

A. A. Berger, *Improving Writing Skills* (1993), deals with producing memos, letters, reports, proposals and 'business documents', and would help any graduate student.

Diane Collinson *et al.*, *Plain English* (1992), is an excellent book for graduate students, which includes an introductory quiz, and chapters on the central topics such as punctuation, each with exercises.

Lee Cuba and John Cocking's *How to Write about the Social Sciences* (1994) is aimed at advanced undergraduates and people doing taught masters courses, but many doctoral students have found it helpful because it deals with searching the literature, framing an argument and technicalities in one slim volume.

Michael Dummett's *Grammar and Style* (1993) is extremely helpful to postgraduates in humanities and social sciences, because it combines ideas on good grammar with clarity of style. As Dummett hates much contemporary social science writing, he includes many 'classic' sociologists in his negative examples.

H. W. Fowler, *A Dictionary of Modern English Usage* (1994), is a classic, and has been reprinted in a facsimile of the 1926 original very cheaply by Wordsworth.

F. W. Frank and P. A. Treichler, *Language, Gender and Professional Writing* (1989), is a thorough guide to non-sexist usage published by the American Modern Language Association.

E. Gowers, *The Complete Plain Words* (1986), was revised by Greenbaum and Whitart for contemporary usage, and students should know of its existence.

John Kirkham's two books, *Good Style* (1992) and *Full Marks* (1993), are specifically for science and technology graduates, and are excellent.

M. H. Manser's *Bloomsbury Good Word Guide* (1990) is much more usable than Gowers or Fowler, and is our reference work of choice because it addresses most of the confusions we find in postgraduate writing – such as the differences between censure, censor and censer (p. 47).

Turabian's classic *Manual for Writers of Research Papers, Theses and Dissertations*, originally produced in 1937, is an essential reference work, but is not designed to be read. There has been a separate British version since 1982, and the most recent edition, the sixth, should be in all university libraries and on students' reading lists.

John Whale's *Put It in Writing* (1984) is a cheerful text which would improve anyone's writing.

Books on writing strategies
The three books on survival as a doctoral student (Rudestam and Newton 1992; Phillips and Pugh 1994; Cryer 1996) all have useful chapters on writing. In Cryer, Chapters 12 and 18 are on writing, in Phillips and Pugh, Chapter 6, and in Rudestam and Newton, Chapter 9.

The book we recommend above all others is Howard Becker's *Writing for Social Sciences* (1980), which is funny, inspiring and packed with ideas that help experienced scholars as well as novices.

Wayne Booth *et al.*, *The Craft of Research* (1995), has five chapters on writing (11–15) which are extremely helpful.

Pechenick and Lamb's *How to Write about Biology* (1995) does exactly what it suggests: guide young scholars in the biological sciences towards professional text production.

Laurel Richardson's *Writing Strategies* (1990) is an autobiographical study of how she wrote about her own research on women who were having affairs with married men, which was published as a best-selling non-fiction book and as an academic journal article. On the way through this account a student can learn a great deal about writing.

R. A. Day's *How to Write and Publish a Scientific Paper* (1995) is a clearly written book which would help any novice academic in science and engineering to submit material for publication.

Harry Wolcott's *Writing up Qualitative Research* (1990) is short and well written, and emphasizes the need to build writing into research from the beginning. It will be of value across a range of disciplines – notably sociology, anthropology, education, health research, human geography and cultural studies.

Reflexive texts on academic reading and writing
There is now a large literature dealing with the rhetoric and poetics of academic writing. Key references include: Edmondson (1984) and Atkinson (1990, 1992) on sociology; Clifford and Marcus (1986) and Wolf (1992) on anthropology; Cameron (1989) on history; Ashmore *et al.* (1994), Bazerman (1988) and Myers (1990) on the natural sciences. Some students find this somewhat introspective material liberating (and it helps them to read and write), while others find it inhibiting because it makes them too self-conscious about their own drafts. This is an area where you need to know your own students before despatching them to the library. Gilbert's (1993) paper on writing about social research is a useful test to see if your students will find this reflexive literature helpful.

References

Aisenberg, N. and Harrington, M. (1988) *Women and Academe: Outsiders in the Sacred Grove*, Amherst, MA: University of Massachusetts Press.

ALSISS (1987) *The Social Science PhD since Winfield: the ALSISS response to the Winfield Report and Subsequent Developments*, London: Association of Learned Societies in the Social Sciences.

Ashmore, M., Myers, G. and Potter, J. (1994) Discourse, rhetoric and reflexivity, in S. Jasanoff, G. Markle, J. Petersen and T. Pinch (eds) *Handbook of Science and Technology Studies*, London: Sage.

Atkinson, P. A. (1981) *The Clinical Experience: the Construction and Reconstruction of Medical Reality*, Farnborough: Gower.

Atkinson, P. A. (1983) The reproduction of professional community, in R. Dingwall and P. Lewis (eds) *The Sociology of Professions*, London: Macmillan.

Atkinson, P. A. (1984) Wards and deeds: taking knowledge and control seriously, in R. G. Burgess (ed.) *The Research Process in Educational Settings*, London: Falmer, pp. 163–85.

Atkinson, P. A. (1985) *Language, Structure and Reproduction: an Introduction to the Sociology of Basil Bernstein*, London: Methuen.

Atkinson, P. A. (1990) *The Ethnographic Imagination*, London and New York: Routledge.

Atkinson, P. A. (1992) *Understanding Ethnographic Texts*, Thousand Oaks, CA: Sage.

Atkinson, P. A. (1996) *Sociological Readings and Re-readings*, Aldershot: Avebury.

Atkinson, P. A. and Delamont, S. (1977) Mock-ups and cock-ups, in P. Woods and M. Hammersley (eds) *School Experience*, London: Croom Helm.

Atkinson, P. A. and Delamont, S. (1985) Socialisation into teaching: the research which lost its way, *British Journal of Sociology of Education*, 6(3), 307–22.

Atkinson, P. A., Reid, M. E. and Sheldrake, P. F. (1977) Medical mystique, *Sociology of Work and Occupations*, 4(3), 243–80.

Bailey, E. P. and Powell, P. A. (1987) *Writing Research Papers*, New York: Holt, Rinehart and Winston.

Barr, B. (1984) *Histories of Girls' Schools and Related Biographical Material*, Leicester: The School of Education of the University of Leicester.

Barzun, J. (1986) *On Writing, Editing and Publishing*, 2nd edn, Chicago: Chicago University Press.

Bazerman, C. (1988) *Shaping Written Knowledge: the Genre and Activity of the Experimental Article in Science*, Madison: University of Wisconsin Press.

Becher, T. (1989) Physicists on physics, *Studies in Higher Education*, 15(1), 3–21.

Becher, T. (1990) *Academic Tribes and Territories*, Milton Keynes: Open University Press.

Becher, T., Henkel, M. and Kogan, M. (1994) *Graduate Education in Britain*, London: Jessica Kingsley.

Becker, H. S. (1980) *Writing for Social Scientists*, Chicago: Chicago University Press.

Becker, H. S., Geer, B., Hughes, E. C. and Strauss, A. L. (1961) *Boys in White*, Chicago: Chicago University Press.

Berger, A. A. (1993) *Improving Writing Skills*, Newbury Park, CA: Sage.

Bernstein, B. (1977) *Class, Codes & Control Vol. 3*, London: Routledge.

Bernstein, B. (1990) *Class, Codes & Control Vol. 4*, London: Routledge.

Booth, W. C., Colomb, G. G. and Williams, J. M. (1995) *The Craft of Research*, Chicago: Chicago University Press.

Bourdieu, P. (1988) *Homo Academicus*, Cambridge: Polity Press.

Bourdieu, P. and Passeron, J.-C. (1977) *Reproduction*, London: Routledge.

Bourdieu, P. and Passeron, J.-C. (1979) *The Inheritors*, London: Chicago University Press.

Bowen, G. and Rudenstine, N. (1992) *In Pursuit of the PhD*, Princeton, NJ: Princeton University Press.

Brodribb, S. (1992) *Nothing Mat(t)ers*, Melbourne: Spinifex.

Brown, C. (1982) *The Education and Employment of Postgraduates*, London: Policy Studies Institute.

Brown, G. (1987) Research supervision, unpublished report of workshop on research supervision, University of Nottingham and Queen's Medical Centre, UK.

Brown, G. and Atkins, M. (1986) Academic staff training in British universities: results of a national survey, *Studies in Higher Education*, II(1), 107–19.

Brown, G. and Atkins, M. (1988) *Effective Teaching in Higher Education*, London and New York: Methuen.

Brown, P. and Scase, R. (1994) *Higher Education and Corporate Realities*, London: UCL Press.

Bulmer, M. and Burgess, R. (eds) (1981) The teaching of research methodology: special issue of *Sociology*, 15(4).

Burgess, R. (ed.) (1979) *Teaching Research Methodology to Postgraduates: a Survey of Courses in the UK*, Coventry: University of Warwick.

Burgess, R. G. (1984) *In the Field*, London: Allen and Unwin.

Burgess, R. G. (ed.) (1994) *Postgraduate Education and Training in the Social Sciences*, London: Jessica Kingsley.

Cameron, A. (1989) *History as Text*, London: Duckworth.

Carter, I. (1990) *Ancient Cultures of Conceit*, London: Routledge.

Clark, B. R. (ed.) (1993) *The Research Foundations of Graduate Education: Germany, Britain, France, United States, Japan*, Berkeley: University of California Press.

Clifford, J. and Marcus, G. E. (eds) (1986) *Writing Culture: the Poetics and Politics of Ethnography*, Berkeley: University of California Press.

Coffey, A. and Atkinson, P. A. (1996) *Making Sense of Qualitative Data*, Thousand Oaks, CA: Sage.

Cole, J. (1979) *Fair Science*, New York: The Free Press.

Collins, H. (1985) *Changing Order*, London: Sage.

Collinson, D., Kirkup, G., Kyd, R. and Slocombe, L. (1992) *Plain English*, Buckingham: Open University Press.

Connell, R. W. (1985) How to supervise a PhD, *Vestes*, 2, 38–41.

Cortazzi, M. (1993) *Narrative Analysis*, London: Falmer.

Cross, A. (1970) *Poetic Justice*, New York: Avon.

Cryer, P. (1996) *The Research Student's Guide to Success*, Buckingham: Open University Press.

Cuba, L. and Cocking, J. (1994) *How to Write about the Social Sciences*, London: Harper and Row.

CVCP (1985) *Report on Academic Standards* (The Reynolds Report), London: Committee of Vice-Chancellors and Principals.

Day, R. A. (1995) *How to Write and Publish a Scientific Paper*, Cambridge: Cambridge University Press.

Delamont, S. (1976a) *Interaction in the Classroom*, London: Methuen.

Delamont, S. (1976b) The girls most likely to, *Scottish Journal of Sociology*, 1(1), 29–43.

Delamont, S. (1976c) Beyond Flanders fields, in M. Stubbs and S. Delamont (eds) *Explorations in Classroom Observation*, Chichester: Wiley.

Delamont, S. (1984) The old girl network, in R. G. Burgess (ed.) *The Research Process in Educational Settings*, Lewes: Falmer.

Delamont, S. (1987) Three blind spots, *Social Studies of Science*, 17(1), 163–70.

Delamont, S. (1989a) Gender and British postgraduate funding policy, *Gender and Education*, 1(1), 51–7.

Delamont, S. (1989b) Citation and social mobility research, *Sociological Review*, 37(2), 332–7.

Delamont, S. (1989c) *Knowledgeable Women*, London: Routledge.

Delamont, S. (1992) *Fieldwork in Educational Settings*, London: Falmer.

Delamont, S. and Atkinson, P. (1995) *Fighting Familiarity*, Cresskill, NJ: Hampton.

Delamont, S. and Eggleston, J. (1981) *A Necessary Isolation? A Study of Postgraduate Research Students in Education*, Cardiff: Social Research Unit, Department of Sociology, University College, Cardiff.

Diamond, P. and Zuber-Skerritt, O. (1986) Postgraduate researchers: some changing personal constructs, *Higher Education Research and Development*, 5, 161–75.

Dooley, P. *et al.* (1981) *Survey of Educational Researchers in Britain*, Birmingham: Aston University Department of Educational Enquiry.

Dummett, M. (1993) *Grammar and Style*, London: Duckworth.

Dyhouse, C. (1994) *No Distinction of Sex*, London: UCL Press.

Edge, D. (1979) Quantitative measures of communication in sciences, *History of Science*, 17, 102–34.

Edmondson, R. (1984) *Rhetoric in Sociology*, London: Macmillan.

Eggleston, J. F. and Delamont, S. (1983) *Supervision of the Students for Research Degrees*, Kendal, Cumbria: Dixon Printing Company for the British Educational Research Association.

Eickleman, D. (1978) The art of memory, *Comparative Studies in Society and History*, 20(4), 485–516.

Eickleman, D. (1985) *Knowledge and Power in Morocco*, Princeton, NJ: Princeton University Press.

Evans, C. (1988) *Language People*, Milton Keynes: Open University Press.

Evans, C. (1993) *English People*, Buckingham: Open University Press.

Fine, G. A. (1983) *Shared Fantasy*, Chicago: Chicago University Press.

Fleck, L. (1979) *The Genesis and Development of a Scientific Fact*, Chicago: Chicago University Press.

Fowler, H. W. (1994) *A Dictionary of Modern English Usage*, Ware: Wordsworth Editions Ltd.

Fox, M. F. (ed.) (1985) *Scholarly Writing and Publishing*, Boulder, CO: Westview Press.

Frank, F. W. and Treichler, P. A. (1989) *Language, Gender and Professional Writing*, New York: The Modern Language Association of America.

Galton, M. and Delamont, S. (1976) *Final Report on PhD/PGCE Chemistry Courses*, Leicester: Leicester University School of Education for the DES.

Gilbert, N. (1993) Writing about social research, in N. Gilbert (ed.) *Researching Social Life*, London: Sage.

Gilbert, N. and Mulkay, M. (1984) *Opening Pandora's Box*, Cambridge: Cambridge University Press.

Goode, G. and Delamont, S. (1996) Opportunity denied, in S. Betts (ed.) *Our Daughters' Land*, Cardiff: University of Wales Press.

Gornik, V. (1990) *Women in Science*, New York: Simon and Schuster.

Gowers, E. (1986) *The Complete Plain Words*, revised edition prepared by S. Greenbaum and J. Whitcut, London: HMSO.

Granfield, R. (1992) *Making Elite Lawyers*, New York: Routledge.

Gray, A. and Flowerdew, R. (1987) Reflections on reform: some implications of the ESRC's new postgraduate policy, *Journal of Geography in Higher Education*, 11(2), 175–8.

Gumport, P. (1993) Graduate education and research imperatives: views from American campuses, in R. B. Clark (ed.) *The Research Foundations of Graduate Education*, Berkeley: University of California Press.

Hacking, I. (1992) The self-vindication of the laboratory sciences, in A. Pickering (ed.) *Science as Practice and Culture*, Chicago: Chicago University Press.

Hammersley, M. and Atkinson, P. (1995) *Ethnography: Principles in Practice*, 2nd edn, London: Routledge.

Hargreaves, A. (1984) Contrastive rhetoric and extremist talk, in A. Hargreaves and P. Woods (eds) *Classrooms and Staffrooms*, Milton Keynes: Open University Press.

Harris, M. (1996) *Review of Postgraduate Education: Volume 1, The Report; Volume 2, The Evidence*, Bristol: The Higher Education Funding Council for England.

Hayhoe, R. (1984) The evolution of modern Chinese educational institutions, in R. Hayhoe (ed.) *Contemporary Chinese Education*, London: Croom Helm.

Heyl, B. (1979) *The Madam as Entrepreneur*, New Brunswick, NJ: Transaction Books.

Hockey, J. (1991) The social science PhD, *Studies in Higher Education*, 16(3), 319–32.

Hockey, J. (1994a) Establishing boundaries: problems and solutions in managing the PhD supervisor role, *Cambridge Journal of Education*, 24(2), 293–305.

Hockey, J. (1994b) New territory, *Studies in Higher Education*, 19(2), 177–90.

Hudson, L. (1977) Picking winners: a case study in the recruitment of research students, *New Universities Quarterly*, 32(1), 88–106.

Jones, D. J. H. (1993) *Murder at the MLA*, Athens: Georgia University Press.

Kadushin, C. (1969) The professional self concept of music students, *American Journal of Sociology*, 75, 389–404.

Katz, J. and Hartnett, R. T. (eds) (1976) *Scholars in the Making*, Cambridge, MA: Ballinger.

Kirkman, J. (1992) *Good Style*, London: Spon.

Kirkman, J. (1993) *Full Marks*, London: Ramsbury.

Latour, B. and Woolgar, S. (1986) *Laboratory Life*, Princeton, NJ: Princeton University Press.

Lathen, E. (1982) *Green Grow the Dollars*, London: Gollancz.

Lather, P. (1991) *Getting Smart*, London: Routledge.

Lie, S. S., Malik, L. and Harris, D. (eds) (1994) *The Gender Gap in Higher Education*, London: Kogan Page.

Lodge, D. (1984) *Small World*, London: Martin Secker & Warburg.

Lynch, M. (1985) *Art and Artefact in Laboratory Science*, London: Routledge.

McAleese, R. and Welsh, J. (1983) The supervision of postgraduate research students, in J. E. Eggleston and S. Delamont (eds) *Supervision of Students for Research Degrees*, Kendal, Cumbria: Dixon Printing Company for the British Educational Research Association.

Manser, M. J. (1990) *Bloomsbury Good Word Guide*, London: Bloomsbury.

Miller, C. M. L. and Parlett, M. (1976) Cue-consciousness, in M. Hammersley and P. Woods (eds) *The Process of Schooling*, London: Routledge and Kegan Paul.

Moses, I. (1985) *Supervising Postgraduates*, Kensington, NSW: Higher Education Research and Development Society of Australasia.

Myers, G. (1990) *Writing Biology: Texts in the Social Construction of Scientific Knowledge*, Madison: University of Wisconsin Press.

Nash, R. (1973) *Classrooms Observed*, London: Routledge.

Olesen, V. and Whittaker, E. (1968) *The Silent Dialogue*, San Francisco: Jossey Bass.

Parry, O., Atkinson, P. and Delamont, S. (1994a) Disciplinary identities and doctoral work, in R. G. Burgess (ed.) *Postgraduate Education and Training in the Social Sciences*, London: Jessica Kingsley.

Parry, O., Atkinson, P., Delamont, S. and Hiken, A. (1994b) Suspended between two stools?, in A. Coffey and P. Atkinson (eds) *Occupational Socialisation and Working Lives*, Farnborough: Avebury.

Parry, O., Atkinson, P. and Delamont, S. (1996) On pedagogic continuity, paper presented at the BERA conference, University of Lancaster, September.

Pechenick, J. A. and Lamb, B. C. (1995) *How to Write about Biology*, London: Harper Collins.

Phillips, E. M. (1994) Quality in the PhD, in R. G. Burgess (ed.) *Postgraduate Education and Training in the Social Sciences*, London: Jessica Kingsley.

Phillips, E. M. and Pugh, D. S. (1994) *How to Get a PhD*, 2nd edn, Buckingham: Open University Press.

Phillips, S. U. (1982) The language socialisation of lawyers: acquiring the 'cant', in G. Spindler (ed.) *Doing the Ethnography of Schooling*, New York: Holt, Rinehart & Winston.

Porter, M. (1984) The modification of method in researching postgraduate education, in R. G. Burgess (ed.) *The Research Process in Educational Settings*, London:
Falmer.

Price, D. T. W. (1990) *A History of Saint David's University College, Lampeter, Vol. 2*,
Cardiff: University of Wales Press.

Richardson, L. (1990) *Writing Strategies*, Newbury Park, CA: Sage.

Rubashow, N. (1986) *Survey of PhD Completion Rates*, London: Makrotest.

Rudd, E. (1984) Research into postgraduate education, *Higher Education Research
and Development*, 3(2), 109–20.

Rudd, E. (1985) *A New Look at Postgraduate Failure*, Guildford: SRHE and NFER
Nelson.

Rudestam, K. E. and Newton, R. R. (1992) *Surviving Your Dissertation*, London:
Sage.

Salmon, P. (1992) *Achieving a PhD*, Stoke on Trent: Trentham Books.

Sayers, D. L. (1972) *Gaudy Night*, London: Gollancz.

Scott, S. (1985) Working through the contradictions in researching postgraduate
education, in R. G. Burgess (ed.) *Field Methods in the Study of Education*, London: Falmer.

Scott, S. and Porter, M. (1980) Postgraduates, sociology and cuts, in P. Abrams
and P. Leuthwaite (eds) *Transactions of the BSA*, London: British Sociological
Association.

Scott, S. and Porter, M. (1983) On the bottom rung, *Women's Studies International
Forum*, 6(22), 211–21.

Scott, S. and Porter, M. (1984) Women and research, in S. Acker and D. Warren-
Piper (eds) *Is Higher Education Fair to Women?* London: SRHE.

Silk, J. (1988) Private affluence and public austerity: motors for innovation in
postgraduate training, *Journal of Geography in Higher Education*, 12(2), 149–75.

Smelser, N. J. (1993) *Effective Committee Service*, Newbury Park, CA: Sage.

Spradley, J. P. (1979) *The Ethnographic Interview*, New York: Holt, Rinehart & Winston.

Spradley, J. P. (1980) *Participant Observation*, New York: Holt, Rinehart & Winston.

Spradley, J. P. and Mann, B. J. (1975) *The Cocktail Waitress*, New York: Wiley.

Startup, R. (1979) *The University Teacher and His World*, Farnborough: Saxon House.

Tesch, R. (1990) *Qualitative Research: Analysis Types and Software Tools*, London:
Falmer.

Torrance, M. S. and Thomas, G. V. (1994) The development of writing skills in
doctoral research students, in R. G. Burgess (ed.) *Postgraduate Education and
Training in the Social Sciences*, London: Jessica Kingsley.

Traweek, S. (1988) *Beamtimes and Lifetimes*, Cambridge, MA: Harvard University
Press.

Turabian, K. (1937) *A Manual for Writers of Research Papers, Theses and Dissertations*,
Chicago: Chicago University Press.

Turabian, K. (1982) *A Manual for Writers of Research Papers, Theses and Dissertations*,
British edition, London: Heinemann.

Turabian, K. (1995) *A Manual for Writers of Research Papers, Theses and Dissertations*,
6th edn, Chicago: University of Chicago Press.

Unwin, D. (1987) The future of postgraduate education, *Journal of Geography in
Higher Education*, 11(2), 173–4.

Valli, L. (1986) *Becoming Clerical Workers*, New York: Routledge.

Vartuli, S. (ed.) (1982) *The PhD Experience*, New York: CBS.

Wakeford, J. (1985) A director's dilemmas, in R. G. Burgess (ed.) *Field Methods in the Study of Education*, London: Falmer.

Weaver, A. and Atkinson, P. (1994) *Microcomputing and Qualitative Data Analysis*, Farnborough: Avebury.

Weiner, M. (1993) *Improving Your Classroom Teaching*, Newbury Park, CA: Sage.

Whale, J. (1984) *Put It in Writing*, London: Dent.

Whicker, M. L., Kronenfeld, J. J. and Strickland, R. A. (1993) *Getting Tenure*, Newbury Park, CA: Sage.

Whitehand, J. W. R. (1966) The selection of research students, *Universities Quarterly*, 21, 44–8.

Whittlesea, C. (1995) Pharmacy doctoral students: thesis writing skills and strategies, unpublished MSc Econ thesis, University of Wales College of Cardiff.

Wilkinson, R. (1964) *The Prefects*, London: Oxford University Press.

Winfield, G. (1987) *The Social Science PhD* (2 volumes), London: Economic and Social Research Council.

Wolcott, H. F. (1990) *Writing up Qualitative Research*, Newbury Park, CA: Sage.

Wolf, M. (1992) *A Thrice Told Tale: Feminism, Postmodernism and Ethnographic Responsibility*, Stanford, CA: Stanford University Press.

Wright, J. (1992) *Selection, supervision and the academic management of research leading to the degree of PhD*, unpublished PhD thesis, University of Nottingham.

Young, K., Fogarty, M. P. and McRae, S. (1987) *The Management of Doctoral Studies in the Social Sciences*, London: Policy Studies Institute.

Zuber-Skerritt, O. and Ryan, Y. (eds) (1994) *Quality in Postgraduate Education*, London: Kogan Page.

Zuckerman, H., Cole, J. R. and Bruer, J. T. (eds) (1991) *The Outer Circle*, New York: W. W. Norton.

Index

The Society for Research into Higher Education

The Society for Research into Higher Education exists to stimulate and coordinate research into all aspects of higher education. It aims to improve the quality of higher education through the encouragement of debate and publication on issues of policy, on the organization and management of higher eudcation institutions, and on the curriculum and teaching methods.

The Society's income is derived from subscriptions, sales of its books and journals, conference fees and grants. It receives no subsidies, and is wholly independent. Its individual members include teachers, researchers, managers and students. Its corporate members are institutions of higher education, research institutes, professional, industrial and governmental bodies. Members are not only from the UK, but from elsewhere in Europe, from America, Canada and Australasia, and it regards its international work as among its most important activities.

Under the imprint *SRHE & Open University Press*, the Society is a specialist publisher of research, having some 60 titles in print. The Editorial Board of the Society's Imprint seeks authoritative research or study in the above fields. It offers competitive royalties, a highly recognizable format in both hardback and paperback and the worldwide reputation of the Open University Press.

The Society also publishes *Studies in Higher Education* (three times a year), which is mainly concerned with academic issues, *Higher Education Quarterly* (formerly *Universities Quarterly*), mainly concerned with policy issues, *Research into Higher Education Abstracts* (three times a year), and *SRHE News* (four times a year).

The Society holds a major annual conference in December, jointly with an institution of higher education. In 1994 the topic was 'The Student Experience' at the University of York. In 1995 it was 'The Changing University' at Heriot-Watt University in Edinburgh and in 1996, 'Working in Higher Education' at Cardiff Institute of Higher Education. Conferences in 1997 include 'Beyond the First Degree' at the University of Warwick.

The Society's committees, study groups and branches are run by the members. The groups at present include:
Teacher Education Study Group
Continuing Education Group
Staff Development Group
Excellence in Teaching and Learning

Benefits to members

Individual

Individual members receive:

- *SRHE: News*, the Society's publications list, conference details and other material included in mailings.
- Greatly reduced rates for *Studies in Higher Education* and *Higher Education Quarterly*.
- A 35 per cent discount on all SRHE & Open University Press publications.
- Free copies of the Proceedings – commissioned papers on the theme of the Annual Conference.
- Free copies of *Research into Higher Education Abstracts*.
- Reduced rates for conferences.
- Extensive contacts and scope for facilitating initiatives.
- Reduced reciprocal memberships.
- Free copies of the *Register of Members' Research Interests*.

Corporate

Corporate members receive:

- All benefits of individual members, plus.
- Free copies of *Studies in Higher Education*.
- Unlimited copies of the Society's publications at reduced rates.
- Special rates for its members e.g. to the Annual Conference.
- The right to submit application for the Society's research grants.

Membership details: SRHE, 3 Devonshire Street, London W1N 2BA, UK. Tel: 0171 637 2766. Fax: 0171 637 2781. email: srhe@clus1.ulcc.ac.uk
Catalogue: SRHE & Open University Press, Celtic Court, 22 Ballmoor, Buckingham MK18 1XW. Tel: 01280 823388. Fax: 01280 823233. email: enquiries@openup.co.uk

HOW TO GET A PHD (2nd edition)
A HANDBOOK FOR STUDENTS AND THEIR SUPERVISORS

Estelle M. Phillips and D.S. Pugh

This is a handbook and survival manual for PhD students, providing a practical, realistic understanding of the processes of doing research for a doctorate. It discusses many important issues often left unconsidered, such as the importance of time management and how to achieve it, and how to overcome the difficulties of communicating with supervisors. Consideration is given to the particular problems of groups such as women, part-time and overseas students.

The book also provides practical insights for supervisors, focusing on how to monitor and, if necessary, improve supervisory practice. It assists senior academic administrators by examining the responsibilities that universities have for providing an adequate service for research students. This is a revised and updated second edition; it will be as warmly welcomed as the first edition:

> One way of providing a more supportive environment for PhD students is for supervisors to recommend this book.
>
> (*Teaching News*)

> Warmly recommended as a bedside companion, both to those hoping to get a PhD and to those who have the responsibility of guiding them, often with very little support themselves.
>
> (*Higher Education Review*)

> This is an excellent book. Its style is racy and clear . . . an impressive array of information, useful advice and comment gleaned from the authors' systematic study and experience over many years . . . should be required reading not only for those contemplating doctoral study but also for all supervisors, new and experienced.
>
> (*Higher Education*)

Contents

224pp   0 335 192149 (Paperback)

THE RESEARCH STUDENT'S GUIDE TO SUCCESS

Pat Cryer

This book is for postgraduate students working for research degrees in institutions of higher education wherever the language of instruction is English. Irrespective of field of study, it will make their work and life more productive, effective and enjoyable.

The Research Student's Guide to Success:

- identifies the skills and strategies which make for success as a postgraduate research student
- offers practical advice which can be readily adapted to meet individual needs
- provides essential support for all research students
- encourages research students to take responsibility for their own progress
- acknowledges both the hardships and the pleasures of being a research student
- builds confidence throughout.

The book is easy to dip into and is written in conversational style. Interest and realism are added through anecdotes, extracts from literature and pithy quotations.

The book will also be useful to undergraduate, diploma and taught masters students doing projects and dissertations.

Contents

Introduction – Registering for a research degree – Preparing for the way of life of a research student – Settling in as a new research student – Towards recognizing good research – Interacting with your supervisor(s) – Keeping records – Planning ahead – Managing yourself and your time – Taking responsibility for your own progress – Cooperating with others for mutual help and support – Producing reports – Giving presentations on your work – Landmarks, hurdles, and transferring from MPhil to PhD – Coming to terms with originality in research – Developing skills for creative thinking – Dealing with flagging – Producing your thesis – Preparing for and conducting yourself in the examination – Afterwards! – Bibliography and references – Index.

240pp   0 335 19611 X (pbk)   0 335 19612 8 (hbk)

WORKING IN HIGHER EDUCATION

Rob Cuthbert (ed.)

Many people work in higher education; few pause to examine their experience. This book offers a unique range of fresh perspectives on higher education work. It analyses who are the workers in higher education, their patterns of employment, and what motivates them. It looks at the changing nature of higher education work, not only teaching and research work by academics but also the growing role of others such as professional librarians and information scientists. And it examines the context for higher education work, by looking at changing patterns of academic culture, professionalism and control. Leading academics, managers and practitioners provide analysis, reflections on experience, case studies and more light-hearted contributions. This book is for anyone who wants to reflect on their experience of working in higher education, for all who study higher education, and for anyone who works *with* higher education and wants to understand it better.

Rob Cuthbert offers us:

- ways of conceptualizing 'working in higher education'
- a range of contributors: academics, managers, consultants, a librarian and information scientist
- fresh perspectives on familiar issues, and fresh writing from familiar perspectives

Contents

Introduction: Working in higher education – Part 1: The workers – Academic staff – Managing the employment relationship in higher education – Does it pay to work in universities? – Which of us has a brilliant career? – Part 2: The work – New liberty, new discipline – Professors and professionals – Managing how academics manage – Work's committees – Geographical transitions – Part 3: The work context – Just like the novels? – Which academic profession are you in? – Autonomy, bureaucracy and competition – Conclusion: All work and no play – References – Index.

Contributors

Michael Bradford, Sheila Corrall, Rob Cuthbert, Sara Delamont, Oliver Fulton, Frank Hartle, R.J. Johnston, Ewart Keep, Ray Lester, Ian McNay, Helen Murlis, Brian Ramsden, Keith Sisson, John Storey, Marie L. Thorne, Gaby Weiner, Richard Winter.

240pp   0 335 19721 3 (Paperback)   0 335 19722 1 (Hardback)